MEAN ON SUNDAY

Second edition, first printing
Copyright © 1973 by Robert W. Wells and Ray Nitschke
Prairie Oak Press edition, with additions, copyright © 1998

Prairie Oak Press
821 Prospect Place
Madison, Wisconsin 53703

Additions typeset by Quick Quality Press, Madison, Wisconsin
Cover design by Prairie Oak Press
Printed in the United States of America by BookCrafters,
Chelsea, Michigan

Library of Congress Cataloging-in-Publication Data

Nitschke, Ray, 1936-
    Mean on Sunday: the autobiography of Ray Nitschke / as
told to Robert W. Wells. -- 2nd ed.
        p.   cm.
    ISBN 1-879483-54-8
    1. Nitschke, Ray, 1936- . 2. Football players--United States-
-Biography. 3. Green Bay Packers (Football team)--History.
I. Wells, Robert W. II. Title.
GV939.N57A3 1998
796.332'092--dc21   98-37872
[B]   CIP

MEAN ON SUNDAY

The Autobiography of Ray Nitschke

as told to

ROBERT W. WELLS

PRAIRIE OAK PRESS   MADISON, WISCONSIN

MEAN ON SUNDAY

CHAPTER 1

Fifteen years. In professional football, that adds up to a couple of hundred games. A few thousand tackles. A lot of hours spent watching game films, doing wind sprints, listening to coaches, sitting in locker rooms waiting to go out on the field on one more Sunday afternoon to try to prove something. Every week during the season you have to prove you're the best. It doesn't matter how well you did last week or last season. You have to prove you're the best all over again. And if the time comes when you don't believe you're the best, you'd better find another way to make a living.

I've always thought I was the best middle linebacker in professional football. And not just because the National Football League picked me as the top man at that job during the league's first fifty years.

I thought I was the best middle linebacker even when I was a rookie, trying to beat my good friend, Tom Bettis, out of a starting job with the Green Bay Packers. I thought so even when I sat on the bench after Coach Dan Devine gave Jim Carter my job.

Whenever I went onto that field, I was the best middle linebacker. I had to be. Otherwise, it wouldn't have been fair, because that center who was trying to block me thought he was the best center who ever lived, and that back who was trying to get past me with the ball thought he was the best halfback or fullback created since the game began.

When that back with the ball was coming at me, he was telling himself: "Nobody's going to stop me before I get a touchdown because I'm the best damned runner in the world." If I didn't think I was the best middle linebacker, how would I stop him?

And if I'm out there, I'm going to stop him. I'm going to hit him. I'm going to let him know I'm still around. I don't intend that he'll make an inch, let alone a touchdown, and then I want him to go back to the huddle shaking his head and thinking about Ray Nitschke. I want him to remember Ray Nitschke even in his dreams.

If you're not a football player, maybe this kind of talk sounds egotistical. But if you've ever played for the pros, you'll understand. There are forty big, bristly egos on each football squad. When two teams run out on the field, there are eleven big egos on one side and eleven big egos on the other. When the coach stands up and talks to his men, he's dealing with guys who believe in their hearts they're the best football players anywhere.

It doesn't make his job any simpler. I've played under four head coaches during my fifteen years with the Packers, and they each approached things differently. But every one of them had to try to figure out how to weld forty over-sized egos into one team. That is, into one brotherhood.

Some of the years, the Packers have been that kind of brotherhood, and some years we haven't. But when we were winning everything—when we were the team that always won when it had to, a team that always took the big ones—we were a brotherhood, a clan, a family. The egos were still there, mine among them, with forty guys each thinking he was the best. But there was a team ego, too.

Our family—that is, the Green Bay Packers—believed it was better than any of the other teams. And it was. And it won.

The coach we had then, Vince Lombardi, was criticized for saying, "Winning isn't everything—it's the only thing." Especially in recent years, some people say winning is over-emphasized. They say football's only a game after all, a form of entertainment like opera or ballet. They say it sets a bad example if you put all that stress on winning.

I don't buy that argument. When a kid is in high school or even in college, there are other considerations besides winning. But when he's a professional, winning is what he's getting paid to do, and if he doesn't win, he isn't doing his job. I think Lombardi was right about that. As a matter of fact, I think he was right about most things.

The fans pay to see you win. That's one thing that hasn't changed in the fifteen years since I came out of the University of Illinois to join the Packers. A lot of other things about football have changed in that length of time, however. The stadiums are bigger. The crowds are bigger. The money is a lot bigger. The interest in football has grown tremendously. The pressures are greater. So are the rewards. I came a few years too early to cash in on the big bonuses—Green Bay paid me five hundred dollars to sign, and I thought that was a lot of money—but I wouldn't trade places with some of the big bonus babies if I could. I came at a good time. I came in time to be part of what I think was the best professional football team in history. I don't believe there'll ever be another that will equal it. I

3

wouldn't trade the chance I had to be there all during those great years for any amount of money in the bank.

Sure, I've played football for money—but not just for money. All during those fifteen years with the pros and during all those games in college and high school, all through those hurts of the body and sometimes of the spirit, I always played football for fun.

Everybody needs to have something he can do well. Ever since I weighed ninety pounds and was trying to understand why God had decided to pick on Raymond Nitschke, I've been working on being able to play football better than anybody else.

When I was born just four days too late to get in on the Christmas celebration of 1936, I was the youngest of three brothers. Growing up, I was the baby of the family. When Bob and Richard and I get together now, I guess I'm still the baby. I've grown some—I'm 6 foot 3 and weigh 235—but they're both bigger than I am.

My birthplace was Elmwood Park, a working-class suburb of Chicago, and I lived there until I went away to college. My dad, Robert Nitschke, had a job with the Chicago Surface Lines. He was of German ancestry, and my mother, Anna, was Danish. I don't really remember him. In 1940, when I was three, he was coming home from a union meeting and his car and a trolley collided and he was killed.

So there was my mother with three heavy eaters to raise by herself. We never had our own home. We lived in a duplex, the Nitschkes upstairs, other people downstairs. It wasn't the best, but my mother did as well as she could. She worked hard. She didn't make much money, but we always had clean clothes and we always had our bellies full.

4

I had a happy childhood, other than not having a father to do things with, although it was pretty tough on my mother to have to raise three boys by herself. It was nip and tuck all the way. My Grandmother Petersen moved in and helped out and took care of the house while my mother went to work for my Uncle Pete. He ran Pete's Place. It was one of those neighborhood restaurants and taverns that serve home cooking. It was always busy, always had a good trade. Factory workers, white-collar people, various kinds of customers. A card game in the back. The same people there every Friday and Saturday night, week after week. Everybody knowing everybody else.

I helped Mother at the restaurant when I got old enough. Peeling potatoes and such jobs. I got a few pennies for helping out, so I always had spending money. My aunt used to take care of me so I had a little change in my pocket.

I was really close to my mother. She was my life. She didn't have much enjoyment out of those years except for her kids, and I was the youngest. She'd work all day in the tavern, and then afterward she might sit at the counter and have a beer and then come home. That was all the fun she had.

Things got so tough financially when I was about six years old that my oldest brother, Bobby, who was just starting high school, had to drop out and get a job. He was fourteen. He got a job with the railroad to help Mother out.

I was in Elmwood Park grade school by then. Later, I transferred to Elm School, which was nearby. My other brother, Richard, went to Proviso High School in Maywood, about five miles away, when he got old enough. Elmwood Park didn't have a high school district, so a kid

5

there had a choice of several different high schools. Because Richard went to Proviso, that's where I went when I got through eighth grade.

Because my dad was dead, my mother sometimes asked my oldest brother to be the family disciplinarian. I remember one time Bob was giving it to me with a belt. I was getting hit in the traditional place, but not just with the belt. I was getting hit with the buckle, and I recall thinking: "You hit me one more time, Bobby, and you're going to have an injured kid brother." But the next one was just a light tap, so it was okay.

Bob grew big early. He says now he can hardly recall a time when he wasn't six feet tall. He thought I was never going to grow. I was a skinny kid. I was always getting into fights with boys who outweighed me by fifty pounds. I was little, but I was aggressive. By the time I got to the Packers, I wasn't little any more, but I still had some run-ins with linemen who outweighed me by fifty pounds.

Even when I was in grade school, sports was the thing I was interested in. I was always playing some kind of ball with my brothers or the neighbor kids. Every spare moment I was out playing basketball, football, baseball, hockey. If you wanted to find little Raymond in those days, all you had to do was head for the nearest playground, because that's where I'd be.

It kept me out of trouble. Mother always seemed to be at work, so I was tearing around loose a lot of the time. But I always had a ball to throw or kick, and I was usually playing with kids who were older. Being little didn't bother me, although I did wish I could catch up with my brother, Richard, who was four years older.

6

I was always competing with him. I was always trying to outdo him. He'd always beat me, but I was always trying to get better so I could beat him. He played a little football in high school and he played fairly well, so he'd beat me at that. In basketball, he'd beat me. In baseball, he'd beat me. I used to get so mad at him. I'd really work hard to be better than he was. My oldest brother was working most of the time, and he didn't do much with sports, except fishing. But Richard was a real sports fan, and he was the one I competed with while I was growing up.

I didn't seem to grow much until I was well along in high school, but size wasn't a big deal with me. I didn't realize how important an advantage size can be in sports, although I did wish I'd grow some so I could be a better player.

So that's how my life was when I started in high school. Everything going along fine, as far as I was concerned. No big problems. Happy. And then my mother went to the hospital.

It was hard to believe. She never took time off from work to be sick. So what was she doing in the hospital? We didn't think too much about it, though. We thought she'd be there for a few days and then come home and everything would be the same as always. Only she didn't come home again. And all of a sudden, everything fell apart.

My mother was only forty-one years old when she died. Still a young woman. She'd never gone to the doctor. If she didn't feel well, she'd take care of it herself. She had been bleeding internally, but she wouldn't go to the doctor. When she finally did, it was too late. She was in the hospital about a week, and then she died of a blood clot.

I was thirteen years old, just starting adolescence, a difficult time in a kid's life even when he's got two parents and a nice house and plenty of money to keep things going smoothly. I'd been all right without a father or those material things the boys in fancier neighborhoods took for granted, as long as my mother was still around. But when she died it was as if the world had come crashing down on my shoulders.

"Why did God have to take my mother?" I asked myself. And I thought: "Why should this happen to Ray Nitschke?"

There was a lot of talk about what would be done with the orphans now. At her funeral, the aunts and uncles stood around discussing it.

"I'll take this one and you take that one," one would say. And the other would say, "I'll take one if you'll take another of the boys." But it turned out that nobody had to take us in.

Bob was twenty-one years old, and he and Richard talked things over and decided they'd stick together and between them they could raise little Raymond, who was now a thirteen-year-old motherless boy with a great big chip on his shoulder because he was feeling very sorry for himself.

So here I was, just starting high school, just starting adolescence, a kid who weighed less than a hundred pounds and who thought nobody cared about him and everybody was against him.

Without a father, I'd had less discipline than most boys get. Now that my mother was dead, too, I grew up without anybody giving me much direction on what to do and what not to do. I grew up with anger seething inside me at the dirty trick life had pulled on me. I had to let that anger find an outlet somewhere, and so I took out my anger on the other kids. I grew up belting the other boys in the neighborhood, and getting belted back.

I didn't have many friends. I was what was called a loner. I went to school, but only because I had to. Afterward, I'd go out by myself and kick a football and run after it and kick it and run after it, just being by myself and away from everybody. If it was winter, I'd go out and shovel the snow off the basketball court in the playground and then I'd stand there, hour after hour, shooting baskets.

Bobby would come home from work and I wouldn't be there. If he wanted me, he'd look over at my aunt's place, and if I wasn't there I'd be over next to the school or somewhere, playing football or basketball. He'd usually find me by myself. I didn't seem to have any buddies. I didn't think I wanted any. They had mothers. All I had was a football. I didn't want anybody—including myself—to know that having a football wasn't enough.

We didn't have a car, so the school and the neighborhood was about all I saw. I never got out in the real country. To me, country was anyplace ten miles out of town. I had no chance to do things like camping or hunting or fishing. Once I decided I'd like to get in on such things, and I signed up for the Boy Scout troop. I went to one meeting. I got in a fight. They told me not to come back.

So I missed out on something every child needs, a chance to explore nature. The only nature I had was a vacant lot with a few trees on it.

Summers, I'd caddy at a golf course. I started when I was ten. On Caddy Day, we got a chance to play, and that started me in golf, which is something I still enjoy.

At one point, I got a job as a carrier boy for the Chicago *Tribune*. I started out with lots of enthusiasm, even though it meant I had to get up at 5:30 A.M. to deliver the papers. But the job didn't last long. I broke too many windows. I'd send those papers flying up toward the porches as if they were footballs and I was going for a long bomb to win the game. You could trail me down the street by the sounds of breaking glass and the yells of customers who didn't appreciate my passing ability. I lost so much money paying for windows I broke throwing Chicago *Tribunes* through them that I had to give up my career. I couldn't afford to be a paper boy.

In the winter, I'd go over to River Forest and get jobs shoveling driveways. In my neighborhood, people shoveled their own, but the River Forest residents could afford to hire it done. Summers, I'd go over to that neighborhood and mow lawns. Around Christmas, some of us would go to River Forest and sing carols. We'd sing until somebody came out and paid us to quit.

In those days, I didn't know anything about the real countryside, but there was a place with a little stream and some trees, and in the warm weather I'd sometimes go down there by myself and walk along, throwing stones in the water and thinking about what I was going to do. I didn't know where I was heading, and there was nobody around to tell me. I didn't think about college—nobody I was close to paid much attention to college, because that was mostly for those kids over in River Forest and such places—and I didn't even think much about what I was going to be when I grew up. But I did think about what I was going to do to prove that I was as good as anybody else. As good as the boys who had mothers. All I could come up with was that I'd play basketball or football or baseball better than they could. Maybe not right now, because I was still a shrimp, but I'd get so I could beat them, and then the whole world—especially Elmwood Park, Illinois—would see that Ray Nitschke amounted to something after all.

Right now, though, I was playing football on the freshman C team. It was a good thing that Proviso High was a big school with about four thousand students—it's since been divided, and the one I went to is called Proviso East, but then it was one big school. It was big enough to have three football teams for the freshmen. If there'd been only one or two, I might not have gotten to play. I was late developing physically, so there was little Raymond, assigned to the C team because of his size, trying to compete with kids bigger than he was. A lot of them were a little older, too. I was thirteen, and I was competing with boys who were fourteen or even fifteen. In grammar school, we'd been divided on a semester basis, and when they decided to change the system, I was with the group that skipped a half year. At Proviso, there were students from a dozen different communities, and a lot of the other kids hadn't skipped a half grade.

Even though some of the other freshmen were bigger and more mature than I was, I fought everybody who looked at me the wrong way. I still had this terrible chip-on-the-shoulder attitude because I couldn't understand why life had pulled such a dirty trick on me, taking my mother. Why was it me who was orphaned? What had I done to deserve such a thing? Why did she have to die—the one who'd given me all that love, the one I loved? So I was against everything and everybody. I just wanted to be left alone.

Sometimes I thought about running away. I might have done it, except for athletics. But as long as I could kick a ball or shoot a basket or, better still, put my head down and tackle somebody to take out my frustrations on the kid who was carrying the ball, I could go on. I was so busy with sports I didn't have much time to go out looking for ways to get in trouble.

I was still feeling sorry for myself. Some of the high school students had plenty of money, and some didn't have much. I was one who didn't have much, and it bothered me. Why should they have a car and new clothes and I didn't? Why should they have nice things and not me? I wanted to catch up to them, and the only way I knew how to do it was to work hard at sports. If one guy did ten push-ups, I'd do fifteen. If somebody would run a mile, I'd run a mile and a quarter. I was always pushing myself, always trying to prove to myself and the others that I was as good as they were.

I got enough to eat, but in every other sense of the word I was hungry. There are some advantages to this kind of hunger. It's helped me all through my career. I haven't lost that kind of hunger yet. I've learned that nothing comes easy, but if you do a little extra you can succeed. There have been times when I've wanted to give up, but then I'd tell myself: "Uh-uh, I'm not going to give up." I didn't figure this out as a kid. I just did it. I was feeling sorry for myself, and I was trying to prove I was equal to anybody.

I was lucky that even in a big school like Proviso I had

some teachers who knew I had problems and tried to help me. I appreciate it now. I didn't then. I thought, "Why are they trying to help me? Why should they bother with me?" I didn't realize until later how great they were.

I had to push myself to go to school. But I went to get away from nothing—what I had was nothing. I didn't have any real roots. There was nothing to come home to after school. I have a lot of love for my brothers—we're grown men now, but when I see them I kiss them, the way you might a father or mother—but when I was in school Bobby was working and Richard was busy and neither of them were much more than boys themselves. So there was a void in my home life.

I had one friend, a boy I went to grammar school with, Roman Strazala. But other than him, I didn't have any real close friends. My first year in high school, I was really struggling. I knew I needed a C average to stay eligible for sports, but after my mother died I didn't really care what happened to me, and I failed a couple of subjects. So when I came back in the fall and was getting ready to go out for the teams they told me I was out of sports during my sophomore year.

That really spurred me on to improve my marks. I'd see the other guys playing and wish I was on the field with them, and I really started studying. I did better and I became eligible for sports again when I was a junior. But even now, I still regret I missed out on that whole year.

I'd been a fullback on the freshman C team—a hundred-pound fullback. I guess I didn't scare anybody when I was carrying the ball. But I didn't back up from anybody either.

By the time I was a junior, I'd gained some weight. I

13

was up to about 170 pounds. And what I wanted to be was the quarterback, because I wanted to be right where the center of the action was. That meant quarterback in football and center in basketball and pitcher in baseball.

The first time the coach noticed me was when he was driving by the field where a bunch of us were playing football during the summer and he saw me throw a pass.

"It went a country mile," he told me later, and he was impressed. That fall I was the quarterback, and before the football season was over, Coach Andy Puplis had a talk with Joe Hartley, who coached freshman football and varsity basketball.

"I want you to do me a favor, Joe. Give Nitschke a try at basketball."

"But Andy, he hasn't been out for it during his freshman and sophomore years. How can—"

"Just give him a try. I want him to play basketball."

So Hartley said he would. He remembered me from when I was a little guy on his C team. When he first saw me he thought I must be wearing my brother's shoes. My feet looked too big for the rest of me. But then he called over another coach, Ray Rice, and told him: "Hey, look. This kid's feet are for real. Take a look at the size of those hands."

He figured with those big hands and big feet that pretty soon the rest of my body would catch up and I'd be big enough to be a pretty fair football player.

There were various coaches and teachers who helped me in grammar school and high school, but the big guy in those years was Andy Puplis, who'd been an All-American quarterback at Notre Dame. I looked up to him. He was a gentleman, an inspiration, not only a very gifted man but a likable guy who wasn't afraid to smile.

By the time I was a high school senior, I'd added another twenty pounds and some more height, and I was not only the quarterback for the Proviso Pirates, but Hartley had also made me the center on his basketball team. He called me a tiger. I may not have been the smoothest center you ever saw. But I had good elbows.

I'd get sore at the coach if he didn't assign me to cover the other team's star player, whoever he happened to be. I felt I had to prove myself every game. One game—it was against the St. Edwards team—I scored thirty-six points, which was the Proviso record until a boy named Dave Roberts broke it in the 1970–71 season.

I'd grown bigger, but I still had the same chip on my shoulder as when I was a ninety-pounder, itching to tackle anybody who looked at me wrong. Puplis had long talks with me about controlling my temper so I wouldn't get thrown out of a game. He tried to show me that it's all right to be aggressive on the football field, but you've got to control your aggression or you hurt yourself and your team.

Puplis gave me quite a compliment. He said I was meaner than any other kid he'd ever coached. Even meaner than Ed O'Bradovich, who went from Proviso to star at Illinois and then with the Chicago Bears. When somebody calls you a mean football player they don't use the word the same way as if they'd called somebody a mean lawyer or a mean plumber. If you're not a football player and somebody says you're mean, you'd be insulted. But on the field, it's a compliment. A mean player is one who enjoys contact and plays hard and doesn't give up. But he's not a dirty player or anything else derogatory.

So I've tried to be as mean as possible whenever I've had my helmet and pads on. The rest of the time, at least in recent years, I've tried to leave my meanness in the locker room with the rest of the equipment after the game's over.

The Proviso football team won three games and lost four the year I was a junior. But the next year, 1953, we did better. We won seven and didn't lose a game, although Highland Park tied us.

Our first four games that year, we won by one-sided scores. The fifth game, which was against New Trier High, was something else. With the fourth quarter half gone, we were behind 29–18. I looked up and I saw some of the people in the aisles, leaving. I couldn't understand why. We had eight minutes left, and we were going to score enough points to win.

I had the reputation of being able to pass a long way— Andy Puplis still talks about the time one of my passes hit a receiver in the head so hard it knocked his helmet off and stunned him. Years later, some of the Packers' veterans used to challenge the rookies in training camp to a passing contest to see who could throw the ball farthest. When all those young hotshots had done their best, the veterans would bring out their secret weapon. They'd give me the ball, and I'd rear back and let it fly. Bart Starr claimed my arm was part bazooka. It was fun to see those rookies' faces when they found out the old bald-headed guy could still throw a lot farther than they could.

But in that high school game with New Trier, with us eleven points behind and the clock ticking along toward

16

the end of the game, this was no time to gamble on long bombs. Using mostly short passes, we gained 153 yards through the air in that fourth quarter, which isn't bad for a high school quarterback. We won, 30–29, so when we played our final game we had a 6–0–1 record and, if we could beat Oak Park, we'd be champions of the Suburban League, the toughest high school league in Illinois.

Late in the game, Oak Park was ahead 19–14 and had the ball on our seven. We were playing at home. There were seven thousand people watching. I'd never heard of the Super Bowl at that point—neither had anybody else, because it hadn't been invented—but playing my last high school game before all those people was just as big an event to me at the time as the league playoffs would be later on.

We stopped Oak Park on our one-yard line, so we had the ball with seven minutes left. I went back in the end zone and drilled a pass to Pete Fiorito on the twelve, which gave us a little room to maneuver, and then we went on down the field, running and passing, with one of the black guys on our team, Fred Keys, making a couple of great catches along the way. We were on Oak Park's one when I handed the ball to Fiorito, and he went through right tackle for the touchdown with 1:03 left, and we were the champions.

I still remember that ninety-nine-yard march. As a little boy, before my mother died, I'd gone to watch the games at Proviso and dreamed of playing against Oak Park. The high school boys looked so big and talented and I sat there in the stands hoping I'd be one of them someday. And now the time had come and we'd won the championship and I thought afterward, "Ray, this is the biggest game of your

17

life." It didn't turn out to be. Still, after all these years, I'm glad we beat Oak Park.

There were some other satisfactions that year, although none to compare with that final victory. After one of the earlier games, the Quarterback Club named me "prep player of the week," and I went around my uncle's tavern showing the customers my name in the Chicago *American* and the article saying I was going to get a certificate at a luncheon at the Morrison Hotel. But the school wouldn't give me permission to cut classes and my uncle, Viggo Rasmussen, had to get dressed up and take my place. I was real disappointed. My uncle was sore about it. He said if he'd known earlier about my being denied permission, he would have gone to the school and done something about it. But anyway, I got my name in the paper and my uncle gave me the certificate, even though he was the one who got to eat the free lunch at the Morrison instead of me.

It was during the 1953–54 school year, when I was a senior, that my oldest brother married Lorraine Klenk. Bob was getting started in the sheet metal trade then. Richard lived with them—he's still a bachelor, working for a beer distributor, and he still lives with them. It seemed more like a real home with Lorraine there.

Things worked out pretty well for me my senior year. Pete Fiorito and I got honorable mentions in *Scholastic Coach* magazine's 1953 All-American high school football squad; we thought we should have been on the first team, but honorable mention wasn't bad. Proviso not only won the football championship, but in 1953 we were state champions in baseball. We had a pretty fair basketball team, too. I remember one game, the Oak Park Huskies decided they could beat us if they went into a stall. But we out-stalled them. At the half, the score was 6–2. Our favor. The last two quarters, we both went back to playing basketball and we won, 41–30.

The championship baseball game with Bloomington was played in Peoria. I didn't pitch that game. I was playing right field. I hit a high, outside fastball that went out of the park. One coach walked it off afterward and said it traveled 560 feet. There was a lot of talk after the game about that homer, although the ground sloped outside the park, so for part of those 560 feet the ball was rolling downhill. It wasn't a turning point in the game or anything—we won by four runs, so the one I made didn't decide anything. But maybe it impressed a few scouts.

After we were state baseball champs, the guys appointed me to throw the coach, Darwin "Doc" Appleton, in the shower to celebrate. That was the tradition. I was six foot one by now and weighed one-ninety, and Doc isn't very big. When he tells the story now, he says I just picked him up with one hand and held him under the shower with his clothes on, but he's exaggerating. Actually, I used two hands.

The only Proviso player named to the *Tribune's* subur-ban league baseball all-stars was Lee Stange, a pitcher. But the paper picked me and a couple of other players for the second team.

If I hadn't been able to play games during this period, it's hard to tell what would have happened to me. Sports was the thing that kept me involved with school. And if it hadn't been for athletics, I would never have gone to college. I would probably have ended up learning a trade or maybe being a factory worker or going into the construction field —some kind of job where you don't need much schooling but can learn as you go along.

Sports was what I lived for in high school because there wasn't much else. My brothers were good to me, but I felt I was somebody who didn't have anything. I still missed my mother and resented having lost her and I was still taking it out on everybody else. That's one thing I liked about football. With the man-to-man contact, it gave me a good way to get things out of my system. It was better than going around the neighborhood, belting everybody.

I had no ambitions outside of sports. I had nobody to look up to and say, "I want to be a doctor or a lawyer or an architect or a mechanic, like him." We didn't have a car, so I never got involved in mechanics. We had balls and bats.

I was one of those kids who'd buy bubble gum and throw the gum away but keep the cards. I had hundreds of those cards. I could tell you all about the baseball and football players—their height, weight, averages. I was a Cubs fan, and sometimes I'd go over to Wrigley Field to see them play. It took maybe an hour and a half to get there. You had to ride several different buses. I was a Bears fan, too, of course. I must have seen my first game when I was thirteen or so, but I followed football long before that. The Bears had some great teams. Like the one in 1943, when I was seven, where Bronko Nagurski came out of retirement to play one more season and Chicago beat Washington for the championship. The score was 41–21. When Nagurski quit after that year, he'd gained 4,013 yards in nine seasons. If you'd asked me in 1943, I could have told you such statistics. I'd read them on my bubble gum cards.

As a kid, you have to have somebody to go with you to see a game, so I seldom got to go. But they were starting to televise the games by the time I got to high school, and I could watch. I used to hope I'd be good enough to play for the Bears, even when I was a shrimp who weighed less than a hundred pounds.

It was hard to get interested in anything in school that didn't have anything to do with sports. I had trouble in English, for instance. One time we were supposed to write a theme, and the teacher kept suggesting topics to me, and none of them sounded good. Finally she suggested I write about the Rose Bowl. Hey, that was a great idea. Sure, I could write about the Rose Bowl, because one of these days, I believed, I'd be playing in it. As it turned out, I never did. But by the time I found out Illinois wasn't going to make it during my college days, it was too late to change my mind about writing that theme for high school English.

I thought about playing in the Rose Bowl, but I wasn't really preparing myself for going to college. I didn't take the right subjects and I really didn't give much thought to what I'd do after high school until I was a senior. Then I considered going into military service or maybe trying to play professional baseball. But I couldn't put everything together and decide what I wanted to do with my life. I just wanted to get through high school. I wasn't looking ahead.

Then I started getting scholarship offers from various universities, and for the first time I could see that college really was a possibility for me, if I wanted to go. I wasn't sure I did. I didn't much care for schoolwork—it was just something you had to do to stay eligible for the games. I liked history, and when I got interested in a subject I did pretty well, but rhetoric and composition were tough. So was math. I wasn't interested in such things, and I just went through the motions.

Now that I was one of the high school's star players in three sports, it helped bring me out socially a little more. I stayed clear of dances and that kind of stuff—I stayed away from girls—but I started going to the pizza parlor and the drug store, the places the other kids went. I began to feel as if I was their equal. Before, I'd felt I didn't have anything to offer.

The reason the college scouts were impressed enough so I'd begun getting scholarship offers was that I'd done pretty well that year as a quarterback. I'd completed 50 of 99 passes for 750 yards and 9 touchdowns, and I'd gained 213 yards running with the ball, averaging about 5 yards a carry. We played defense as well as offense, and I'd made a lot of tackles, although Coach Puplis kept complaining I was too eager to get in on the action. I'd leave my assigned position too early. Sometimes they'd float a pass over my head to a receiver I was supposed to be covering.

With scholarship offers coming from different directions, I finally woke up to the fact that I had a decision to make. Puplis was the one who really helped me make it.

"Go to college, Ray," he kept telling me. "Make something of yourself. Take advantage of your God-given ability."

I looked up to him. I decided that if the coach said I should go to college, maybe he was right.

Because I was one of thirty-three high school players picked for an all-state football squad, I got to eat dinner at the executive mansion in Springfield with Governor

William G. Stratton—the school let me go to this one, so I didn't have to send my uncle. All of us on the squad also went to Champaign-Urbana to hear a talk by the governor, but the speech I paid more attention to there was given by Ray Eliot. He was the Illinois coach and one of my heroes. We got to meet the entire Illinois football squad. Pete Palmer, "the Illini's singing tackle," sang a new song called "Illinois" and introduced the homecoming queen, Margie Burger, and the nine coeds of her court, who gave us autographed pictures of themselves.

We began to get the idea that the people at Illinois would like to have the thirty-three best players in the state decide to become freshmen there. The trip made going there seem like a pretty good idea, but I still wasn't sure. I had a chance to go into professional baseball and start earning money, besides not having to study any more English or math.

The St. Louis Browns would give me three thousand dollars just to sign my name, and that seemed like all the money in the world. Nobody I knew had ever cashed a check for three thousand dollars. If I didn't grab the chance now, maybe I'd never get that much money in one lump the rest of my life.

The Browns weren't the best team—in fact, a lot of years they were the worst, although they did better after they moved to Baltimore and became the Orioles—but getting a chance to play in the big leagues appealed to me. I'd always enjoyed baseball. It's an individualist's game. Compared to football, it's easy. Football is part individual effort, but it's more work and a lot more physical.

But Andy Puplis said not to sign with the Browns.

"Get yourself an education, Ray. Make something of yourself."

I hated to pass up that bonus check, but I could see he was right. But even after I'd decided to go to college, I still wasn't sure where. Some schools wouldn't consider me because of my C average, but there were plenty of places that wanted me to play football for them. I visited Miami and some other colleges, but I finally decided on Illinois.

When I was a high school sophomore, J. C. Caroline was a senior there, and the Illini had a fine team. Puplis said he'd sent other boys there and Eliot had taken good care of them. But the main thing that sold me on Illinois was that it was in the Big Ten. So if I made the team and we won the championship, I'd play in the Rose Bowl. That was the No. 1 game, and I wanted to be the quarterback and win it, which would show all those kids back at Proviso that Ray Nitschke was as good as anybody when he had a football in his hand.

CHAPTER II

When I enrolled in the University of Illinois in the fall of 1954, I was a real selfish guy who didn't have much love for anything or anybody. I worried about myself. I didn't have much interest in anybody else. I stayed away from people, and they stayed away from me.

I wasn't really prepared for college. I'd never done much homework in high school, and I didn't have any idea how to study. It took me a year to learn. Everything moved so much faster. The classes were so much bigger. You didn't have a chance for the same kind of personal relationships with the teachers I'd been used to.

I was on a football scholarship that gave me a full ride —room, board, and tuition, with a job in the Athletic Association laundromat that paid about fifty dollars a month for spending money. A good share of the other sixty guys on the freshman squad were on full or partial scholarships, too.

For half of my first semester, I roomed with Jan Smid, a senior who was captain of the football team and an All-American guard. He grew up around River Grove, where his aunt and uncle had a restaurant, so I'd known him and his family. He was a good guy. He helped me get oriented to the school. Later he was drafted by Green Bay, but he got hurt in training camp and that was the end of that.

I'd majored in physical education because I wanted

to study something I was interested in and I didn't want to try to be something I wasn't cut out to be.

I'd been a big shot my last year or two of high school, but in a school like Illinois it's hard for a freshman to be anything more than a face in the crowd. This took some getting used to, and so did the idea that being a student athlete could be a disadvantage to you as well as an advantage. People assume that if you're a football player you get a free ride in the classroom. It didn't work out that way for me. There were a few classes where being an athlete helped— the profs knew who you were, and you got some special attention. But there were other teachers who put you down as a dumb jock as soon as they heard you were a football player, even before you'd opened your mouth. Some teachers, especially in the physical education department, took a special interest in me when I was playing regularly because they wanted to be sure I'd stay eligible. But others were tougher on us than they were on the rest of the students. I guess it all averaged out, but it didn't add up to the kind of free ride for football players you're always hearing about. There was one prof who made me sit all by myself in the back of the classroom because I played football.

That bothered me some, but what bothered me more was learning to study. I had to take English, and I'd had trouble with that even in high school. I had to really work at it, but I had even more trouble with botany. The only tutor I had in college was hired by the Illinois Alumni Association to help me get through that course. I couldn't get it through my numbskull—all that stuff about plants. The only thing I knew about plants was that my aunt cooked some of them and served them in her tavern. The customers there didn't care to know anything about the plants' private lives.

I might be having trouble in some of the classrooms, but on the football field things were going pretty well. I was the quarterback of the freshman team. People said I wasn't the most graceful fellow who'd ever played that position, but it was hard to bring me down when I had the ball. One sports columnist wrote that I "didn't run to daylight—he ran to flesh." I remember one game that year when I was returning a punt. A big tackle from the other team hit me so hard you could hear the "thunk" all over the field. The impact knocked me back a step, but I was still on my feet. The tackle fell, arms outstretched, like a piece of tall timber. I still remember the astonished expression on his face as he looked up to watch me going by.

Bobby Mitchell, who went on to star for the Washington Redskins, was another of the freshmen, and he had great speed and hands even then. He and I would go out on the practice field and I'd fire long ones to Bobby, who'd grab them deep in the end zone. We were practicing for next year when we'd be sophomores and eligible to play for the varsity and I'd be able to throw passes like that to him in the games. I was still making plans to be an All-American quarterback.

But Ray Eliot was making some plans, too. And our plans were different.

Getting ready for that 1955 season, the coach was having quite a run of problems. Joe Gorman, the No. 1 fullback, had been ruled ineligible. Then Don Kraft, Joe's replacement, had to have his appendix out two days after practice started. Some years later, Vince Lombardi made a medical breakthrough by proving he could get a player back in the lineup only ten days after an appendectomy. But Dr. Lombardi wasn't around Illinois, and Ray Eliot was going into a tough season with only one fullback, Danny Wile. He needed someone to back him up.

It was early in my sophomore year when Eliot called me into his office and said: "Ray, which would you rather be: the second-string quarterback or my first-string fullback?"

My heart sank. I could see where a question like that was leading.

"Coach," I said, "I'd rather be the first-team quarterback."

But the way Eliot saw it, I was no better than third in line in the quarterback competition. He had two veteran quarterbacks, Hiles Stout and Em Lindbeck, and he didn't think I could beat either one of them out of a starting job. I thought I could—in fact, I was sure in my own mind that I could. But he was the coach.

"Ray," he said, "as of now, you're not a quarterback on this team. You're a fullback."

So there went my dream of quarterbacking a team in the Rose Bowl. I was so disappointed I did something that big, tough, hard-nosed college football players aren't supposed to do. I sat there in his office and cried.

Looking back on it now, I can see that Ray had another reason for switching me. In those days, college players had to play both offense and defense. The fullback played linebacker when the other team had the ball, and the coach knew I enjoyed contact, an attitude you watch for in picking your linebackers. He said after watching me in practice that I was "a vicious player." He meant it as a compliment.

So that's how I became a linebacker. I was still thinking

offense, but I enjoyed getting out there on defense and knocking a few people down.

Now that I was eighteen years old I weighed a little over two hundred pounds, about double what I'd weighed the last time I'd played fullback. That had been on the freshman C team at Proviso. It had been a long time since I'd had to get down in a three-point stance. As a quarterback, I'd been handing off or throwing the ball or maybe running with it. Now all of a sudden I was putting one hand on the ground and coming out of a three-point stance, and I had a tough time getting used to the change, especially going laterally. I didn't have real quickness off the snap as a sophomore or even a junior. It took me until my senior year at Illinois before I had the natural feel of going in either direction or going forward, depending on the play.

I think one reason I lost out on a chance to play quarterback was that the coaching staff hadn't been sure I'd be able to play at all. After my freshman year, my grades were so low that I had to go to summer school to try to bring them up so I'd be eligible. I carried the maximum number of credits, nine. I've never studied as hard in my life as I did that summer. I really bore down, and it paid off because I finally passed English and botany. But the coaches weren't sure how I was going to make out scholastically, and at spring practice before my sophomore year, when I worked out with the varsity, I was no better than third- or fourth-string. I didn't work out with the two top teams, and I didn't have much chance to show what I could do as a quarterback.

The last two years of college, the success I had begun to have in football made me a little more confident, and I did better with my schoolwork. It wasn't until then that I felt

I really belonged in college. It wasn't until I was a junior that I started getting away from my old habit of feeling sorry for myself.

Our opening game my sophomore year was against California. Eliot had decided to add the belly series to his T formation offense. The play began as if the fullback were going to smash into the line with the ball. The quarterback would shove the ball in the fullback's belly, sometimes letting him keep it and sometimes withdrawing the ball and pitching it wide to the halfback or keeping it himself. To make the belly series work, the fullback has to be a good actor. He has to make the other team believe he has the ball when he doesn't have it. Eliot had originally planned to save the belly series until the third game so he could spring it as a surprise on Ohio State. But he changed his mind and told us to use it in the opener with California.

Danny Wile started the game at fullback, but before long the coach put me in. I was told afterward that I ought to get an Oscar for acting. I kept getting tackled by half the California team while somebody else was carrying the ball. On one play, the movies showed California's left tackle charging toward the quarterback, then stopping and going after me. When he finally realized I didn't have the ball, he whirled again and got knocked down by one of his own men. Meanwhile, Lindbeck was passing to Bob DesEnfants for a thirty-four-yard gain.

I did well enough against California so Eliot let me start against Iowa State. We'd beaten California by a touchdown, and we came out fast against the Iowans. I was too eager. Early in the game, I fumbled twice. It made me sore at myself, and the next time I got the ball I hung onto it. In fact,

I scored three of the six touchdowns we made in beating Iowa State 40–0. The newspapers started calling me the "Proviso Pounder." When I went to classes the following Monday, quite a few people had heard of Ray Nitschke.

Some of the sportswriters had picked Illinois to win the Big Ten that year, so there was a lot of interest in the next game. Ohio State was in the middle of a thirteen-game winning streak. The Buckeyes had won the title in 1954, so if we could beat them we might be on our way to the Rose Bowl. But they beat us, 27–12.

Unfortunately, I didn't play in that game or the next one, which was against Minnesota. I'd pulled up lame with a charley horse in practice, so Wile moved back in as fullback. I was well again for the Michigan State game, though. That gave me a chance to chase Earl Morrall, who was showing some of the ability as a quarterback he'd later demonstrate with the pros. We were leading by one point in the third quarter, but we lost, 19–14.

It was a frustrating season. Instead of winning the championship and a chance at the bowl, we wound up with a 5–3–1 record over-all and 3–3–1 in the Big Ten. Ohio State went unbeaten and took its second straight championship.

I remember how I felt that year in the Purdue game, which came after the one we lost to Michigan State. It was raining. The field was muddy. When I was on defense I'd look across at this offensive tackle, and he was so big that even though he was down on a three-point stance and I was standing straight up, he was looking me square in the eye. After the first quarter, they brought in another offensive tackle, and I thought life might get a little easier. But I

31

looked over and this guy was bigger than the first one. He started knocking me around, and I was getting wetter and muddier with every play, and I got to thinking: "What am I doing out here?"

But I survived, which gave me something to look forward to. Next Saturday, we'd get a chance to play Michigan. All they'd done was win six straight games, and the week before they'd gained 289 yards in the air and made 3 touchdowns on passes. They had a kid named Ron Kramer, who was supposed to be something special in pass catchers. He was, too, as I found out when we played together a few years later at Green Bay.

But that afternoon when we were sophomores, Ron didn't have much of a day. In fact, he caught only one pass all afternoon. At one point, Michigan tried four straight passes from our sixteen-yard line and missed them all. When we'd finished the game the score was 25–6 in our favor, which was the worst beating Michigan had taken from Illinois since Red Grange helped whip them 39–14 in 1924. Our pass defense held them to three completions out of twenty-two.

Michigan had to play most of the game without their halfback, who was their best runner. In the first quarter, he and I met on our twenty-one-yard line. He didn't come to for several minutes, and they carried him off on a stretcher. He wasn't seriously hurt, but Coach Bennie Oosterban didn't send him back in.

As a fullback, I was being used mostly as a blocker. I needed to develop more finesse as a runner, and that took time. It wasn't until my senior year that I felt I'd developed into a pretty good running back.

Even though I was getting to be well known around the campus because of my football, I still wasn't really acclimated to college life. I was a big-city boy in what I considered corn country. When people heard I was from a Chicago suburb, they thought I had to be a tough guy. So I was trying to live up to my bad-guy image, and I made some problems for myself.

I'd stayed away from beer in high school, but in college it seemed as if everybody was drinking it, and I wanted to be like the rest of them. But I couldn't handle it. A few beers and I'd get belligerent. I'd say the wrong things to the wrong people. Stupid, immature things. Nothing real bad or malicious, but I'd get in a fight here and there. I didn't realize that I was a guy who just couldn't handle alcohol, that I should leave it to the ones who can handle it or think they can. To me, it was firewater.

It was while I was at Illinois that I started smoking, too. This was before the government made the tobacco companies print health warnings on packs of cigarettes, but any athlete knew smoking was no way to keep in shape. But somebody dared me to try a Chesterfield, and I did. I had to inhale it right away, of course—if you're going to do something, go all the way—and it made me sick. But pretty soon I was lighting up with the best of them, and it took ten years to get rid of the habit. Then I switched to pipes for a while. I'd buy a new pipe every couple of weeks. Before long I realized I was spending a lot of money on pipes, I was scattering tobacco all over the house, and I wasn't really enjoying all the bother. So I quit tobacco entirely. It would have saved me a lot of trouble if I'd just been smart enough not to have to prove what a big shot I was when that fellow in college dared me to light up and inhale.

Trying to be one of the boys and hanging around taverns in Champaign did have one good effect. I'd been going mostly to Kamm's Annex, the place some of the other players went, but one day I wandered into the Tumble Inn, and while I was there I met the man who ran the place, Al Herges. We hit it off. He took me under his wing. He treated me as part of his family. He became a guy I really looked up to, a father image for me. I hadn't been aware of it, but I was looking for somebody like that who could give me something I'd been missing. He had a wonderful family, and I grew to love them all. There was his daughter, Nancy, and two younger boys, Butch and Peter, and Al's wife, Lorraine. They knew I had no real home life and they let me feel I was welcome, so I always had a place to go. It helped me to get away from that big school with all its pressures and frustrations and just relax with a fine group of people like that.

Every Sunday, I'd go over to the Herges' house and eat a big meal, and afterward we'd sit around and talk. I wanted to let him know I appreciated all this so once, when I'd gone home over the weekend, I brought back all my baseball cards, the ones I'd collected all through grade school and high school. Al collected them, too. I had two shoeboxes filled with those cards, and I gave them to him.

"Someday football teams will have cards like this," I told him. "Then you'll see my picture on one of them."

"Sure, Ray. Sure I will."

Al was kidding when he said that. But I wasn't.

If I was going to get my face on any cards it wasn't going

to be because my team was setting any records, however. My junior year we won only two games. We lost five and tied two. It's not a season the alumni do much bragging about. Still, we had one game that year I like to remember. It was against Michigan State. MSU was ranked No. 1 in the country, and Illinois must have ranked about No. 998. The writers said we were twenty-one-point underdogs.

We didn't feel like twenty-one-point underdogs when we ran on the field that afternoon, though. Morrall, MSU's quarterback, had been getting a lot of publicity, and he deserved it. But we'd proved to ourselves the year before that we could handle his passing game. We thought we were pretty fair football players, too, no matter what the sportswriters said. Even after we were behind 13–0 at the half, we went into the dressing room convinced that we could still win.

In the third quarter, I got a chance to carry the ball instead of block, and I got through the line and went for thirty-eight yards. Before long, our halfback, Abe Woodson, went over for a score. He made two more touchdowns in that second half while we were holding the No. 1 team in the country to no points. We won, 20–13. This game showed me something: A team that's ready to play to its full capacity can beat another team on a particular afternoon, even if the other team is supposed to be three touchdowns better.

It was in that 1956 season that I lost my four front teeth. When I'm introduced to somebody from Ohio State, I always think of that day in Columbus. I slip out my front plate and give the Ohio State alumnus a big smile, and I tell him: "That's what your school did to me."

He usually laughs, but sometimes he takes a step back, too. I'm not really sore about it any more, though. At the time, I felt differently.

That afternoon in Columbus, I figured I was too tough to wear a face mask, and I was running down the field after the opening kickoff when this big guard came over and blocked me. With his head, right in the mouth. Two of my upper teeth went flying, and two more were hanging by the roots.

During a time out, somebody shoved a wad of cotton in my mouth and I went on with the game, spitting blood all over the field.

"How am I going to look with no teeth?" I kept thinking. "How am I going to look with no teeth?"

I played the whole sixty minutes that day, but I didn't have a good sixty minutes. As normally happened in Columbus, we got beat. After the game, the rest of the guys headed for the dressing room and the fans shuffled along toward the exists, but I went back on the field. I started scrounging around, looking for my teeth. Somebody asked me what I wanted them for.

"I want them because they're mine," I growled, still walking around, looking for them.

I never did find them, though. Maybe they're still there.

In college, we played a six-man line with two linebackers. We didn't have a middle linebacker. I was always over a big tackle or a big guard. By the time I was a senior, I'd grown to 6 foot 3 and I weighed 225 pounds, only ten less than now. But some of those linemen in the Big Ten outweighed me by seventy-five pounds. I had to learn how to deal with them on defense.

The fans didn't pay much attention to defense then—they hadn't been educated by watching those TV closeups and instant replays we have now. But the coaches and the players knew how important defense was in winning games, and I was beginning to get a reputation as a pretty fair linebacker. I didn't know a lot of the things then that I know now about doing the job, but I had enthusiasm, and I was usually in on the play. My senior year, I was the team's leading tackler. And each time I tackled somebody, I tried to make sure that when he got up and walked away he'd remember he'd met Ray Nitschke. And I don't mean socially.

Some of them remembered those tackles for quite a while. Len Wilson, the Purdue halfback, told a sportswriter, "I've never been hit as hard in my football career as Nitschke hit me," and another player described what happened when I had the ball and he tried to tackle me:

"All I remember is waking up in the locker room twenty minutes later."

The coaches let me carry the ball more in my senior year, and I wound up with a 6.2 yards-per-carry average and a total of 386 yards rushing, sixth best in the Big Ten. I made a good share of those yards in the games against Colgate and Northwestern. I almost didn't get a chance to start that Colgate game. I'd been demoted to second string after we lost the season opener to California, and Jack Delveaux, who later played in the Canadian League, was supposed to start in my spot. But he got hurt in scrimmage, and I got my job back. The thought of having come so close to sitting on the bench made me try a little harder. I wanted to show Ray Eliot he'd made a mistake by not realizing that one thing Nitschke wasn't was second string. The first time we got the ball I went through center for thirty-two yards, and a little later I ran for a touchdown from the eleven.

I made three touchdowns altogether that day, including one on a pass I caught in the end zone. Late in the game, the coach took pity on the Red Raiders and started emptying the Illinois bench, but we beat them 40–0.

In one practice scrimmage that year, we were playing the third team. They got close to our goal line, and on fourth down the ball went to Delveaux, who was still hoping to get my job. I wasn't about to let him score. I stopped him on the one. So that gave us the ball with ninety-nine yards to go for a touchdown.

"All right, you guys," Ray Eliot yelled. "If you score from there, I'll buy the milk shakes."

What he had in mind was a sustained march—short plays through the line, sideline passes. But we were thirsty. On the first play, Dick Nordmeyer and Percy Oliver opened a hole off right tackle and I went through it, then cut to my left and started pumping my legs as hard as they would go downfield. Eddie DeLong was the safety. He saw he was going to have to try to stop me all by himself. He tried, but I gave him the stiff-arm and went over the goal. This wasn't the kind of ninety-nine-yard march the coach had in mind, but he had to buy.

In our last game of the season, we used exactly the same play. We had a 2–4 record by then and Northwestern was 0–6, so about all we had to prove was which of the two Illinois schools was better. Eliot decided to play ball control and let me do most of the carrying.

The day before the game, I got to talking with a sportswriter named Bert Bertine from the Champaign-Urbana

Courier, and I told him I wished I could have just one long touchdown run before my college career was over. Thanks to the same play that won us those milk shakes, I got my wish.

We weren't on our own one this time, but we were eighty-four yards away from the Northwestern goal line. The quarterback handed me the ball and I went through tackle. A guy named Nick Andreotti had me for a moment, but I got loose and took off. There were a couple of good blocks that helped, including one at midfield by Rich Kreitling, and I made it all the way. That run was the longest from scrimmage by an Illinois player since Buddy Young gained ninety-three yards against Great Lakes Naval Training Station's team in 1944.

I made another touchdown from the three-yard line in that Northwestern game and had a hand in a third—I got near the goal, but then I fumbled, and Kreitling picked up the ball and went in to score. Altogether, I made 170 yards that day, the most I'd ever made. It was a good way to finish off a college career.

I'd been hoping to be picked as an All-American. When I was a senior, I really felt I deserved it. But the school wasn't pushing me for it. I went to the publicity man and asked him to tell me confidentially why not.

"Well, Ray," he said, "we just don't have a chance to get two All-Americans this year with a record like ours. And there's another fellow we want to push."

The other fellow was Rod Hansen, a fine offensive and defensive end, a real fast player. He didn't make it either, though. He was picked for the All-Big Ten team and I was picked for the second team. It was quite a letdown.

I'd wanted to be an All-American ever since I was a little kid, reading the sports pages and dreaming of playing in the Rose Bowl. We never got to the Rose Bowl, and I wasn't picked as an All-American. But in my own mind, I thought I was one. And that was important to me.

I did make one list. Paul Brown, who was with Cleveland and who was the most successful coach in the country, included me in his roster of college seniors the pros would most like to get. He said I was the top college linebacker. Brown's list was backed up by a lot of scouting by men who knew football. It didn't agree with the lists of All-Americans picked by sportswriters, but it meant something.

Another coach who thought I belonged with the best college players was Otto Graham. He picked me for the College All-Stars, along with some guys I'd get to know a lot better in future years. That was quite a squad of college boys. It included guys like Jim Taylor, Alex Karras, Jerry Kramer, Lou Michaels, Dan Currie, and Wayne Walker. We played the Detroit Lions, the National Football League champions. And we beat them, 35–19.

I also played in the Senior Bowl on a team that was coached by Joe Kuharich of the Redskins. That was the first time that game was on national television. It was also the first time I got paid for playing a game I'd been involved with ever since I was old enough to lift a football.

So now came the time when we waited, like wallflowers at a dance hall, to see if some pro team would ask us to play. I had enough confidence in myself to believe I'd be drafted, and I hoped the call would come from Chicago. I'd been a Bears' fan so long. I'd thought how great it would be to run out on that field with that team instead of watching them on TV. But I guess George Halas didn't want me, because when the draft came I was passed over on the first two rounds by everybody. On the third round I was drafted, but it wasn't by the Bears.

Green Bay? I knew about the Packers because they played Chicago, and I knew there was a little town up north somewhere that had a football team. But when I got word that I was the twenty-seventh college senior picked in the draft and that I'd been chosen by the Packers, I had to get out a map to find out where Green Bay was.

CHAPTER III

After fifteen years of playing for the Packers, I know where Green Bay is now. It's where my home is. But after the 1958 draft, I wasn't at all sure I wanted to go there. Not that I had much choice. In those days, if you wanted to play pro football you either played with the NFL team that drafted you or you went to the Canadian League. It wasn't like two years later, when the NFL began competing with the new American Football League and everybody started throwing big money around.

I'd felt hurt when the Bears didn't draft me, but they had such linebackers as Bill George and Joe Fortunato. Teams draft for positions where they're weak. I wondered why the Packers had picked me because they were pretty strong at linebacker, too, with guys like Tom Bettis and Bill Forester.

I believed I could play in the NFL. All I wanted was a chance. But I wasn't sure the Packers wanted me very much. Lisle Blackbourn, the coach, saw me after the North-South Shrine game and offered me a contract, but it wasn't much of a contract. It was for something like seven thousand dollars, and all the other players were talking about getting more than that. I wondered what Blackbourn was trying to pull. It seemed like he was belittling my ability, and I knew I could make his team. I wasn't too impressed with Coach Blackbourn.

He wanted me to sign the contract right then. He acted like he was doing me a big favor.

"No, coach," I told him. "I'm not going to sign right now."

I'd also been drafted by the Toronto Argonauts. After my experience with Blackbourn, I decided I'd better go up to Canada to see what they had to offer. I made plane reservations. Then I called Jack Vainisi, an administrative assistant and talent scout for the Packers.

"I'm flying to Toronto," I told him.

"Hold everything, Ray. I'll be right down there. I'll meet you in Chicago and we'll have supper together and talk things over."

So we had a good meal, and he was the one who kept me from going to Canada. The contract I signed was for only a little more than the one Blackbourn offered, but Vainisi agreed to give me five hundred dollars cash just for putting my name down on that piece of paper.

That five hundred dollars seemed like a large sum of money. But it wasn't just that. I liked the way Jack had come down to see me. It gave me the feeling that the Packers were really interested in Ray Nitschke after all. If it hadn't been for that, I might never have gone to Green Bay, and things would have turned out a lot differently.

If I'd been a couple of years younger and had come along two years later, I would have made out a lot better financially. But I can't complain. I was pleased with that five hundred dollars. I could appreciate that kind of money. I didn't know any better.

A five-hundred-dollar bonus was probably the going rate at the time for third-round draft choices—anyway, I hope it was. My contract was about average. I didn't consider it too bad. I knew that seven thousand dollars a year was more than most schoolteachers were making then—all those teachers of botany and English and things like that.

The Packers hadn't drafted me as a fullback. They'd picked Jim Taylor for that job. I thought I could play fullback for them—I couldn't run the ball as well as some, but I could catch passes and block. I thought I could play offense. But I recognized that linebacker on defense was my best position because of my size, range, aggressiveness, and ability to follow the ball instinctively.

In college, we didn't have a middle linebacker. But I knew that was the job that would suit me. It was the focal point of the defense. I've always liked to be in the middle of things, which was why I'd been disappointed when I couldn't play quarterback in college. I thought I could handle the middle linebacker's job. I have good range and enough agility. I'm not extremely fast, but I'm fast enough. The main thing in playing that position is to be quick on your feet.

A year or two before I got there, the pro teams had changed from a five-man line to a four-man line. This gave the middle linebacker more responsibility. He had to be big enough to stop the run but quick enough to cover short receivers.

In college ball, you were primarily interested in stopping the run because there wasn't so much passing. With the pros, the linebacker's responsibility for defending against the pass was much greater.

I knew the Packers hadn't done too well the season before. In fact, before I reported to training camp, Blackbourn had been fired, and Ray "Scooter" McLean was coach. But it was a professional team, regardless of its won-lost record, and it was something for a young guy who'd been a fan to know he was going to be on the same squad as people like Jim Ringo, Bill Forester, Dave Hanner, and Bill Howton— not to mention a 235-pound player named Tom Bettis, who was starting his third season. Bettis was the one I had to beat out if I wanted to be a first-string middle linebacker, which was exactly what I planned to be.

There were some second-year men I recognized, too. I knew Ron Kramer from having played against him, and I'd read about Paul Hornung when he was Notre Dame's Golden Boy and getting his name in the Chicago papers. The first-string quarterback was Babe Parilli. Bart Starr was starting his third year, but nobody paid much attention to him. It didn't seem likely that he had much of a future in pro football.

Before Liz Blackbourn got fired, he'd said he might use me as a defensive end or a linebacker. He told a sportswriter the main thing about me was that all the scouts had called me a "mean cuss." But McLean didn't give me a tryout at end. He did have me working out as an outside linebacker part of the time, but middle linebacker was the place I wanted to play.

Before I left the Illinois campus, I bought myself a four-year-old Pontiac, putting three hundred dollars down. That left me two hundred dollars from my bonus, so after the school year ended and I was on my way to Green Bay, I drove past Herges' house. Al's son, Butch, was out in the yard, shooting baskets. I handed him the two hundred dollars.

"Buy your mom, your brother, your sister, your dad, and your aunt some clothes," I told him, and drove off.

He didn't want to take the money. But I figured I'd eaten at least two hundred dollars worth of groceries those Sundays I'd gone over there for dinner and the chance to enjoy a little family life. I have a pretty fair appetite at the table. My wife says now that I don't eat food, I inhale it.

So I drove into Green Bay in my '54 Pontiac, and I can see now I came on too heavy. Here I was, a big-city slicker. Here I was in this little town, and I didn't realize that being a football player in Green Bay is different than being one in Chicago. I didn't know you couldn't do the things you could get away with in a big city. I didn't realize how important the Packers were to the community. My ego was big, and I made a fool of myself.

I was still a loner. I was all for Ray Nitschke. I didn't worry about anybody else. I had a selfish attitude about everything and everybody.

I must have looked funny walking around Green Bay because I didn't have my feet on the ground. I talked too loud. I got too boisterous. After a game, I'd sometimes get too much alcohol under my belt and I'd get obnoxious.

In Chicago, the attitude was that if a fellow wants to be a jerk, let him be a jerk. But in Green Bay, if a player acted like a jerk they were concerned about it. The people there didn't want you to act that way because it reflected on their pride and joy, the football team. It took me a while to realize the impact the Packers have on the community and how many people in Green Bay are sincerely interested in the team's welfare.

I was being a big shot—a big spender from the big city.

Actually, I was small fry. I'd get too many drinks and get loud. Drinking always brought out my childhood frustrations, my inferiority complex that went back to the feeling that God had pulled a dirty trick on Ray Nitschke by taking his mother just when he needed her most.

That chip on my shoulder would swell up from the alcohol inside me. If anybody looked at me the wrong way when I started drinking, I'd think he was infringing on my privacy. He could have been thinking of something else entirely. Maybe he couldn't care less whether I was around, but I'd think he was giving me a wrong look, and I'd start something with him. If he was smiling, I'd think he was laughing at me. It was a childish attitude—literally childish. It was my childhood complex coming out.

After the season began and the Packers started losing, week after week, there were a lot of stories about how we were doing all of our best playing after hours. When you're losing, people start looking for reasons. We were a group of young, aggressive males, and we were old enough to go to bars. If you're losing and people see you in a bar, they figure you're drunk. When you're winning, they don't say anything. But when you're losing, you're all a bunch of drunkards.

I wasn't really doing that much drinking—I don't need more than a drink or two to get obnoxious—but the hassles I kept getting into didn't help the team reputation any. There has to be an alibi when you're not doing well. I don't think it was alcohol that kept the Packers from winning that season. I think we would have had the same record if we'd all trained on nothing but buttermilk. We had some good players, and sometimes we'd put our game together and play well. But we wouldn't play well for a full sixty minutes. There were a lot of games that year when we'd do fine for the first half or even the first three quarters, and then we'd die.

To win, everybody on a team has to play together, and the Packers weren't doing it. There were different factions on the team. There was a Texas faction, a veterans' faction that ignored the rookies, and some other factions. There were four or five guys here, four or five guys there. And then off to the side somewhere there was this loud kid from Illinois, Ray Nitschke.

I wasn't in any of the factions. I was a faction all by myself. I was all for Ray, not worrying about anybody else. I was kind of an outcast. The veterans didn't like my attitude. I'd come to Green Bay with my mind made up that I wasn't going to take any bull from anybody.

I wanted to make the ball club. I wanted to be a pro. I wanted to make good. I wanted to show the people back at Proviso and my relatives and everybody who knew me that I was good enough to be a professional football player.

I still lacked maturity, on the field and off. I wasn't close to being a solid citizen. I didn't have anybody to love or to love me, and I took it out on people—the ones I met in bars as well as the guys carrying the ball on the field.

In spite of all this and in spite of the Packers having their worst season in history, 1958 was a good year for me. I was learning. I was experiencing new things. I was finding out that I didn't have to make all the hits—just my share. I was discovering that in the pros you take care of your own responsibility and then, after you've done that, you can move over and help make the tackle. I was too exuberant, too excited, too interested in getting to the ball carrier and making the stop myself instead of taking care of my own responsibility first.

Getting away from that attitude took experience and study and watching other people play. Gradually, I began putting things together. Football is not only a physical game, it's a process of learning. I'd see one guy who did one thing well and another who did something else well, and I kind of put my game together, trying to take the best from what the others were doing and put it into my own pattern of play.

It takes a professional at least three years before he really gets the feel of what he's doing; in the case of a quarterback, it takes even longer.

The hardest thing for an aggressive player to learn is to take care of his own assignment, even when it takes him away from the ball. You must fight down the temptation to get in on every tackle. You have to be consistent so your teammates know where you're going to be and can depend on you, because that's how a team develops the cohesion it needs.

Learning to play defense in the pro league isn't simple. I've always felt that the best football players are on defense. The offense knows exactly when that ball is going to be snapped, where it's going to be, who's going to be carrying it. It's up to the defense to react to whatever the offense throws at it, and that's a bigger challenge, not knowing what to expect. The defensive man has to diagnose the play, defeat his blocker, and get to the man with the ball. The offense has the advantage, so it's a great challenge to the defense to stop them.

I was too cocky as a rookie. I was fancy free and not worrying about anything. I didn't take anything from anybody. Looking back on it now, I can see I was something of a jerk.

I've always felt it took me longer to mature than is normal. In fact, I'm still maturing, still learning to adapt myself and my personality to people, learning to communicate and to be more receptive, to be more concerned with other people.

I think that most athletes—maybe 99 percent of them— get the feeling that they're better than anybody else when they're in high school or college. As a young player, I really thought I was hot stuff. I wanted people to like me and respect me, but I didn't know how to go about it. Young players get spoiled. If they're stars in school, they get a lot of publicity, a lot of attention, and they aren't ready to handle it.

They get patted on the back so often it affects their egos. A young player has a lot of temptations. You're in the limelight, so people want to be seen with you. They're always buying you drinks, buying you meals. The women, because you're well known, want to go out with you.

In high school and college, the school has some control over what you do. But when you're a rookie on a pro team, you're on your own. Nobody really cares about you. Management's attitude is that if you don't perform you will be replaced. Anybody can be replaced. So there are a lot of temptations when you first come into the league, and a lot of players find they can't handle them.

In school, you have to study in your spare time to stay eligible. But when you're a pro, you have more chance to get involved in the kind of stuff that you'll regret later. A lot of people get to believing that professional football is a fun trip. I can think of players who would have been great athletes if they'd taken care of themselves. Instead, they got too involved with alcohol or women or both. To be good at his job, an athlete has to discipline himself. And not just on the field. He has to discipline himself in his social life, too.

I wasn't handling myself too well off the field that rookie year of mine. But I had the determination to succeed, and that saved me from getting into more trouble than I did. I had a goal in mind, and the goal wasn't to set a new indoor record in the Fox River Valley, for most arguments started in barrooms. My goal was to make the team and become a starter.

I came on pretty strong. A lot of the veterans resented an attitude like that. A rookie has to prove himself, and when I got to Green Bay the veterans weren't too receptive even to the other new men, the ones who said, "yes, sir" and "excuse me." The rosters were smaller then. There were only thirty-six men on the squad instead of forty. If one or two rookies survived the cuts it was considered a big deal. And that year there were four of us who made the squad: Dan Currie, who'd been the first-round draft choice; Jim Taylor, Jerry Kramer, and me. So that meant four old-timers would have to leave. It didn't make us very popular, because some of the veterans were worried about leaving, and even the ones whose jobs were secure resented having to say goodbye to some of their friends who were being pushed out of a job by one of the young kids.

I went through the usual routine for rookies, including having to get up and sing. Making a first-year man stand up and try to carry a tune was part of the treatment then, as it is now. It's not a matter of hazing a young guy. It's a way to break the barrier that always exists between the veterans and the new men by letting a rookie show everybody who he is and where he went to school. On the field, you let your muscles do most of the talking, and there's no chance to get to know people well, even if you've just run into them full speed. The singing makes the young fellow feel he's part of the group.

And it seems like the ones who are a little bashful on the podium are apt to be bashful when it comes to tackling somebody. The better singers are apt to turn out to be the better players. One thing I've noticed over the years: If a rookie has a good day on the practice field, he sings better.

What you're trying to do is create the feeling that the team is a family group. With a large number of young men, each with his own ideas and most of them with big egos, that's not easy to do.

Before a rookie finds a place in the family, he has to be accepted by the veterans. That has to come from the veterans themselves. They're likely to accept those rookies who produce much quicker than the ones who aren't doing a job.

I've always had a mean streak, and it helped me when I went to camp with the Packers that first year. I had my mind made up that I was going to play pro ball, and if Green Bay didn't want me, I'd make it somewhere else. Before the last cut that summer, I went to Scooter McLean.

"If you're going to cut me, coach, let me know now so I can go someplace else."

"No, Ray. We're going to keep you."

Normally, the Packers kept only four linebackers, but that year they kept five—the fifth one was me. I was on all the special teams—kickoff return teams and the rest—and I think that's probably how I made the club. They like an aggressive player on those special teams—the suicide squads—and aggressiveness was something I had going for me.

McLean was a real nice guy—so nice that some of the players took advantage of him. Scooter had been an assistant for years and now he was trying to coach the same men he'd played cards with, his old friends. But a head coach has to be a little aloof. He has to be a disciplinarian. McLean just didn't have the stern kind of leadership that it takes to handle all those big egos that wear uniforms on a football team.

It was an embarrassing year for the Packers, with a season's record of 1–10–1. But I wasn't on the spot the way the coach and the more experienced players were. As a rookie, I didn't feel the pressure from the community and the fans, even though I started at middle linebacker because Bettis got hurt in the first exhibition game.

I tried to play with aggressiveness, which was what they said they wanted, but I wasn't going about it the right way. I was all over the field. I was out of position a lot of times. Playing middle linebacker was a whole new experience for me; it's a job that takes a lot of practice. I'd be hitting the wrong people.

As a rookie from Illinois, starting his first regular-season game against the Bears, I was especially enthused over the opener that year. It was a great feeling, running out on the field, even though when I was a kid I'd always hoped that when it happened I'd be wearing a Chicago uniform. I was playing opposite a big center—he must have been six foot seven—and I felt like a shrimp. I don't know if I hit the right people that afternoon, but I sure hit a few of them. I hope they came off the field knowing Ray Nitschke had made his debut.

The Bears beat us, 34–20. We tied the Lions, but the Colts won the next game. Washington was next, and I was still a starter. The Redskins' quarterback was Eddie LeBaron. A player his size would have trouble making the team now because the defenders are so much taller and faster, but in 1958 the little guy was a marvel. He was the most deceptive ball handler I've ever seen. You couldn't find Eddie behind all those beefy linemen, and you never knew where the ball was. You'd see it snapped and then Eddie would disappear, and before you knew it somebody was catching a pass or running down the field. He had great timing—not only in the way he handled the ball but in the way he got into the pro league before so many big, fast players arrived and started chasing quarterbacks.

The Washington player I had the most trouble with that Sunday afternoon in 1958 wasn't LeBaron but a back named Johnny Olszewski. He had a great game. He made 156 yards, and I was the one who got blamed. I was making tackles six feet past the line of scrimmage, so I don't think the fault was all mine—he must have done pretty well with our linemen, too. But I was the one who bore the brunt of the criticism, and the next week I was on the bench. Bettis' knee had healed, and he came back and finished out the season. I felt I was the fall guy. I didn't think that losing to Washington was all my fault. But you have to go with how the coaches feel.

54

The week after I lost my starting job we beat Philadelphia, which gave us a record of 1–3–1. Some of the fans started talking about how the team was finally starting to play together and might not do too poorly in the final standings. But the next game was with Baltimore, and after the Colts got through with us there wasn't much room left for optimism. The score was 56–0. We never lost that bad again in 1958, but we didn't win again, either.

You can get into the habit of being a winner and you can get into the habit of losing. You can go out on the field with the attitude that you'll do your best but there's no way you're going to win. The 1958 Packers had a loser's complex. Everybody lacked that little extra spark. We lost a lot of games in the last few minutes because of guys believing that they just couldn't win.

I was still trying to find my way. I was kind of wandering, looking for something but not knowing what I was looking for. I know now I was looking for somebody to share my life, to understand me and to love. But at this point, I wasn't really doing anything to improve myself—except on the field. There, I was learning something about my job and I was proving to myself that I could play with the best of them. In a way, I was proud of myself that year, although it wasn't a season where there was much reason to be proud if you worked for the Packers.

Professional football was different in those days. A fellow in Green Bay or Milwaukee could decide at noon on the day of the game that he'd like to see some football, and he could go out to Lambeau Field in Green Bay or County Stadium in Milwaukee and buy all the tickets he wanted.

If it was a nice day, the fans would turn out. If it was cold or rainy, they'd stay home.

It isn't that way now, of course. The only time there's an empty seat, even if it's twenty below, is if the ticketholder died. Even then, one of the relatives will probably skip the funeral and use the seat.

In 1958, Lambeau Field held only thirty-six thousand, compared to fifty-four thousand now. It started as a horseshoe and now it's a bowl. All around the league, the size of the stadiums has increased, and every year there are more people at the games. There are other differences, too. In 1958, we stayed at nice enough places when we were on the road. But there were hotels that didn't want our business. They preferred not to be associated with football players. We were looked on as a rough, tough bunch of brutes.

The dressing rooms were smaller then. Now they're much fancier places—carpets on the floor, stereo music, all of the most modern equipment. The hotels and motels all want us, because it's good for business to have us around. The football player's image has changed. He's a college graduate who's articulate, poised, suave, worldly—at least, that's the image people have of him.

In 1958, you could take off your helmet and put on regular clothes and nobody knew you. Today, it's amazing how often people recognize you on the street. It's like you were a movie star. With my bald head and horned-rim glasses—not to mention when I put in my front teeth after the game—I look a lot different away from the stadium, but people seem to know me just the same.

The big difference is television. In 1958, the games were on the tube every Sunday afternoon as they are now, but the audiences were smaller. The game was just starting to catch on big with the general public. You always had fans, but nowhere near as many of them then as now. Football was just on the verge of moving past baseball as the nation's most talked-about sport. Now it has arrived. All the tickets are sold long in advance at all the stadiums. The broadcasts of the games have high ratings—not only on Sunday afternoons but Monday nights. The players have become celebrities. It's a bigger responsibility than we had before because of the bigger audience and the greater spectator interest.

In 1958, the salaries for starting players ranged from sixty-five hundred dollars to maybe fifty thousand dollars. It's hard to tell what some players are making now with all these bonuses and their various clauses, but I'd guess the range is from ten thousand dollars to a hundred thousand dollars, not counting the bonus, with perhaps a few making over a hundred thousand.

But in 1958, I didn't know football was on the threshold of a new era, a more exciting era. All I knew after the season was over was that we hadn't done well in the standings, but it had been a good year for Ray Nitschke. I could play in the league. Now I didn't have to take a back seat for anybody.

CHAPTER IV

When Vince Lombardi took over the team for the 1959 season, he brought us together. Regardless of how many games we lost in '58, there was a lot of ability on that ball club, and he brought it out.

I'd been called up for active duty by the Army Reserves during the summer of 1959, so I missed Lombardi's first training camp. That meant I missed the hardest part of the year. The coach really tore into the players. Some of them passed out from heat prostration, and everybody worked harder than he'd ever thought possible.

If Lombardi hadn't decided to go into coaching, he could have opened up a dieting salon. Emlen Tunnell, a crafty old-timer from the Giants who came to Green Bay to play another season for Vince, tells of what happened that summer when Lombardi decided there was too much flab on several of the players. He singled out three of them: Tom Bettis, Dave Hanner, and Jerry Helluin.

"You guys got two weeks," he yelled. "Each of you take off twenty pounds or you're on your way home."

If you've ever tried to drop twenty pounds in fourteen days, you know it isn't easy. But Bettis and Hanner came close enough to satisfy the coach. Helluin didn't, which is one reason why most Packers' fans won't recognize the name. When the two weeks was up, he was out.

Bettis was the fellow I had to beat out for the middle

linebacking job. Except for some fast dieting that summer, I might have become a starter for Lombardi quite a bit sooner than I did.

A man can get used to almost anything except getting hung, so the players lived through those first Lombardi practice sessions. As Phil Bengtson said, almost all of them survived and "nobody vomited after a couple of days." I'm told that the squad lost an average of twelve pounds per man during training, but they found out they could take anything Lombardi could dish out. It made anything the opponents could do to them during the season seem like nothing at all.

I finished my Army training and met the team during the exhibition season. When I caught up with the Packers at Greensboro, North Carolina, the equipment manager gave me a word of advice.

"Watch yourself, Ray. Don't do anything you're not supposed to be doing. This Lombardi is really tough."

So here I was after six months in the Army, trying to establish myself all over again with a new coach. I thought the Army had me in pretty good condition. But I soon found out that the Army was one thing but Lombardi was something else. I wasn't in the shape he wanted me in, so I started working extra hard to catch up to the rest of the players. The practice sessions were much tougher than anything I'd experienced. The ones we'd had under McLean were a breeze by comparison.

I was young. I got myself in shape fast. But Lombardi didn't seem to be very impressed. Except for playing on the special teams, I didn't get a chance to play in the games in

Lombardi's first season. That left me disappointed and disgruntled, although I tried to joke about it.

"Just call me 'the judge,'" I told everybody. "All I do is sit on the bench."

If I'd been through training camp, things might have been different. But Lombardi didn't have any idea of what kind of football player I was. All he had to go on was the movies from the previous season, and that didn't mean too much because he had his own approach to football. I wanted a chance to prove to him that I was capable of playing. But once a season has started, a coach doesn't try to use everybody. He goes with the ones he has the most confidence in. You have to build a team's unity, and you don't do that by changing the lineup unnecessarily.

So he went with Bettis as his middle linebacker. Tom was probably the best friend I had on the team. He'd grown up not far from where I did, and we had a lot in common. I really liked him. I was sorry that he was playing my position. It was a shame, because I intended to get myself off that bench and put him on it.

I got sore at Lombardi because he wasn't playing me. I wasn't getting a fair chance to show what I could do. But that year on the bench helped me. It's good to sit down and find out that somebody else can play football, too. You discover that you're not the whole team, all by yourself. That year was part of my education.

The only time I got to play was late in the game when we were so far ahead or so far behind that it didn't matter. Even that was better than nothing. I'd sit there, collecting splinters, hoping we'd score a lot of points early in the game so I could go out on the field. But sometimes I wouldn't get a chance to go in even when the score was lopsided. I remember the Washington game. It was the fourth quarter. We were ahead 21–0. There was no way the Redskins were going to beat us, and I kept expecting the nod, but it didn't come. Finally, with only a few minutes left, I went over to Bengtson, who handled the defensive team.

"How about putting me in?"

"No," Phil said. "We want the shutout."

It wasn't a remark that did much for my morale.

As long as I had to sit there on the bench, I decided I might as well try to learn something. I watched how the other players handled their jobs, and I tried to pick up pointers. I paid special attention to the linebackers—ours and those who played for the other teams—but the player who really exemplified the type of athlete I wanted to be was another second-year man, Jimmy Taylor. The Packers had some great players then and I've known some great ones since, but Taylor was in a class by himself. In fifteen years with the pros, he's one of the toughest men I ever played against—and we were on the same team.

When we played against each other, of course, it was in practice, but that didn't make any difference to Jim. He was a man with great pride. He'd refuse to go down when you hit him. You had to hold him and yell for help.

He'd hurt you when you'd tackle him. He was as hard as a piece of granite. He had such strong legs. He had the attitude that he was going to run with that ball, and if you got in his way, look out. He was a tiger, the most determined man I ever played with, and I was glad he was on my side and I didn't have to go after him except in practice.

Getting ready for those Lombardi two-a-day practice

sessions, he'd lift weights in the early morning and again before we went back to practice in the afternoon. Those two-a-days were real drudgery, and the rest of us felt we didn't really need any more exercise than Lombardi dished out. It was something to see a guy who'd go out and lift weights during that annual period of agony. Taylor really pushed himself. But it paid off. He became one of the game's greatest fullbacks.

Here was a man without too much natural ability who wanted to be the best football player in the world. He showed me what could be done just on determination and desire. He played as if he were convinced there was no one in the world better than he was. He'd sting everybody. Sitting there and watching during that 1959 season, I decided that if Jimmy could play that hard when the Packers had the ball, I could play that hard on defense.

That is, I could if that damned Lombardi ever put me in. All I was doing was running down the field on kickoffs and punts. Back at Proviso, the kids might think their alumnus was a football player. But all he was right now was "the judge."

The way I felt about the coach not playing me didn't blind me to the fact that Lombardi was a different breed of leader than we'd had before. All those factions that had existed in 1958 disappeared when he got to Green Bay. He moved out the guys who'd been creating problems, and by the time his first season started he'd created a healthy atmosphere where nobody was satisfied unless we won. There wasn't room on a Lombardi team for cliques.

Henry Jordan has been quoted as saying that Lombardi treated everybody equal—like dogs. That was one of the jokes that went around, but it's true that he treated us all the same. He didn't care about your religion or your politics or your color or anything else. What he was interested in was whether you were willing to give 100 percent of your talents to the Green Bay Packers—or maybe 110 percent.

Under Lombardi, we never had any serious racial problems, the way some other clubs had. We had some real fine blacks on the club, fellows who were real gentlemen—guys like Willie Davis and Willie Wood and Herb Adderley and others, not only fine players but fine people. If we had any racial problems, I didn't know about them.

The Packers were the first NFL team to have blacks and whites rooming together on the road. That attitude was one of the reasons for the team's success. The black players had some problems in their off hours, living in a small city like Green Bay where there weren't too many places they liked to go to relax. But they learned to accept this. And it was a two-way street. I think Green Bay learned a lot from the ballplayers about not judging people by their skin color.

Lombardi made everybody on his team feel like part of one family. We'd work together, play together. There weren't different factions creating problems. If you can get an entire group involved, you've created something strong. If you have everybody running out on that field with the attitude that there's nobody going to beat you, you're hard to beat.

Lombardi knew football, but every coach knows football. His special asset was his ability to handle men. He got the most out of us. He knew our personalities. He studied our characters. He knew how to handle each individual. He knew when to be harsh and when to let up a little. His timing was perfect.

He really worked at coaching. He surrounded himself with good people, but he was the one who set the tone and made everything work. He said the strength of any group is in its leadership, and he showed us that this is true. We were a strong team under Lombardi because of his strength. He didn't want to be anything but a winner. He was determined to prove that he was the best football coach in the world, and to do that he had to create the best football team in the world. He'd waited a long time for his chance. He'd coached in a little parochial high school in New Jersey, then been an assistant at Fordham, West Point, and with the Giants, waiting all those years for a chance to show what he could do. When he took over the Packers in 1959, he wasn't going to be satisfied until he proved we were the best team and he was the best coach. And he did prove it, too.

Even while I was serving my term as judge on the bench, I liked his attitude that there was nothing like winning. If you're going to go into something, you might as well do anything you can within the rules to win. I don't like losing any better than Lombardi did. It leaves a bad taste in my mouth. If we lose, I don't care how well I've played, I hurt inside.

Lombardi disciplined himself, and he disciplined his disciples to aim for an impossible goal, perfection. We'd beat a team 49–0 and go in the locker room and find out he wasn't even close to being satisfied. We'd made mistakes he didn't think we should have made.

Each game, week after week after week, was the most important game ever played in the history of the world. He never let us think about the game two weeks ahead or look forward to a big playoff somewhere down the road. The next game—that was the one the coach was worrying about, so it's the one we worried about.

I've played, as I've said, under four Packers' coaches and some others in college and high school, and all of them have known a lot about the game. But the ones who do a great job are the ones who act as the team's leader, the man who sets the tone. If the coach is organized, everything falls into place. If he has self-discipline, the team has discipline. If he's dedicated, the team is dedicated. Everything revolves around the head coach. He sets the example. He's the one who has to make the team go.

We had a much better season in 1959 than in 1958. We won seven games, six more than under McLean. I couldn't feel I'd contributed much to the improvement, but somehow I felt I'd finally found a home. When the season ended, a lot of players caught the first plane out of town, but I decided to stay in Green Bay.

I'd always considered myself a big-city boy, but now I didn't want to go back to the big city. Other than my brothers, who had their own lives to live, I didn't have anything to go back to there. As long as I was making my living in Green Bay, I decided I might as well settle there. It wasn't that far from Chicago if I wanted to visit, and it was a pleasant area, nice people, the whole bit. I decided I was going to be a small-town boy and I've never regretted it.

Players come from all over, but they soon identify with the city where they're playing. Football is not just another job. If you play for the Packers, even though you may have grown up in New York or Chicago or Los Angeles, you get to feeling like a Fox River Valley native. When you go to Manhattan or some such place, you feel like a country boy who's going to try to whip those big-city boys on the football field. It's always a joy to beat somebody like Chicago or New York and prove that while Green Bay may not have as many people or skyscrapers, its football team is better. Playing for Green Bay, you're representing all those small towns and cities everywhere in the country. That's why playing for the Packers is something special.

Some players don't like Green Bay because there are fewer opportunities to make money on the side. Big-city athletes are more likely to get a crack at doing commercials and finding off-season jobs. But there's another side to the situation. In what other city in the league can you live five minutes away from the practice field? Where else can a well-known player have his name in the phone book without getting woke up by drunks who want to talk football at 3 A.M. or guys who want to tell him how he should have played the game? In what other league city can you live on ten acres in the country, the way I do, and still be close to everything—the stadium, my friends? For that matter, how many football players can go away from their homes without worrying much about locking the doors and expect to find things the same when they come back? You have better control of your family in a place like Green Bay. You know everybody. You may not have the choice of outside jobs that you'd have in a bigger place, but if a man is qualified, he can find plenty of things to do in a place like Green Bay.

So even though I wasn't happy about not playing that first season under Lombardi, I was glad I'd been drafted by the

Packers. As it turned out, my timing was perfect. If I'd come ten years earlier, it would have been bad news. The way it was, I got to Green Bay just at the right moment to be a part of the Lombardi era of football, a time that will probably never be equaled no matter how long the game is played. It has all worked out perfectly.

But this is hindsight. During 1959, waiting there on the bench, I wasn't satisfied with the situation. And the 1960 season started the same way. The only time I got into the games was on the special teams. I'd hoped two terms on the bench would be enough, but here I was, starting another.

We began the season by losing a close one to the Bears. But then we started to put things together. We beat Detroit, Baltimore, San Francisco, and Pittsburgh. But then we played the Colts again and lost by two touchdowns. We won from the expansion team, Dallas, then got beat by the Rams. Los Angeles won by only two points—33–31—and Lombardi wasn't happy about that. He wasn't happy at all. Our next game was with the Lions on Thanksgiving Day, and when we went out to practice, the coach called me over.

"Ray," he said, "the middle linebacking job is yours. You go out there. You do the best job you possibly can. We're going to sink or swim with you."

That was what I'd been waiting for ever since I got benched after the Washington game in 1958. Lombardi wasn't going to be sorry. Tom Bettis was my best friend, but I made up my mind that he was going to have to collect those bench splinters from here on out. There was no way he was going to get his job back.

There was locker room talk that there'd been an argument between Bettis and the coach and that was the reason Tom was benched. I don't know whether there's anything to this or not—I never asked Tom about it. I hoped I'd been given the job because the coach felt I'd developed into a player who could handle it a little better. I went out there with a plan in mind: I was going to be the meanest player on that field. A lot of players are mean one play, then slack off for the next three. Ever since I was in high school, people had been calling me mean. Now that I was a starter on Lombardi's team, I intended to live up to that compliment.

Even before he made me a starter, the coach seemed to be convinced that I was a hard-nosed guy. It was in September when we were practicing, and it was a real humid day. Lombardi told us we could take off our helmets and shoulder pads. We put them on the ground next to a tall steel structure that had been built between the two practice fields. People called it the photographers' tower, and it's true that the cameramen used it, but the main reason it was built was so Lombardi could stand up there, twenty-five feet in the air, and watch the plays and yell down at us.

The practice went on. I could see there was a big thunderstorm coming up. Those big, black clouds were moving in fast from the west, and the wind started blowing hard. We were out there in our T-shirts, and when I got a chance I ran over to the tower and started putting on my shoulder pads so the padding wouldn't get wet when it started to rain. I put on my helmet, too. That turned out to be a lucky thing because all of a sudden a big gust of wind came along and the tower tipped over and collapsed and I went down under about a thousand pounds of steel scaffolding. Everybody came running, including the coach.

"Who's that guy on the ground?" he yelled.

"It's Nitschke."

Lombardi looked relieved.

"Nitschke? He's all right. Everybody back to practice."

Apparently the coach felt that it would take more than half a ton of steel to dent my head. It was the first time I'd ever been tackled by a tower, but he was right. I wasn't hurt much. The scaffolding bounced off my shoulder pads, knocking me down, and a big bolt went right through my headgear, stopping just short of my skull. There's about an inch of space between your helmet and your head, and most of this space is taken up by a sponge liner. The hole in my helmet was about four inches above the left temple. I was lucky. If I hadn't put my helmet on, I might have spent the rest of the season in the cemetery.

As it was, I was able to kid about what had happened. I told some of the reporters that my bald head saved me. I said I'd put the helmet on so it wouldn't get wet.

After Lombardi left, some of the guys dug me out from under the tower, and I went back to practice. My ankle hurt some—I'd strained it three weeks before in practice, and being at the bottom of that steel pileup hadn't improved it any—but I didn't say anything about it. Lombardi didn't pay any attention to what he called small hurts, so we learned to ignore them, too. The way we understood it, as long as all your legs and arms were still attached to your body, anything that happened to them was a small hurt.

We lost to Detroit my first time out as a starter for Lombardi. But he'd said I was his middle linebacker, and he kept me in for the rest of the season. We beat the Bears the next week, and then came San Francisco. Playing the

Forty-Niners gave me a chance to spend a frustrating afternoon chasing Hugh McElhenny.

We won. But McElhenny's ability to shift from one gear
to another while he was moving, and his open-field running
were something to behold. He was in his ninth year, and I
felt sorry for those people who'd been in the league and had
played him when he was really coming into his own. He had
a great change of pace and a remarkable ability to change
direction just as you thought you had him. After the game, I
went up to Bengtson.

"Boy, I really had a bad game. I didn't hit that McElhenny
once."

"Well, Ray, you aren't the first and you won't be the last.
He's done that to linebackers before."

Bengtson had coached at San Francisco before he came to
the Packers to help Lombardi, so he'd had a chance to see
a lot of McElhenny. Hugh was one of the most beautiful
runners you'll ever see play football. It was a great opportunity to play against him.

The collapse of the steel tower wasn't the only close call
I had in 1960. The other one came just before our last game
of the season. We had to beat the Rams in Los Angeles to
win the Western Conference. Before the game, we were
staying in Santa Monica, and I went out by myself to unwind. I was in a restaurant near our hotel. I knew about
Lombardi's rule against sitting at the bar—he didn't object
to having a drink, but he didn't want to see one of his players
perched on a barstool—but I decided to take a chance.

So I ordered and was minding my own business when
in walked Lombardi, Phil Bengtson, and Norb Hecker,
the defensive backfield coach. It was too late to duck, and

I'm too big to hide. They walked right past me and what could I say but, "Hi, coach," and hope for the best? I noticed the red was creeping up the back of his neck, but Lombardi didn't stop. He stalked over to a table, and the three coaches sat down. Lombardi reached out for a bowl of unshelled peanuts and started squeezing them. He wasn't eating any, just squeezing them and watching the shells shatter.

I knew I was in trouble, and I told the waiter to bring the coaches a round of drinks on me—one Scotch, one bourbon, and one beer, because that's what they liked. I just wanted to show everybody I was a nice, friendly guy. But for some reason when the waiter showed up with his tray and told them the drinks were on Nitschke, Lombardi just got angrier. He jumped up and walked out, the other two shadowing him. As he passed my stool he didn't even look at me. But he spoke to me.

"You're all done. You're through. Get out of town."

He meant it, no doubt about that. My only hope was that when he cooled down he'd reconsider. The coach got sore easy but sometimes, if you avoided antagonizing him, he'd forget what he was sore about an hour later. But I wasn't feeling very optimistic about my future with the Green Bay Packers. I could think of some other people who'd been sent on their way fast when Lombardi got down on them. It looked like that drink I'd ordered might be the most expensive one I'd ever drunk.

At the time, of course, I didn't know what was going on with Lombardi after he left the restaurant. But Hecker said later that Bengtson kept pointing out to the coach that he needed me and Lombardi kept saying, "Get rid of him."

But finally Phil won the argument. Lombardi wouldn't back down all the way, but he agreed to leave it up to the ball club. The squad met the next day, and the vote was 39-0 in my favor. So I stayed. But if there'd been a healthy linebacker in reserve for that last game of the 1960 season, my career with the Packers might have ended while I was on that barstool in Santa Monica.

We beat the Rams, which gave us an 8-4 record. That was only one game better than in the coach's first season, but it was good enough to put us into the championship playoff with Philadelphia.

Lombardi had been offered the job of coaching the Eagles before he came to Green Bay, but Philadelphia had refused to give him a five-year contract, so he'd turned it down. Buck Shaw had accepted the job and had done well. Like the Pack, the Eagles had climbed from last place to first in their conference. In fact, they won two more games in 1960 than we did.

It was the day before Christmas when we ran out on the turf in Franklin Field in Philadelphia. This was a real big game for me, my first playoff. The National Broadcasting Company was paying two hundred thousand dollars to televise it—a lot of money, it seemed then. Now it would pay for about a one-minute commercial on a Super Bowl telecast.

The Packers hadn't been in a championship game since 1944, and sixteen years is a long time, so this was a big game for the team, too. I thought at the time that we were ready, but it turned out we weren't as ready as we should have been. We were a young team, just on the verge of being a great team. We had a lot of great players. But we never quite put our game together that afternoon.

We played them toe-to-toe all afternoon, but the Eagles made a couple of key plays that changed things. They ran back a kickoff fifty-eight yards in the fourth quarter, setting up the winning touchdown. They made some receptions that kept their long marches down the field going. Their defense played an outstanding game.

We led 6–0 halfway through the second quarter on two Hornung field goals—Paul had been the league's high scorer with 176 points during the season—but then Norm Van Brocklin hit on a couple of passes, and the Eagles made a touchdown. The next time he got the ball, Van Brocklin hit Pete Retzlaff for a forty-one-yarder, and even though we finally stopped them on the fifteen, they got a field goal to pull four points ahead. We each scored a touchdown in the last quarter but we lost, 17–13.

Afterward, I felt I was getting most of the blame for losing. Van Brocklin told the reporters that the Packers' middle linebacker had been out of position a few times and he took advantage of it. I felt I'd played as well as I could at that stage of my development, although I did make some errors by being too aggressive. I made some mistakes I wouldn't make in future championship games. It was a big game, and I didn't really know how to get ready for it. But that game helped me in the future. I was able to prepare myself better for other playoffs.

Philadelphia had an experienced team, a cagey bunch of veterans. In a game like that there really is a difference between a veteran team and one that's made up of young players. It's not just another afternoon. There's a tremendous amount of pressure built up by all the publicity. All those sportswriters coming from around the country, all those TV interviews, all those people calling you from everywhere—there's a lot of pressure on you as well as on the organization. Players with experience can handle that kind of tension much better. When you're young, you don't have the self-discipline to control your feelings.

As I say, I felt as if I were the one being blamed for losing the championship, and whenever we got in another game where the stakes were high—and we got in plenty of them as the years went by—I felt I had to prove something. I had to prove that losing to the Eagles hadn't been my fault.

But Lombardi never made me the fall guy that day. He understood that even if I'd played a bad game, some of the others had let him down, too. He knew I was a young, aggressive player and that I was going to improve and wouldn't make the same mistakes again. As he said to us once in the locker room: "You will make mistakes—but not too many of them if you're going to play for the Green Bay Packers."

The coach expected you to learn from mistakes, but he didn't want you to brood about them. So the one he blamed for losing that Eagles' game was himself. Early in the first quarter, we'd pushed our way down to the Philadelphia six after Bill Quinlan intercepted a pass. Lombardi always used to say that when you got close to the goal line you must not come away without some points. But when we were on the six, he decided to gamble on getting seven points. The kicking unit was waiting for his signal, but he didn't give it. Instead, he told Starr to hand the ball to Taylor. He had confidence that Jim was not going to be stopped when he had his first chance to score in a championship game.

And even if he didn't score, we were only two yards away from a first down. If he made only those two yards on that fourth-down play, we'd have four more chances to get across the goal line.

The linemen did what they were supposed to do. They opened up a hole big enough for a fullback to squeeze through. But Taylor's foot slipped. The hole closed. The score was still o–o.

After the game, there were a lot of players Lombardi could have blamed. Hornung, who missed a field goal from the thirteen. Max McGee, whose punt in the second quarter went only thirty yards, giving the Eagles position so they made their first touchdown. Ray Nitschke, that rookie Van Brocklin had decided to take picks on. Instead, the coach blamed himself.

"I made the wrong guess," he said, talking about that decision not to kick a field goal from the six-yard line. The way he figured it, if we'd come away with three points then we would have been behind only 17–16 late in the game when we had the ball within field-goal range. As it was, we needed a touchdown, and the Eagles stopped Taylor on their nine-yard line as time ran out.

You had to respect a coach who could admit when he was wrong. It took me a while to understand Lombardi. When he'd come out with compliments about this player or that, it bothered my pride. I'm like most players—I enjoy seeing my name in print and knowing the coach has said nice things about me, even though that isn't what motivates me basically. But Lombardi didn't think I was the kind of player who needed compliments, and I guess he was right. The important thing to me was how I felt about my own game. As long as I thought I'd done well and that the coaches and other players respected me, I could get along without compliments.

I got a big kick out of Lombardi's attitude toward football. He treated every game as a championship game, so that when we did get into a big game we'd be ready to play. He never really felt happy about any part of any game he ever coached. Even when he was looking back at it after the season was over, he was never happy about it. Nobody is pleased with a defeat, but Lombardi was never pleased with a victory, either. He stayed on us all the time. Even if we'd won, you'd think we'd lost from the way he'd talk about the game and your part in it. He was critical all the time.

On the other hand, he never let us feel that we were beaten. He always said that the clock just ran out too soon. I really think that was true a lot of times—it was true of that 1960 Eagles' game, for instance. But as it was, we'd lost our first chance for the league championship since 1944, and none of us felt good about it, even though we were $3,105.14 richer. That was a losing player's share in 1960.

During the off-season, I spent part of my time at my brothers' house. Richard was still living with Bob, and the three of us really enjoyed a chance to get together again. I have a lot of affection for those two big guys.

I guess a lot of people who ran into us in the bars around Chicago that summer wouldn't have described us as affectionate, however. The way Bob tells it, "We never looked for trouble, but a lot of guys in Chicago and the suburbs wished they'd never seen us."

I'd have a few drinks and I'd see somebody looking at

me the wrong way, and the first thing you knew, he and his friends would have eight hundred pounds of Nitschkes on their hands. But we didn't get into any serious trouble. As I've mentioned, the theory around Chicago is that if a man wants to act like a jerk, let him act like a jerk.

I was a starter on the best team in the Western Conference now. Around Green Bay, at least, people knew who I was, and some of the players around the league had met me often enough with my shoulder pads on so they remembered Ray Nitschke. I had money in my pockets and I wasn't a poor orphan boy from the wrong side of the tracks in Elmwood Park any more. But I still hadn't found anybody to think about except myself. I might be six foot three and old enough to vote, but I wasn't mature. I knew something was wrong. Here I was, doing what I'd always wanted to do, having the first real taste of the kind of success I'd been working for all my life. But it wasn't enough. Trying to prove I was the best middle linebacker in the world wasn't enough. But I didn't know what else I was looking for or what to do about it.

I wasn't really happy, and when I got back to Green Bay for the practice sessions I found that Lombardi wasn't happy either. Even though we'd lost the playoff, we'd won the conference, and that made us winners, which was what he'd been saying he wanted us to be. But it just gave him one more thing to worry about. He said the other teams were all out there waiting to knock us off. And they might do it, too, he said, because when players win "there's a tendency to get fatheaded." We weren't more than a few minutes into our first practice before it was plain the coach wasn't going to tolerate any fat, between the ears or elsewhere. He didn't ease up a bit. In fact, he said some of us might not be around long unless we got down to work.

"No matter what a player did last year, if he can't do it this year he has to go"—that was how he put it.

There'd been rumors that the coach wasn't going to be back that year. As a New Yorker, he'd always wanted to coach the Giants, and he'd been offered the job. But the AFL was raiding NFL rosters, and around the league, club owners were talking a lot about loyalty and how wicked it would be for a player to jump a contract. Lombardi still had three years to go on his agreement to be the Green Bay coach and general manager, so even if he could find a way out of that contract it would hurt football. And that may be why he was back on the job and yelling at us again, looking for ways to improve the team, such as hiring a star backfield man from Michigan State, Herb Adderley. Bill Austin, one of the assistant coaches, had the job of signing Herb, and the story is that he had to fight a scout from the Canadian League in a parking lot before Adderley put the contract on the hood of a car and wrote his name.

Looking back, it's easy to see that the 1961 season was the first where pro football really came into its own. For the first time since the league was organized, it was hard to buy a seat for any game at any stadium, even if the teams that were playing were fighting for last place. The Packers, of course, were in contention right from the start, and even though Lambeau Field had been enlarged, it wasn't big enough. The official capacity was now up to 44,450, but the average attendance that year was 45,145.

If any of us were fatheaded, as the coach said, and thought this was going to be an easy year, it wasn't long before we changed our minds. It was one complication after another. Like Hawg Hanner's appendix. The doctor said it had to come out, and the big tackle got Lombardi's reluctant permission to miss one game. But ten days after he was on the operating table he was back in the lineup. As Jerry Kramer pointed out later, Lombardi had a high pain threshold—"none of our injuries hurts him a bit"—and Hanner's appendectomy pained the coach only when he had to put a substitute into the defensive line.

Kramer broke a leg midway in the season, which was another complication in our plan to win the championship, and then the Army stepped in and proved that it outranked the coach. Hornung, Boyd Dowler, and I were in the Reserves, and when the Berlin crisis got hot, President Kennedy decided he needed us more than Lombardi did. I was with the 32nd Division, along with a lot of other men from Wisconsin. My pay was $85.80 a month. The Army put me to work carrying sacks of potatoes—I guess they thought I had the muscles for an important assignment like that. But first we ran into a little problem. The quartermaster couldn't find a uniform shirt to fit me, and the Army had to make me one with an 18½-inch neck.

I carried those potatoes so well that the Russians finally gave in and the crisis at Berlin ended, but not in time to suit Lombardi. The Army let us go back for some of the games by taking weekend passes, but having three of his starters miss all those practice sessions didn't make things any simpler for the coach.

I hadn't changed from my football helmet to an Army helmet until the season was half over, and after I was safely in Fort Lewis, Washington, Lombardi said something complimentary about me to a sportswriter.

"He has learned his keys," he said.

That may not sound like high praise to anyone but a middle linebacker. But one of the things a man in that job has to learn is to read the other team's offense by noticing the moves of certain opponents—in other words, keying on them. The coach also said I'd cut down on my mistakes. He'd always told us that if we had to make a mistake, "make it with abandon," and I guess I'd done that. But with experience, I was making fewer of them. I knew this without anybody having to tell me. Still, it was nice to hear that the coach had said it, even if he did wait until I was in the Army.

We'd lost the opener to the Lions, but then we won six in a row, all by one-sided scores. The Colts beat us midway in the season, but we came back to win five of the last six games to end up with a record of eleven wins and three losses, giving us the conference title again. This time the Giants were representing the East, and Lombardi wanted to show his old hometown that he'd created a team that was the best in the world.

I'd played all but two of the games that season in spite of being in the Army. Because I didn't have a chance to practice during the week, Bettis and I alternated at middle linebacker. Hornung, Dowler, and I were all back in Green Bay for the playoff, the first one ever held there. In the old days, the Packers had won four conference championships, but as it happened, none of the title games had been held in Green Bay, and there were banners and posters all over town bragging that this was "Titletown, USA." I had a week's pass for the Christmas holiday, and when I got home the town was covered with snow and full of enthusiasm, and I could sense that the Giants weren't going to have a chance against us.

The players were ready. You can tell a lot by the players' attitude toward practice. If a team is sloppy during the week, it's not going to have a good game on Sunday. But this time there was a singleness of purpose, a feeling that we weren't going to be denied the championship two years in a row. I felt sorry for the Giants, but not very.

Lombardi had done his part. The practices were crisp and precise. The team had reached a high point. Because I'd missed so many practices, I wasn't as prepared as I might have been, but I felt I'd be all right, playing one quarter then out a quarter, besides being on all the special teams.

When we ran out on that field it was a pleasure to be a part of it. It had been below zero for several days, and the New York sportswriters were calling Green Bay the Siberia of the league, but I hardly noticed the cold. I knew this was going to be one of the great afternoons of my life.

The Giants' quarterback was Y. A. Tittle. He'd been given the special treatment a star gets if he plays in New York. Bart Starr still wasn't getting credit for being one of the great quarterbacks. But a lot of people changed their ideas about him that afternoon. Our offense really dominated the game. Tittle was a good quarterback, all right. But this wasn't his day.

Every quarterback is likely to do certain things in certain situations, and we had the advantage of having a defensive coach who knew all about Y.A.'s habits. Bengtson had been with San Francisco when Tittle was breaking in there, and he told us what patterns the Giants' quarterback liked, what receivers he was apt to throw to in certain situations, what plays he was likely to use when his team was on the right hashmark and which ones when it was on the left hashmark.

It gives the defense an advantage if it has learned the opposing quarterback's habits. If you know he has the habit of trying to hit the wide receiver when he has a certain field position, for instance, that's the time you'll have double coverage of that man. Before any game, the defensive players study certain things about the quarterback they'll be playing against. When's he likely to go to his tight end? Does he usually hit his halfback on first down or second down? Which player does he look for when he has to hit on third down or give up the ball?

So it's a battle of wits between you and the quarterback. He'll try to mix things up and throw you off, but in general he'll follow certain patterns that have worked for him in the past. It's the same in any game. In basketball, a player has certain places on the floor where he's most confident of hitting the basket. If he needs one basket to win, he's going to try to get the ball at that favorite spot. In football, every quarterback has certain receivers and certain plays he likes in a certain situation. If you really study an opposing quarterback, you see that his game falls into a pattern. So you follow the percentages. He won't always do what you expect. But if he does it only 55 percent of the time, you'll be in the right defense more than half of the time.

One thing the defense must try to do is take away the opponent's best play. With Tittle, it was the long bomb down the middle. He'd stung a lot of defenses with those. So we kept those bombs in mind when we ran out on that frozen field to prove we could stop him and bring the title to Title-town.

Lombardi had a special feeling about New York. He loved the place, and he wanted to beat it. He really had us ready to play. No team that has ever existed could have out-scored us that afternoon.

Almost every time we got the ball, we moved it steadily down the field, using up the time before we went in to score. We didn't get any points in the first quarter, but four seconds after the next period started, Hornung went over for a touchdown, and then it was all downhill. The offense really took it to the Giants that afternoon. The defense wasn't really on the field long enough to get tired.

I remember Ron Kramer, our great tight end, had the Giants' middle linebacker on him all afternoon. But it was a great day for Ron. He caught two of Bart's three touchdown passes, with my fellow soldier, Dowler, catching the other. Meanwhile, when the Giants got the ball it was usually one, two, three, and out. Tittle tried twenty passes. Ten of them were caught, but four of the catches were made by Packers. I intercepted one myself, after somebody else had tipped it. Finally, New York brought in Charlie Conerly, and he hit on four of eight, but he couldn't score on us either. We won, 37–0.

How great it was to be part of that day. It's hard to de-scribe the feeling I had for this group of young men. We were just putting our talents all together in one smoothly functioning team—Ringo and Starr and Hornung, Taylor and Willie Davis, Willie Wood and Henry Jordan and on down the list. Not long ago we'd all been strangers to each other, and before Lombardi came some of us were going

83

one way, some another. But now we were a single unit made up of many parts, each part doing its share and feeling confident that the others would do theirs. All season, the team had been teetering on the brink of greatness. Now, all of a sudden, it had arrived. It was one of those afternoons that couldn't be improved on. I was just happy that I'd been there and had a chance to do my part.

Afterward, Norb Hecker, who coached the defensive backs, violated Lombardi's theory that Nitschke was someone who didn't need compliments. Hecker said my tackling had inspired the defense.

"It sort of rubs off on the rest of the men and makes them want to hit harder," he said. "You know how it is when you're in a fight and someone on your side gets in a big punch? It swings things your way. That's the way it is when Nitschke flattens someone."

I enjoyed seeing in the paper that Bengtson was saying nice things about me, too. He said those jarring tackles had an effect on the opponents.

"It gets so they want to know where Nitschke is lined up on every play—they become quite conscious of his presence."

Well, great. That's always been my idea on defense. Make those other guys conscious of Ray Nitschke's presence. I think Y. A. Tittle was one of those who remembered me after that afternoon. I got to him once just as he released the ball. I hope he recalled that meeting every time he faded back to pass from then on.

Those of us who played for the Packers remember 1961 as the year we brought Lombardi his first league championship. But that game takes second place in my memories of

that year. I've said that this was the season when the
Packers found a new unity of purpose. It was also the year
when Ray Nitschke finally grew up and found a little unity
of his own.

I'd gone into a restaurant in Green Bay and I saw this
girl, working as a waitress there. Her name was Jackie
Forchette. She'd lived on a farm in Ewen, Michigan—that's
on the Upper Peninsula—and when she grew up she went
to California. She was there about five years, but then her
father got sick and she wanted to be closer to home. Green
Bay is about two hundred miles from Ewen, but there
aren't many places to get a job in between. So there she was.
When I saw her, I knew I had to meet her.

But she didn't want to meet me. She'd heard about Ray
Nitschke, the rowdy, the tough bully, the man you want to
stay away from because if he has one drink, look out. That
was the reputation I had because after a drink I'd get too
loud and boisterous and maybe a little vulgar—just one of
those guys who are bad to be around. In those days, I used
to worry that I might have bad breath—there must be some
reason why everybody got up and left when I walked into
a place.

So I had trouble getting a date with Jackie, but I wasn't
about to give up. Finally I arranged for a girl I knew to in-
vite her out to dinner. Then I just happened along, accidentally. Even after we talked and she could see I wasn't
always so obnoxious, she wasn't sure about me. She says
now it took her about two weeks before she decided I
wasn't the kind of bully she'd been led to expect and that
I was more of a man than I wanted people to think I was.

As for me, it was love at first sight; she didn't think so at first, but I thought so. We got married that fall, and it was a turning point in my life.

I'd gone through a long period when everything was "I" and forget about you. But something had been lacking. I'd been struggling within myself. I didn't care what anybody thought or have any real confidence in myself or any real purpose in my life. I didn't worry about anybody as long as I had three meals a day, a place to sleep, and a chance to tackle people who were running my way with a football. But now I'd finally outgrown that adolescent attitude. I wasn't just thinking about myself any more. Even Lombardi was pleased.

"The best thing that ever happened to Ray was getting married," he said.

And who was I to argue with the coach? Even though Jackie confessed something to me after we were married. She admitted that from living in San Francisco so long, she'd rooted for the Forty-Niners when I first knew her. But I guess every girl is entitled to one mistake.

We knew Jackie couldn't have children, so from the first we planned to adopt some. We adopted John in 1963 and Richard in 1966 and Amy in March of 1972. Having a family really solidified my life. Not having anyone to love or to love me had been what I was lacking. My wife and then the children brought it all together, brought it into focus. Now I wasn't just concerned with myself. It was something I needed: to care for somebody, to worry about somebody else.

People could see the change in my personality. Starr, for instance, said I mellowed after I got married—not on the field, where I wasn't hired to have a mellow personality, but off the field. I wised up and gave up drinking entirely. I decided I was one of those people who shouldn't have even one drink. I didn't need it that much. I didn't need it as medicine. I didn't require it to have fun. In fact, I never really enjoyed it.

It wasn't a case of Jackie saying, "Hey, Ray, cut it out." It was just that I finally put everything together and told myself: "You've got a long way to go and you can't just keep on doing foolish things and making a jerk of yourself. Now you don't just represent yourself. You represent your wife, your family. So wise up and set a good example and become a man."

Getting married, settling down, gaining responsibility for someone besides myself, having someone to love and, later, adopting the children—all these things were enough motivation for me to quit making a fool of myself. Besides, it had been aggravating to keep getting into those stupid little fracasses over nothing because I didn't know when to stop or have the maturity to control my behavior. Now I finally was willing to admit that my body and alcohol didn't get along. I'd taken those drinks to be a big shot, but it was really a depressant. I didn't have to drink, but I had to learn that the hard way.

Some say liquor tends to exaggerate your mood: If you're feeling good it makes you feel better, if you're feeling bad it makes you feel worse. But with me, even if I was feeling good when I started, it always turned out to be nothing but bad news. I was never a big drinker, but I just couldn't handle the stuff. Every time I'd overindulge I'd get into those fracasses and there'd be bad feelings and I'd wake up the next morning knowing I'd done stupid things.

But now my life was different, off the field as well as on. Among the players, we'd discovered a feeling of respect for each other and confidence in each other that made us hard to beat. Now I had that feeling of unity in my personal life, too.

It was great. I don't know that I would have told this to Lombardi or Bengtson or anybody on the team. But even if we hadn't beaten the Giants that December day, 1961 would have been a great year.

CHAPTER V

Lombardi seemed to worry more when we were riding high than when we were having hard going. After we'd whipped the Giants so decisively, we went to summer training camp feeling like the champions we were. But what the coach wanted us to feel was hungry.

"I don't want to seem ungrateful," he said. "I'm awfully proud of you guys, really. You've done a hell of a job. But sometimes you just disgust me."

Before Lombardi took over the Packers, you could get an argument in any bar in Chicago or New York about whether a place the size of Green Bay belonged in the league. Now people were talking about a Packer dynasty. We'd had almost the same starting lineup since the middle of Lombardi's first season—I was one of five starters who hadn't been on the first team then, along with Willie Wood, Ron Kramer, Willie Davis, and Herb Adderley.

We won every exhibition game in 1962, and we kept up the momentum after the season started. When we went to Detroit for the Thanksgiving Day game, we had a record of ten wins and no defeats. Only two of the games had been close. Earlier in the season, we'd beaten the Lions by only two points, and the week before that Thanksgiving game we'd won from the Colts by four. After that other game with Detroit we weren't taking the Lions for granted, particularly because they were in second place in our conference, but we'd come to believe that no one could beat us. We didn't have as much physical ability as people gave us credit for, but we had this belief in ourselves. When you have that, you generally win.

I felt that my marriage had made me a better football player. I wasn't taking all those bruises only for myself. I had a happy family life, and it helped me go about my job. My family was the most important thing to me because of not having had much of a family life when I was a boy. We were planning to adopt our first son and I thought about that and how I was going to give him the things I'd lacked when I was a child.

So everything was going well for me and for the team. In the first three games, we'd allowed only a total of seven points. The defense couldn't keep up that average, but our team dominated the league. Every game we went into we knew we were going to win. The only question was by how big a score. Lombardi has said that that 1962 team was his greatest, but that's a hard thing to judge. It depends on the level of competition, the opponents' injuries, your injuries, what kind of a schedule you draw. But going into that second game with Detroit it seemed as if everything had fallen in place.

But sometimes you can go into a game where ten of the guys on your side of the field are having a good day and the eleventh is having a bad day, and that can make all the difference. In that Lions game, the one player who wasn't able to play up to his usual ability was Fuzzy Thurston.

One of his parents had died. He'd missed a whole week of practice. That was bad enough, but his assignment that day was to block Roger Brown, a great player and a real tough pass rusher. Fuzzy didn't want to let us down. He wanted to play. He played as well as he could under the circumstances. But Starr got creamed eight times in the first half, including once when they caught him in the end zone. After two quarters, the champions of the world were behind, 23–0.

We adjusted our defense in the second half and held Detroit to one field goal while our offense was scoring two touchdowns. But we lost. It was the only game we lost all year. After the season was over, people kept asking what had happened at Detroit. Lombardi said it was "coaching stupidity," for not changing our game plan fast enough to adapt to the Lions' changes. But one reason was that Thurston was out there when he was not at his best, through no fault of his own. Fuzzy wasn't as prepared for that game as he would have been if it hadn't been for the death in his family. He couldn't get emotionally aroused to play the way he'd played in other games. Fuzzy was a great guard. He usually played with all the zeal it takes. When he had that bad game it was because he was emotionally sapped from the funeral.

Every time we came on the field to try to hold Detroit that day, it seemed we were in the hole. The Lions had all the momentum. We'd been playing great football all season, but that day we had a letdown. It's hard to get emotionally prepared for every game, and that's one reason you have upsets in football. But losing in Detroit helped us the rest of the year. We were determined it wouldn't happen again, and it didn't. The next week we regrouped. Not only did Thurston regain his form, but so did a lot of other people. We took out our embarrassment over that Lions game on the Rams, beating Los Angeles 41–10. When the season ended, we'd won thirteen and lost one, making us the first team to have thirteen wins since the 1934 Bears. During the season our offense scored 415 points and our defense allowed only 148.

So now we'd taken three conference titles in Lombardi's first four years, which gave us a chance to play the Giants again and try for a second straight league championship. New York's record was almost as good as ours—they'd lost only two games. Their passing game was something you had to treat with respect. They'd scored thirty-five touchdowns with passes during the season. We'd made only fourteen that way, although with Taylor and Hornung on our side we didn't need to rely on throwing the ball as much. Besides, Starr's pass completion record of 62.5 percent was better than Y. A. Tittle's, and Bart had thrown only nine interceptions compared to twenty for the Giants' quarterback.

Taylor had gained 1,474 yards that season, the best in the league, and the Packers made more yards on the ground than any other team. Taylor had a 5.4 yards-per-carry average, which shows how hard he was to stop, and Hornung was just as competitive. Paul was one of the smartest ballplayers I've ever known. He always seemed to be in the right spot at the right time. The bigger the game, the better he played, which is a sign of a good football player. When he was inside the ten-yard line, nothing was going to stop him. He had this fierce attitude that he was going to get that ball over the goal no matter what anybody did to stop him. He did everything well—block, run, catch the ball, kick—so he was an all-around threat. But his biggest asset was his competitiveness. He could smell that goal line. Lombardi always said the test of a man's character comes inside the ten-yard marker, so Paul must have had a lot of character.

Near the goal line, the defensive alignment tightens up. The offensive team doesn't have as much freedom to move or to use a lot of its pass patterns. It can run only certain plays, and the defense knows it. So down near the goal it is the defense, not the offense, that has the advantage. The area it has to cover is smaller. You know that the quarterback isn't going to throw the pass forty or fifty yards, because that would put it up in the cheap seats. Screen plays aren't too likely, because you need room to manipulate. The defense has fewer things to think about, so it can react faster.

The offense gets tested inside the ten, but the defense gets tested, too. You find out which players can stiffen their backbones and stop the attack when one small mistake will give the other team six points.

In those early Lombardi years, we played mostly man-to-man coverage, even when we weren't near the goal line. Now there isn't a team in the conference that plays strictly man-to-man, but we used to when Lombardi was around and the Packers were winning consistently. It was man-to-man coverage with variations—one time you'd cover one man, the next time you'd cover a different one to keep them guessing.

Everybody says the best pass defense is a good pass rush and we had one, but other teams blitzed more. We believed we could beat the other team by reacting to whatever play it wanted to try. If it was a pass, everybody on the defense knew the other guy would be in his proper position. We had real unison on the defensive team. Once the pass was thrown, everybody reacted to the ball instead of standing around and watching. The other team always knew what our defense was going to be. It was as though we told them, "We're going to be in this defense, but to beat us you'll have to outexecute us."

It was part of Lombardi's philosophy to keep football simple, to do basic things better. On defense, we all had confidence that the other ten men knew what they were doing. Each player was motivated by a determination not to let the others down. Our success was built on pride of performance, pride in ourselves and in the team. That's something that has to be built up through experience and a lot of hard practice. We believed that the other team's offense couldn't play well enough to beat us. It might complete some passes, but we weren't going to let that quarterback complete enough to win. The opponents might make some gains on the ground, but they weren't going to gain enough yards to do them any good. We knew we weren't going to outsmart anybody. You don't outsmart anybody at the professional level. What we planned to do was try to be in the right position for every play and then to execute better than the other team did.

To listen to Lombardi, you would have thought that he considered offense the most important part of his teams. The offense was his pride and joy. But he knew that if the defense didn't get the ball enough times for the offense, the offense wasn't going to have a chance to win. In the early years, he concentrated on building up a good defense, because you win on defense. The team that gets the ball the most is going to win. That's the job of the defense—to get that ball.

Lombardi was more offensively oriented, however, and it was Bengtson who ran the defense. He was the same kind of student of the game as the head coach. He made it basic and simple. He made us believe in what we were doing. He wanted us to practice hard and get enough confidence in ourselves to do our jobs. He was a quiet, dedicated man, a fellow I admired. Football knowledge just flowed out of him. I learned more football from Phil than from any other coach I've ever had.

Lombardi was volatile but Bengtson was a cool customer, a man who demanded excellence and worked hard to try to get it. Lombardi was always blowing up, but Phil usually kept his poise. If he did get angry, you knew it. His voice got a little louder. But mostly he didn't say too much.

When he did talk, I listened. He tried to show me that you really have to study the game and apply yourself, off the field as well as on. You have to study yourself. You have to study your opponent—his personality as well as his moves. You have to study how the offense reacts to you and how you react to it. He wanted me to be a more knowledgeable player. He'd look at a movie of a game and say, "Ray, you're not doing this right, you're not doing that right." He'd show me the fine points, and he made me a smarter player. He'd see I wasn't getting to a certain spot the fastest way, for instance. He'd see things I'd overlook. He made me more aware of my role in the total pattern of the game.

Before we'd get into a big one, like that 1962 playoff in New York, Bengtson or Lombardi would walk up to me on the sidelines and say:

"Give us some hits right away, Ray. Get the boys started hitting."

That suited me. I'm the kind of guy who has to start a game off by making some good hits. Over the years, the games I've done well I've started off at full speed, all out. The ones I've played poorly I've gone out there and pussy-footed around for a while, not being aggressive enough. I was glad that the coaches felt I could be an inspiration to the other defensive men, get them in the right frame of mind to be mean. Before every big game when I'd get that order to make a couple of good hits right away I'd take it as a compliment. It made me feel special.

The first few plays of any game are always the hardest. You ought to get it over with and hit somebody right away. You've got all those pads on and you've got to use them. The faster you get involved, the better off you're going to be. If you stand aside politely and let John do it, you're in trouble.

Lombardi really wanted that 1962 New York game—he wanted all of them, but this one more than most—and he wasn't happy with the way we were getting ready for it. Four days before the playoff, we were practicing and he was standing on the sidelines yelling at us, and finally he shouted:

"Hit those guys. Hit those guys like they're Giants."

That was fine with me. I looked over at all my friends on the offensive team, and they looked just like Giants. When the ball was snapped, I really let Jim Ringo have it. I popped him good. His head stayed attached to his shoulders, but just barely. His neck wasn't in such great shape, though. He had such a severely pinched neck muscle that he almost missed the championship game.

I was sorry that he was hurting. But when I popped him, I couldn't see Jim Ringo under that Green Bay helmet. To me, he was Ray Wietecha, the Giants' center. It was Wietecha I was busting, although Ringo claimed it was him who got hit.

When we ran out on the field that afternoon in New York, Lombardi told me as usual to start hitting people, and I did. It was a miserably cold day, and it's harder to get started under such conditions. But Bengtson always said the first five or ten plays dictate how the other team is going to play you, and I went out there with my mind made up that the Giants were going to play us with the idea that we were going to be hitting them hard.

I guess the Giants had the same idea. When we had the ball they were really going after us. Especially Taylor. To beat us, they had to stop him, and the whole New York team began working him over, gang-tackling him. He'd get the ball and grind out a few yards, those stubborn legs of his pumping up and down and a snarl on his face, and then he'd go down under a pile of guys like Jim Katcavage, Andy Robustelli, Erich Barnes, and Sam Huff. Especially Sam Huff.

I like contact. If you don't like contact, you don't belong on the football field. But what they were doing to Jimmy went beyond the proper bounds. It got out of hand. He was getting beaten up something awful. It was the officials' business to handle things like that, but they didn't do a thing about it.

The ground was frozen. When you hit it, you might as

well have been playing on cement. It was a terrible day—unbelievable. Playing for Green Bay, you expect cold weather, but that day in New York was the coldest I've ever experienced. It was the only game I've ever played where I didn't really want to go out there and play. It was so cold it wasn't any fun.

The field was bad and the wind was blowing hard—hard and icy. It was coming off the ocean, and it was so piercing it went right through your uniform and pads and underwear and maybe even your skin until it rattled your bones. My hands were numb. My feet were numb. The quarterbacks couldn't pass well because of the wind, and everybody's hands were so cold it was easy to fumble.

I recovered a couple of them. We punted and I was running down the field when Phil King lost the ball. All of us started scrambling for it, and Forrest Gregg got it. I couldn't tell who had it, so I was still down there, grabbing.

"Who is it?" Gregg asked from under the pile.

"It's Nitschke."

So he gave me the ball and I got credit for the recovery. I ended up with two fumble recoveries and a deflected pass. The deflection came in the first quarter, with the Giants on our fifteen. I looked across the line and tried to read Tittle's mind. We were going to blitz. It wasn't something the Packers did often, but the Giants had done most of their scoring during the season through the air, and it seemed like a good time to gamble. When Y.A. took the handoff and moved back, I headed for him. I batted a blocker out of the way. Tittle was back in the pocket and I was still going and he was cocking his arm to throw and the ball was in the air. I put my hand up, which is what you're supposed to do. I felt the ball hit. I tried to twist around to grab it, but there was no need. Dan Currie had the ball and he had an open field ahead of him. But his trick knee threw him on the forty, and we didn't get the touchdown.

Our first score came in the first quarter, when Jerry Kramer kicked a field goal—Hornung was hurt, although he started the game, so Jerry had to take over even though he'd never kicked a field goal except in practice. We got close enough for those three points mostly on Taylor's determination. Early in the game, he set the pattern. When he got the handoff, he headed straight for Huff, who had a reputation as a tough linebacker. Sam drove him out of bounds, and as they skidded across the ice he was using his knees and elbows on Jimmy as fast as he could.

When Taylor got up, he was groggy. I saw him staggering. He leaned over, coughing blood. But he went back to the huddle and grabbed Starr's arm.

"Give me the ball," he said.

When the ball was snapped, Bart gave it to the fullback. He headed straight for Huff. He hit him like a bull moose, knocked him down, trampled him into the icy ground, and kept going. Even those New York fans cheered.

All day, he defied the Giants. He'd get smashed to the frozen turf with half the defensive team piling on top of him, and when he got up he'd turn and snarl: "Is that as hard as you can hit?"

Late in the half, we had the ball on the Giants' seven, and Starr handed it to Taylor again. He pushed and shoved and dodged his way over for the only touchdown we got all day. So at halftime we were leading 10–0.

I should have felt good. We'd held the best team in the

99

East scoreless. But all I wanted to do was get warm. I couldn't wait to get inside. You could hear all of us panting, trying to catch our breaths, and everybody lined up to get some hot bouillon or coffee. Lombardi and Bengtson started talking—the rest of us were saving our breath—and all of a sudden I heard a big yell, the kind of sound a player makes when he's in agony.

It was Taylor. He'd carried the ball at least fifteen times in the first half, and he had a big gash near his elbow. He was in the back room getting sewed up, and he was really in pain. Here's the toughest player on our team, maybe the toughest player in the league, and he's yelling, and all I could think was: "How are we going back out there and play two more quarters?"

Hearing a guy like Jimmy scream like that was horrifying, and it looked like we were going to have to try to beat the Giants on that frozen field without our key player. But they finished sewing him up and taped his arm and he went back out and you'd never know anything had happened. He started carrying the ball again and climbing out from under those pileups, shaking his head and snarling and daring them to hit him again. Before the day was over he'd gained more than ninety yards, every one of them tough yards.

When we went out after halftime we were all a little numb. One of the second-stringers even forgot to bring his helmet. When he saw the guy who played ahead of him get shaken up on a play he started looking around for it, and he couldn't find it. He sent an attendant running back to the locker room for the helmet. He got it before he had to go in, but it looked for a couple of minutes like he was going to have to play the way the players did in the old days, bareheaded. That would have been something to see in a game like that and on a field like that one.

It wasn't a good day for New York's passing game, which was what they depended on. Tittle was a fine passer and he had some good receivers, but the wind was really swirling around Yankee Stadium, and it wasn't Y.A.'s kind of day. We had a better ground game than they did, and it paid off. New York gained 291 yards to our 244, but we held them when they got near the goal, and the only score they made all day came on a blocked punt. The ball bounced back in our end zone, and Jim Collier fell on it for a touchdown. Kramer kicked a couple more field goals in the second half, and we beat them 16–7.

After the game, even Huff had nice things to say about Taylor. He said he wasn't human.

"No human being could have taken the punishment he got today," Sam said. "Every time he was tackled it was like crashing him down on a cement sidewalk, because the ground was as hard as pavement. But he kept bouncing up, snarling at us and asking for more."

One of the defensive backs, Dick Lynch, agreed that Taylor "never stops defying you" and defended Huff against people who were criticizing him for roughing up Jimmy.

"The middle linebacker keys on the fullback, and that's why Sam was in on him so often," Lynch said.

The middle linebacker does key on the fullback a lot of the time. But the movies showed that Sam had played in a way that justified all those letters he got complaining that he'd been a dirty player. The cameraman got one real fine shot of Huff giving Taylor's head a twist after Jimmy had been stopped, for instance. And Huff wasn't the only one. At one point, Jim and Robustelli squared off and were ready to start throwing punches until we got them apart.

The Packers' offense had played a fine game, considering the conditions. But this time it was the defense that won the championship for us. It was the kind of day when the team with the better defense is bound to win.

After the game, the New York writers claimed that Green Bay has an advantage when it plays in cold weather because we were more used to it. That's what always happened after we won a big game under frigid conditions. But I don't think the cold gave us any kind of edge. Like the players on the other teams, the Packers came from all over the country. Nobody likes playing in the cold. I grew up in the Chicago climate, which isn't much good for growing oranges, but I'd like to have it sixty degrees with no wind every day we have to play. I don't like it when it's a hundred degrees and humid. I don't like it when it's real cold. But you have to play the game, no matter what. That's part of football.

You play in warm weather or cold weather or when conditions are ideal. Unlike most team sports, football isn't played under controlled conditions, except in a few cases, like the Astrodome. If it rains, you play wet. If it snows, you play in the snow. If it's icy, you skid around on the ice. If it's cold, you have to get used to the cold, and if you play for Green Bay you have to get used to it more often than if you're with a team from a warm climate. You have to get used to it, but you don't have to like it.

I don't think the weatherman won that game for us in Yankee Stadium. I think we won it ourselves, and after it was over, as Henry Jordan said, "We can hold our heads high and our wives can go shopping."

Like the other wives, Jackie got her choice of a color television set or a stereo console from the Packers—the year before, Lombardi had ordered that all the wives be given mink stoles when we won the championship—and each of us got $5,888.57 as our winning share. The Nitschkes also got a new car. *Sport* magazine gave me a '62 Corvette for being "the player who did the most to bring the championship to his club." It was a great satisfaction to know that a defensive man was getting some credit for a change, even though one of those two fumble recoveries I made against the Giants deserved a big assist from Forrest Gregg.

I'd gone into the locker room after the game just happy because we'd won the game and the championship—and because now I could finally get warm. There was no way in the world I figured somebody was going to come up to me and say I'd been picked as the most valuable player.

So it was a pleasant surprise, but it didn't mean as much to me as it might have a few years earlier. Now I was more interested in getting the respect of my teammates and the coaches than I was in what outsiders thought about me. Earlier in my career, I'd been selfish, but I'd found out there's no place for a player who keeps thinking about nobody but himself. It's a team game, not an individual game. The old saying that you're only as good as your teammates is true. When you win a championship, it's because of forty guys, not just one or five or ten.

Now we'd proved we were champions again. But I knew what Lombardi was thinking. He was thinking about next season, when he'd have us out there trying to prove we could win three titles in a row. Until we did, he wouldn't be satisfied. And if the coach wasn't satisfied, we wouldn't be either because he wouldn't let us.

And that was fine with me. Sure we'd won thirteen of fourteen games, plus the playoff. We'd taken the worst the weatherman and the Giants could throw at us and proved we could win. But we'd lost to Detroit. Even in the games we'd won, we'd made mistakes. Lombardi wasn't going to be content until we played perfect football every minute of every game. Because nobody human could do that, I knew we had some more big challenges ahead of us, and the game would keep on being frustrating—and fun.

CHAPTER VI

At the Pro Football Hall of Fame in Canton, Ohio, there's a diary kept by Fats Henry when he was at Washington and Jefferson in 1916, and the December 4 entry is one any player can understand.

"Don't know what to do," it says, "since football is over."

I never kept a diary, but if I'd had one at Proviso or Illinois or during my early years with the Packers, I might have written down something like that during the off-season. But now those days were gone. I had a family. I didn't have to sit around waiting for football to start again, killing time by having a few drinks and getting loud and maybe starting some trouble. I had a wife and finally, after all those months of waiting for the red tape to unwind, we had adopted our first son, John Raymond Nitschke.

Looking at the little guy, I knew he was going to change my life. Now I was a father as well as a husband. I'd taken one additional step away from the kind of man I'd been, a step toward my maturity.

Of course, you can't afford to forget football entirely in the off-season. I kept up my physical conditioning that winter, as I always do. I caught myself thinking about what was going to happen when the 1963 season began, especially after April 17, when Commissioner Pete Rozelle announced we'd be getting along without Hornung. Paul had bet on football games, and now he was suspended. So was Alex

Karras. Five other Lions got two-thousand-dollar fines for betting on us in the playoff with the Giants. They'd won fifty dollars apiece, but the commissioner saw to it that they lost money on the deal.

So we were going to have to try for a third straight championship without the man who'd scored the most points for us. No team had won three league titles in a row in the modern era of football; in fact, the way the draft was planned, to give the weaker teams a chance to get stronger, there was a built-in handicap against one club dominating the game. But Lombardi wanted a third championship to prove it could be done, and the rest of us had long since been convinced that winning was not only more fun than losing but more profitable for everybody concerned.

Lombardi picked up some fine college talent in that year's draft: Dave Robinson, Dan Grimm, Marv Fleming, and Lionel Aldridge, all future stars. But there was no way of completely filling the gap that Hornung's suspension had left.

The season didn't start out well, either for me or the club. I've almost never been hurt enough so I can't play, but that year I got injured practicing for the All-Star game and I was home in traction, watching it on television, when we lost 20–17 to the college boys. When I got hurt, the coach moved Ken Iman from center to middle linebacker, and he'd never played the position before. It's not a job you learn overnight. I felt we lost to the All-Stars because I didn't play.

The Packers never seemed to draft anybody for middle linebacker, but I was glad they didn't. I would have felt bad for the guy, having to spend all his time on the bench. I was the established man in that position, and nobody was going to get my job. I wasn't just going out and hitting people now. I'd come to realize that the big play is getting rid of the fellow trying to block me, then getting the man with the ball, and I'd learned how to go about that assignment pretty well.

I had four keys to watch: first of all, the opposing center, then the fullback and the two guards. I paid special attention to these four in watching game films, studying their habits and tendencies. The coaches pointed out things, too, and Henry Jordan and Dave Hanner, the defensive tackles, would give me suggestions on what to watch for—they were good men at reading keys. For instance, if one of the guards wasn't putting much weight on his fingers in the three-point stance, I'd look for him to go back to block for a pass. If he leaned to one side or lined up with one foot slightly behind the other, he was probably going to pull out to lead a sweep or off-tackle play. But if he put his weight forward on his hand, look out. He was going to fire straight at me, and I'd get ready.

Bengtson called the defensive plays from the sidelines with hand signals. As defensive captain, Bill Forester passed the word to the rest of us when he saw what the coach wanted us to do. But as middle linebacker it was my job to call out what formation the other team was in because I was in the best position to see it.

"Blue right," I'd yell, or "red left" or "brown right" or "double wing" or sometimes "shotgun." My call told the defense what we were going to do a second later when the ball was snapped, because our defenses were automatic, depending on the other team's formation.

By now, I'd reached the point where the other players had confidence in me. They hadn't at first. They didn't know where I was going to be—they figured I'd be running around out in center field some place, hitting just for the sake of hitting. But now we had respect for each other's abilities. I had more experience now, but it takes more than that. A lot of knowing what to do out there on the field isn't so much experience as it is instinct. It's like when you're driving a car and all of a sudden the driver up ahead spins out of control. If you have to stop and think, "now I will lift my right foot off the accelerator and put it firmly on the brake pedal and then I will take my hands and twist the wheel slightly to the right," it'll be too late to avoid getting mixed up in the accident by the time you get all those things sorted out in your mind. You've got to react first and think about it later.

Our defenses were all prearranged, so that on any given play I'd know whether I should go in after the quarterback, drop back to guard a pass receiver, or help stop a running play. The other ten defensive players knew where I'd be, and I knew where they'd be. Everybody liked to know where Nitschke was going to be operating so they'd know where their help was coming from.

After that embarrassing loss to the college boys, we started putting our game together, and we won all the rest of the exhibitions. Our opener for the regular season was with the Bears. The game started out well, with Jerry Kramer kicking a forty-one-yard field goal in the first quarter. But then Chicago got three points, too, and when we got the ball back our offense started having all kinds of trouble. Starr had thrown only nine interceptions during the entire 1962 season, but Chicago intercepted four passes in that first game of 1963. We never found out if Hornung's replacement, Tom Moore, could smell the goal line from the ten-yard line the way Paul could, because the closest we got all day was the Bears' thirty.

It wasn't one of my better games. My knee got hurt when I was chasing a receiver and was blocked from the side. And I got caught offside, which is something that almost never happened to me. I stepped across the line and Mike Pyle, their center, snapped the ball before I could jump back. It was smart football on his part. When they walked off those five yards, I was angry—not at Mike, at myself.

It's hard to win a game when you can't get inside the other team's thirty, and Chicago beat us, 10–3, not a very encouraging start to what we hoped would be our third championship season in a row. We did better the next Sunday. Against Detroit, Moore scored two touchdowns and gained over a hundred yards, and we won by a one-sided score. Then we took the next eight games, giving us a 9–1 record, before it was time to head for Wrigley Field to take on the Bears again.

Chicago had an identical won-lost record, and the week before they'd held the Los Angeles Rams to a total of eighty-eight yards, so we knew we were in for a rough afternoon. We had to go into this showdown game without Starr —his hand had been broken a month earlier in St. Louis.

But we still had confidence in ourselves. We'd always been able to win the big games in the last few seasons, and we'd come to expect we'd be able to win them every time. But it didn't work out that way. Our offense couldn't get anywhere against those tough Chicagoans. It seemed like

I'd hardly gone to the sidelines before it was time to run out there again and try to get the ball back. By the time Moore finally scored a touchdown in the fourth quarter, we were behind 26–0. So when we left for home we were in second place.

But we weren't out of it. The next Sunday, the Bears were tied while we were winning from San Francisco. And now Starr was back in action again. When we played Detroit on Thanksgiving we were still hoping to catch the Bears before the season was over. If we could keep winning and somebody knocked off Chicago, we'd be back in a tie for the lead.

But the Lions weren't cooperating. It was a tough game all the way. We couldn't pull ahead until the fourth quarter, but then Starr hit Ron Kramer for a touchdown, and we led 13–6. I ran out on the field knowing all we had to do was hold the Lions for a few minutes more and we'd have the game.

On the next play, Tom Watkins was trying to block me, and I hit his helmet a good crack with my forearm. I felt something snap, and it wasn't Tom's neck.

"My arm's broken, guys," I said, back in the huddle. "I'm taking myself out."

"Oh, no you aren't, Nitschke," Dan Currie said. "Wait until this series is over."

So I stayed in, trying not to let the Lions know I was hurt. But I wasn't going to hit anybody with that arm. It was numb. There was no strength left in it. But even with only one arm to use, I got in on the next couple of plays. In fact, in one of them I got in far enough so I got my nose broken, too.

Our guys almost got to Earl Morrall on that one, but he

shoveled the ball to Nick Pietrosante, the fullback, and I helped stop him on our thirty-six. But enough was enough. I got out of there and Forester moved over to take my place with Dave Robinson, the rookie, moving in as right linebacker. But that was a makeshift arrangement, and the Lions went on to score. The game ended in a 13–13 tie.

It was a disappointing game. The previous year, we'd had the best field-goal percentage in the league, hitting on over 70 percent, and earlier in the '63 season Jerry Kramer had kicked fifteen of twenty-four, including four in one game. But this time our kicking was off. He'd missed a field goal from the ten, and one of his attempted points after touchdown was blocked.

Lombardi was apt to go easier on us after a loss than after a win—he knew we already felt bad enough when we'd blown one. He said the tie with Detroit didn't matter because for us to win the championship somebody would still have to beat Chicago. We now had a 9–2–1 record and the Bears were 10–1–1. If either the Forty-Niners or the Lions could beat Chicago while we were winning our last two games, we'd be tied in percentage and get another crack at the Bears in a playoff.

We won our last two games, all right—I was on the sidelines with my broken arm—but Chicago didn't lose. So our 11–2–1 record was only good enough for second place and a chance to play the Browns in Miami in what the coach called "a rinky-dinky game for losers," the Playoff Bowl. We beat Cleveland, but that wasn't much consolation. We'd had our chance to win three championships in a row and we'd come close, but close wasn't good enough.

If Hornung hadn't been suspended . . . if Starr hadn't

been hurt . . . if Jim Taylor hadn't been hampered by injuries and an attack of hepatitis . . . above all, if we'd only managed to rise to the occasion and win just one of those games with the Bears. . . . But as it was, we weren't champions any more, and that meant we had to come back next season and start proving ourselves all over again.

So when we reported to training camp at St. Norbert College the next summer, we knew what to expect. Lombardi was even tougher than usual, if that's possible. He'd wanted those three titles in a row, and he could have had them except for those Chicago games. The second time we'd played the Bears in 1963, we couldn't have beaten them if we'd had blackjacks and brass knuckles, but that first game had been close and could have been won. Losing it was the biggest disappointment of my career. It didn't please the coach very much, either.

So here we were again, the alarm clocks nudging us out of bed at 7:00 A.M. in time for seven-thirty breakfast, which you ate whether you were hungry or not. It was always a quiet meal. A lot of the players were still half asleep. Then there was time to study plays before the bus took us to the practice fields. The morning session was scheduled for 10:00 A.M., which meant that if you weren't out there running three laps around the field by 9:30 A.M. you were considered late, according to Lombardi Standard Time.

The morning drill lasted ninety minutes, and they were busy ones. The session involved a lot of running, and finished up with ten minutes of sprinting, all-out, so we'd end our first daily practice hot and sweaty and out of breath.

Then I'd go over with the other guys and inhale lunch, and then it was time to get the ankles taped for the second time that day and go back to the practice field wearing helmet and shoulder pads. During the morning, shorts and T-shirts were okay. But the afternoon drill ended up with a scrimmage where we'd knock heads together.

There were a lot of close friendships among the Packers. But when we got out there for those Lombardi-style scrimmages, there was no such thing as friendship. If somebody tried to get past me with the ball, he got knocked on his tailbone with as much abandon as if he'd been playing for the Bears.

I always tried to arrive for those summer sessions in good shape, a little under my playing weight instead of over. But some of the guys would shed as much as ten pounds in just one day. And when the last session was finally over we didn't ride back to the dressing rooms. We walked. And it was all uphill.

The day wasn't over yet, though. After dinner, there would be movies of the previous day's scrimmage, and the coach would give us new plays or show us how one play had looked at different times from different angles. You might see the same play run as many as fifty times. If you'd made a mistake in running it, you'd sit there wishing the projector would move a little faster when it came to that part of the film.

Lombardi didn't make his training camps so exhausting just because he liked to hear us pant. He knew that the time to get tired is in practice, not on Sunday afternoons when the season has begun. If you get fatigued in practice, there's no harm done. If you get tired in a game, you lose. So his training camps were far and away the most strenuous part of football for his players. He really worked us hard, not only physically but mentally. He knew that a well-conditioned player is not only able to play better, but he's less likely to get injured. He believed that a team that's really in shape wouldn't lose.

By now, my broken arm was in fine shape and I was ready to go. Sitting out those final games of 1963 had been frustrating. I'm not used to being too injured to play. I've been very fortunate to be able to take so many licks over fifteen years without getting hurt very often. I've had all the minor things a football player expects—abrasions and bruises and calcification problems with bones—but I'm blessed with a strong body, and that broken arm in the Detroit game was the only injury I'd ever had that I considered serious—unless you want to count losing those four front teeth to Ohio State. I've had a knee hurt off and on, but not so I couldn't play. I've always had a high pain threshold. Some people can't play with pain, but even though I think I feel it as much as they do, I try to concentrate on what I'm doing on the field and forget about the misery. You know the pain is there, but you try not to worry about it. If you start thinking about how much you're hurting, it bothers your play. Maybe it slows you down, but you do the best you can with whatever your body has to offer at the time.

All during that 1964 training camp we were looking forward to our opener, when we'd get a chance at the Bears, who'd shoved us into second place the year before. When the game began, we jumped right out to a first-quarter lead when Max McGee scored on a pass. Then in the second quarter, Moore made a touchdown on another Starr pass, and before the game was over Hornung celebrated his return to action by booting three field goals. We won, 23–12.

Hornung had really worked hard to get back in shape after that compulsory year's layoff. The coach had started him jogging a mile a day and running up and down the stadium steps twice, but before long Paul was jogging a mile and a half and running the steps three times. And this was before training camp even started. When the season began, he was ready to run and to block, and in that opening game it looked as if he could still kick the ball, too.

But kicking is a funny thing. Good kickers are as scarce as good quarterbacks. Anybody can kick accurately in practice, when everything's going well and he has the wind behind him. But to kick in front of a big crowd when you need the points to win and the wind is blowing wrong and the other team is crouched there a few feet away, ready to rush you and try to block the ball—that takes a hell of a guy to do it consistently. Not too many kickers can withstand this kind of pressure. And after that 1964 opener, something went wrong with our kicking game. The next two Sundays we lost because of missed extra points. Then we played the Colts and Hornung missed five field-goal attempts and we lost again, 24–21.

Something had to be done. Lombardi talked Ben Agajanian into leaving his sporting goods business in Los Angeles long enough to come to Green Bay to try to cure whatever was wrong with Hornung's and Kramer's kicking. Ben said it might be a loss of confidence, which made sense. If you've missed as many kicks as they were missing that year, you're bound to lose your confidence. Paul and Jerry worked with Agajanian and they improved a little, but when the year ended, our inadequate kicking game was the main reason why our record was 8–5–1, the worst since Lombardi's first year in Green Bay.

To win, you must have somebody who can make a field goal when you need it. The kickoff is important. So is punting. These are things you take for granted in the pros, but if I were coaching, one of the things I'd emphasize would be the kicking game. I've seen too many games lost over the years for lack of good kickers. The fellow who boots the ball may not be on the field more than a couple of minutes all afternoon, but how his toe meets the ball can make the difference between winning and losing. In 1964, with a little better kicking we would have won our first six games instead of losing three of them, and our final record would have been 11–2–1.

But kicking wasn't our only problem that year. Taylor made over one thousand yards again, and Starr was league champion quarterback, but our great center, Jim Ringo, wasn't with us any more, and he was hard to replace. When Ringo went to the Eagles, Bob Skoronski took over his job. But then Fuzzy Thurston got hurt, which meant Gregg had to move from guard to tackle, Skoronski took Forrest's place, and Ken Bowman, an eighth-round draft choice, became the starting center. Ken became a fine player, but it took a while and we missed Ringo, an all-pro at the job. Then there were other complications later in the season— Jerry Kramer went to the hospital, and for a while it looked as if he'd never be back. After they removed some wood splinters he'd been carrying ever since he was a small boy, he fooled everybody, including the coach, and returned to play as well as ever. But by then the season was over.

According to the story they tell about Ringo, he'd hired a lawyer to do his negotiating for a better contract. Now a young guy gets an agent as soon as he learns how to pick up a football, but in those days the coach wasn't used to dealing with outsiders. He didn't want to get used to it, either. When Ringo's attorney showed up, Lombardi excused himself and went out of the room to make a phone call. A few minutes later, he came back.

"I believe you've come to the wrong city," he told the lawyer. "Mr. James Ringo is now the property of the Philadelphia Eagles."

I always had some differences of opinion myself with Lombardi at contract time, but I did my own arguing. I rather looked forward to it. Our discussions would get pretty loud. Each year, the girls in the office would see me go into his office and sit back waiting to hear the yelling start. We'd get sore at each other. But it was all part of the game, and as long as I was the one doing the yelling instead of some lawyer who didn't know a red dog from a pink poodle, Lombardi never sent me to Philadelphia.

Even with that disappointing 1964 season, the Packers had won more games than any other team in the league since Lombardi arrived in Green Bay. But everybody started talking about the Green Bay dynasty in the past tense. The team was getting old, the sportswriters said. It was over the hill.

If just three or four more kicks had gone over the crossbar in 1964, those same guys would have been claiming the Packers were so good the team ought to be broken up to give the rest of the league a chance. But instead they were sitting at their typewriters explaining how we'd started skidding down the shady side of whatever hill it was they were talking about. I noticed that six of us made the Pro Bowl squad in '64, though. One of them was a middle linebacker who wasn't feeling a bit older than his age, which was twenty-seven.

I don't know why they built up that "over the hill" nonsense after we'd finished second two years in a row. We still had some good football players, so it was just a matter of time before we'd come back. I never thought we were on the wrong side of any hills, but I did think it would be a good idea to find a kicker. That thought occurred to Lombardi, too. He gave the Giants a third-round draft choice for a veteran, Don Chandler. New York figured Don was over the hill, I guess. But during his first season with us he made seventeen out of twenty-six field-goal attempts. The fellow the Giants used in his place made four of twenty-five.

In spite of all that shouting in Lombardi's office, my contract wasn't settled as early as usual as the next season approached, and I told a reporter I was playing out my option.

"They're paying the rookies too much and forgetting the veterans," I went on. "I'm worth more money."

I'd told the coach the same thing in a louder voice, but when the reporter asked him for verification, Lombardi denied I was playing out my option.

"Nitschke says he is," the newsman said.

"Oh. Well, nobody on this ball club plays out his option until he's talked to me for the last time."

Lombardi got sore at the reporter when he printed the story, although he didn't ban him from the Packers' dressing room the way he did a year later when Ken Hartnett of the Associated Press wrote that Taylor was playing out his option. It took an order from the commissioner's office to get Hartnett back through those dressing room doors.

The coach and I finally resolved our differences over my contract. Being picked as an all-pro middle linebacker the year before may have helped me a little in the arguments. But it didn't make me satisfied with the way I was playing. I've never been satisfied—not with any game, any play. I've always thought I could do better. After every game, heading for the dressing room, I was always wishing I could replay the game and do a better job.

It was in 1965 that Dick Butkus came along and began getting a lot of ink as Chicago's great middle linebacker, which he was and is, but I was glad to see that the young man had some respect for his elders.

"Nitschke is the greatest," he said. "I'm nowhere near that good."

That was a friendly thing to say. But I knew when we played the Bears again, Butkus would be running around out there and knocking people down and trying to prove he wasn't No. 2, even if he was trying harder.

We had a lot of injuries on the team. There had to be changes in the offensive line, the forward wall that's supposed to protect the quarterback. It developed a few cracks. In the first nine games, Starr was thrown for losses forty-three times. It had been a long time since a Packer quarterback had been treated that way.

Taylor was hurt. Hornung was so ineffective that he was benched. But we still had our tough defense. Sometimes, when the offense couldn't score enough points to win, we'd take over that job, too. Like the first Baltimore game. In the second quarter the score was 3–3 when Herb Adderley intercepted a Johnny Unitas pass and ran forty-four yards for a touchdown. Then late in the game, after the Colts had taken the lead, 17–13, Adderley recovered a fumble. Zeke Bratkowski came in and hit McGee for a touchdown that won the game.

Our running game wasn't effective enough to play ball control, but Starr and his receivers were doing well, and we were unbeaten after six games. Then we ran into the Bears, and we weren't unbeaten any more. The next week, the Lions beat us, too. The week after that, it looked as if we were going to have to settle for a 3–3 tie with the Rams until Lionel Aldridge recovered a fumble with a minute left and Chandler kicked a field goal.

Later in the season, however, we lost to the Rams, and after eleven games we were a game and a half behind the Colts. But then Baltimore lost to the Bears in a game that put Unitas out for the season with a knee injury, so when we played the Colts for the second time that year we were only half a game back.

If we could win, we'd take over first place. So this was a money game, and Lombardi decided to bring his money player off the bench. Hornung came through as of old. He scored five touchdowns, and we won. So all we had to do was beat San Francisco in the last game of the season and there was no way Baltimore could catch us. Even if the Colts beat the Rams, their season's record would be 10–3–1, and ours would be 11–2–1.

Judging from the record, we shouldn't have had any serious trouble with the Forty-Niners. But when you put on your pads and helmet and run out on that field, you aren't playing against the statistics. You're playing against eleven other guys who are good at their jobs, no matter where their team happens to be in the standings. On any given day anybody can beat you, especially if the other team has a quarterback like John Brodie. If he's having a hot afternoon, he's about as good as anybody.

With sixty-seven seconds to play, the Packers and San Francisco were tied. Even a tie would give us the championship. But then John brought down that great arm of his, the ball sailed into a receiver's hands, the Forty-Niners scored, and instead of Green Bay having the conference title, we had to get ready for a playoff with Baltimore—because now our season's records were identical, the Colts having beaten the Rams even though Unitas' team had no one to play quarterback but a halfback, Tom Matte.

Gary Cuozzo was Unitas' replacement, but he was taken out of the game with us with a shoulder separation. Matte hadn't called signals since he played for Woody Hayes at Ohio State. At Los Angeles, he taped the plays to his wrist so he could remember them. He didn't gain a single yard passing, but the Colts took the Rams, 20–17. You had to admire a team that could rise to a challenge like that.

But now we had to play them in Green Bay. There had been a ten-inch snow. The roads were still bad. But the stadium was filled, of course. It's always filled, but this was a game that no one wanted to miss. It would decide whether the Packers would be back on top, where we belonged. It would show whether a team playing without a regular quarterback could beat us. As underdogs, the Colts could play with that abandon Lombardi was always talking about.

On the first play of the game, Starr threw a pass to Bill Anderson, and Lenny Lyles knocked him down. The ball skidded along the frozen field when Bill fumbled. Don Shinnick grabbed it and headed for our goal line. Starr was one of those who tried to stop him, but Jim Welch threw a block and Bart had to leave the game with injured ribs. So the game had barely started and we were behind seven points and had lost our best quarterback.

The defense held Baltimore to one field goal the rest of the first half, but the closest we got to a score was the one-yard line. Hornung tried and Taylor tried but neither could shove his way for those three feet. On third down, Zeke Bratkowski fumbled. Baltimore recovered. At the half we were behind, 10–0.

It was a hard-hitting, bruising game that afternoon. The Colts might have the league's only nonpassing quarterback, but they had a good offensive line and some hard-running backs. It was an uphill battle for us, but the defense kept going out there and getting the ball back for Bratkowski, and finally he hit Carroll Dale with a pass and we had seven points. We went back out again and got the ball for Zeke and he took the team close enough to try for a field goal. Don sent it wobbling toward the goalpost, and what happened next depends on whether you're a Colts' fan or a Packer backer. The Colts claimed it didn't go between the uprights. But the officials said it did, so the score was tied, 10–10.

That's how the fourth quarter ended. But this was a play-off, so there had to be a winner. We came out for sudden-death overtime, and before long the Colts had the ball on our thirty-seven. Their kicker, Lou Michaels, was warming up his leg on the sidelines. But Matte wanted to get the ball a little closer to the goal before Lou tried the kick that could win the championship.

In a spot like that, a quarterback likes to go with his best man, and that meant Lenny Moore. Lenny was a back who was really quick on his feet. If there was a tiny opening, he'd find it. It was amazing how he could cut and change directions at the line of scrimmage. He looked skinny, but when he got near the goal line he'd lower his shoulder and really bang into you. He was a hard target. He'd keep his feet moving like pistons—boom, boom, boom, up and down—a real elusive player with grace and speed and the ability to evade you.

But this was one time we couldn't afford to have Lenny get away from us for even a short gain. We made up our minds to stop him. I didn't have to look over at the other guys—I knew they were where they were supposed to be and that they were just as determined as I was that the Colts had gone far enough.

Matte took the ball from the center. He shoved it into Moore's hands. Lenny's legs started pumping—boom, boom, boom—but they didn't pump very long. We came roaring in, knocking aside blockers, and hit him a yard behind the scrimmage line.

On the next play, Matte kept the ball. We smeared him for a two-yard loss. It was only third down, but in two plays the Colts had been moved back from the thirty-seven to the forty, and their coach decided not to take a chance that they'd be pushed out of field-goal range entirely. He sent in Michaels.

Lou has kicked plenty of forty-yarders in his time, and if he made this one we'd lost the championship. You always try to block a field-goal attempt, and you hope you get lucky. But mostly you try to make the kicker conscious that there are eleven mean tigers heading his way and he'd better not dally about getting that ball in the air.

I put myself right on the nose of the Baltimore center, and when he snapped the ball I gave him a little extra push. I wanted to throw the timing off. You never can tell for sure, but I thought afterward that I'd had something to do with Michaels missing that kick. The ball was short and to the right. When we took over on the twenty, the score was still tied.

Bratkowski connected for 248 yards with his passes that afternoon, demonstrating why people called him the best backup quarterback in football. Now he went about moving the ball down toward the Colts' goal. One of the passes that helped us make three first downs in that overtime was an eighteen-yarder to Bill Anderson, who'd been picked up by Lombardi after Washington released him. Anderson's catch was a big help, even though we discovered later that he'd been knocked groggy halfway through the fourth quarter and played in that overtime without knowing where he was or what was going on, operating strictly on instinct and habit.

People find it hard to believe that a thing like that can happen, but it's happened to me. It's a funny feeling. When you come to, you're in the middle of a football field—you don't know where—with the crowd yelling, and you don't even know who's playing or what you've been doing for the past few minutes. But you've made the moves so often in practice that you can go through them when your brain is blacked out.

So Anderson could catch a pass while he was out of his skull. But luckily, Bratkowski knew what was going on, and he kept moving the team downfield until finally Taylor was stopped on the eighteen. It was fourth down. Chandler came in. He didn't miss. We'd won the Western Conference title again, giving us the right to play Cleveland and Jimmy Brown.

Lombardi once said that Brown was "the greatest player of all time," and there's no question that he was a gifted athlete. Before that 1965 championship game, I spent the week thinking about how I was going to play him. He was the key to Cleveland's offense, so we had to stop him. It was easy for me to get myself keyed up against a player like Brown.

Jimmy was a fullback, but he ran more like a halfback. That was how Cleveland used him. Normally, a halfback is the one who runs the wide plays, the speed plays, and he needs more deception and more breakaway speed than a fullback usually has. Most fullbacks are the bruising type of player like Jim Taylor, a fellow who can hit the line and make it bend. The Bronko Nagurski or Clark Hinkle type of guy. By the 1970s, we began seeing more combination halfback-fullback types of runners. But in 1965 it was more unusual to see a fullback like Brown who was better going off tackle or around the end than through the line, a fullback who played the position with great finesse. He had speed. He was adept at using his blockers. He was the smartest runner I've ever played against. Brown didn't just take the ball and start running with it and hope things worked out. He knew where his teammates were, where his help was coming from, who was going to block for him.

He knew how each defensive player was going to attack him. For certain opponents, he'd just drop his shoulder and run over them; for others, he'd use his forearm to protect his legs; for still others, he'd use finesse and quickness to outrun them. He had a sixth sense that told him how the defense would react. Then he'd react accordingly. He was an artist—a brilliant football player who could not only beat you physically but mentally.

We didn't play Cleveland often while Brown was there, but when we did we usually did pretty well against him in spite of all his talents. He didn't run away from us. From noticing where and how he'd line up, we had a pretty good idea of what kind of plays the Browns were going to run. We keyed our defense off him.

Paul Brown was the coach at Cleveland then, and everything he did was done for a purpose. He didn't care whether an opponent knew what he was going to do or not. Like Lombardi, he said, "We'll outexecute you," and that's what his players tried to do. But we were out on that field, too, and it seems as if we were always ready to outexecute his team instead.

But if you were playing against a team coached by Paul Brown you had to be especially prepared and extra alert. If there was any coach Lombardi ever admired, it was Brown. He is one of the great coaches of all time. When we played his team we knew we had to be ready, because he'd have his players ready. And in those years when we played Cleveland he not only had his usual well-coached team, but he had Jimmy Brown.

To overcome the great talent of a fullback like that, it takes more than one man. The whole defense has to fulfill its responsibilities on every play. Any time he gets the ball, a fellow like Brown can run for six points, so we concentrated on stopping the long gains. We didn't expect to stop him from making some yardage, but we weren't going to let him make the big gain that can break a game wide open. If our defense slackened for just a moment, we knew Brown was going to be off and running for that goal line. So we couldn't afford to slack off.

I don't know how Brown played me—I'm sure he had his own theories about me, just as I did about him. I don't think he ever tried to run over me. I'm as big as most of the backs and I'm strong enough, so I've never been overpowered. I suppose it was a matter of studying how I reacted to a play; each middle linebacker reacts differently to a particular stimulus. I react to a sweep differently than Butkus or Tommy Nobis, for instance. Being the exceptional player he was, Brown would know how I'd react to a sweep or an off-tackle play or a drive up the middle. He'd know these things before the game began. Then he'd rely on his natural ability to carry him the rest of the way.

I don't think he ever fooled me, but I know he was reacting to what I did on defense. I spent a lot of time watching films, studying Jimmy Brown. He didn't run just to be going somewhere. He ran with a purpose, an aim. To stop him, you had to do your job a little better than normal. So it was more of a challenge playing against a man like that.

In fact, it was fun. I'd like to play every week against a superior player like Brown. It would make me get up for the game a little bit more. A great player like that can embarrass you. So if you have any pride in yourself, you do your job with a little extra effort. I made it a point to be extra ready when we were going to play against a team with a star back like Brown.

Before the playoff with Cleveland, I concentrated on him. I talked to myself about Jimmy, getting myself emotionally ready for the challenge I knew was ahead.

"Brown's your responsibility," I told myself. "Here's a big challenge. Are you big enough to handle it? Are you a big enough man to stop him? You're big enough and you're strong enough, but can you do it?"

That's the way I always approached a game where I was going to compete against someone like Brown or Sayers or Leroy Kelly. I'd get myself keyed up. I'd make up my mind that he wasn't going to make yards against Nitschke the way he'd made them against other teams.

Lombardi probably gave some thought to Brown that week before the playoff, too. But he had other things to worry about. Starr, Hornung, Taylor, and Boyd Dowler were all hurting—not enough to keep them out of a game like that, but they were hurting. Bart's ribs were still sore. There was a question of what would happen if he got hit there again.

It wasn't long after the game started that Cleveland started a little scientific investigation of that interesting question. Several of the Browns rammed into Starr's right side, where his bruises were. Standing on the sidelines, I winced when he got hit. But Bart didn't let on that it bothered him at all.

Dowler didn't do bad for an injured man that day, either. He caught five passes. That's a pretty good day's work even for a receiver who's feeling fine.

It had snowed, then rained, then snowed again on the

day of the game, so Lambeau Field wasn't in great shape underfoot. This may have helped slow Brown down, although those of us who had to chase him were using the same turf he was. After the game, Jimmy said he'd spent the afternoon "running into people I'm usually able to avoid." He didn't mention any names, but I knew one baldheaded fellow who'd been thinking all week about how to be sure of running into him.

At one point, Cleveland had third down inside our thirty-five and had been moving the ball pretty well. On the next play, the quarterback got ready to throw a pass to Brown. He'd gone through my zone of defense, so I had to cover him man to man. Running down there with him toward the end zone, I kept thinking: "I can't let this guy make a touchdown!" I knew he was much quicker than I was. But I had an angle on him, and I'd expected he would come into my zone, and when the ball nearly got to where he was reaching for it, I threw up my arm. I felt it hit. I saw it bounce away. I felt a lot better.

Knocking down that sure touchdown pass was one of the big plays of the game and one of the biggest plays I ever made in a championship playoff. But it wouldn't have happened if I hadn't anticipated the pass pattern. I'd been thinking about Cleveland's tactics in general and Brown in particular all week, and I figured he'd be the receiver because they always went to him in key situations.

You might think that a linebacker doesn't belong that deep in the end zone, but I was there because I had to be. Brown was my man to cover once he went through a certain area of the field past the line of scrimmage. He was my responsibility, and I wasn't going to let him score an easy one.

The first half of that game was close, but in the second half the defensive team really bore down. We held that great Cleveland attack to exactly fifteen yards rushing and eleven yards passing in the last two quarters. During the entire game, the Browns had the ball for thirty-nine plays, and our offense had it for sixty-nine. When you control the ball that much, you'll win. And we did, 23–12. After two years in second place, we were on top again.

There were eighteen men on the squad who hadn't been with the Packers when we won the championship in 1962. So we voted to have championship rings made as an official souvenir of the season, even though that meant some of us would have to decide which of three rings to wear when we took our wives out for a steak.

CHAPTER VII

Before the 1966 season started, General Manager Lombardi agreed to give Coach Lombardi enough of the Packers' money to grab off the year's prize rookies, Donny Anderson and Jim Grabowski. Lombardi had once worked for twenty-two dollars a week, so he knew the value of a buck. But he parted with a million dollars for those two college boys, hoping they'd be our new Taylor-Hornung combination in a few years.

The NFL bidding war with the AFL was nearly over—Congress had granted the leagues a partial exemption from the antitrust laws so there could be a common draft of talent and the owners could end their battle of the checkbooks. But there was one final bidding battle, and such players as Anderson and Grabowski got the benefit of the competition.

I'd signed for a five-hundred-dollar bonus, remember. I won't say there wasn't a twinge of jealousy in my heart. But I decided what the hell, it wasn't my money. If that million dollars was going to keep the team at the top of the heap, why not spend it? Some veterans said, "Why should guys who've never helped Green Bay get this kind of money instead of giving it to somebody who's earned it?" But most of us felt: More power to them. The new players might as well get it as somebody else. The Packers still had to compete with the AFL for the best players that year, so Lombardi had to come across with the better offer or lose out.

Before Lombardi got to Green Bay, the Packers couldn't have spent a million dollars on players, because that was more money than they took in during a year. But the Packers had changed, the league had changed, football had changed. Green Bay got as big a share of all that loot from TV as New York, and there was never an empty seat in the enlarged Lambeau Field. The club was now taking in about five million dollars a year. Its 1,698 stockholders, who'd chipped in to keep the team alive in the lean years, had agreed never to take any dividends. So all the profits could be plowed back into the business. And our business was to win.

Jim Taylor was one of those who got restless over all that big money being passed around to younger players. When Lombardi wouldn't pay him what he wanted, he decided to play out his option. That meant that 1966 would be his last year in Green Bay.

The new crop of rookies might be richer than I was when I drove my used Pontiac to Green Bay in 1958, but they soon found out that they weren't in for a soft life. Like the rest of us, Anderson started sweating it out on the practice field that summer, and one hot day he asked one of the older men where he could get a drink of water.

"Water?" the veteran said. "There hasn't been any water around here in eleven years."

When I came to the Packers, football was making money but it wasn't throwing much of it around. People like Anderson and Grabowski got out of college at just the right time, when the AFL and NFL were fighting for personnel. A veteran player was bound to think about what he'd do with six hundred thousand dollars if he'd gotten it instead of Anderson. That's an interesting figure, with all those pretty zeroes. But the people at the bank didn't mind seeing me come in by now, either. I was doing all right financially, and I decided if those two guys could help us win championships, more power to them. I won't say money isn't important. You need it to take care of your family. But it's never been the most important thing. I've never played football just for money. It has always been fun to play, giving me a chance to get out on that field week after week and test my skills and my body and my courage against the best.

Football wasn't the most important thing to me now, though. Lombardi used to say the most important things were your religion, your family, and the Green Bay Packers, and I could go along with that. But it was my family that had really solidified my life, and it ranked quite a distance ahead of the team. It was growing. John was three years old—we'd gotten him when he was three months—and in 1966 we adopted a brother for him. Richard was only ten days old when Jackie and I brought him home.

Those two boys and, later, their sister, Amy, made my life so much more interesting and worthwhile. Now there was not only the give and take of two people being married. Now there were four of us—later, five—and I would look at those kids and think of how someday they would develop into the kind of adults who'd make it a better world. As it was, the children made it a better world for a big, tough linebacker named Nitschke. They were so innocent and truthful and honest.

I wondered sometimes when they were babies if having a football-playing father would make it harder for my boys when they got old enough to go to school. I guess it has made things a little difficult for them at times. The other kids in school may have felt that because Ray Nitschke was a bruising kind of player, the little Nitschkes would be tough guys. Because I played aggressively, everybody expected the children to be that way. The other children didn't realize that because a father's tough doesn't mean his children necessarily have to be tough. Mine aren't. They've had a different life as my sons than I had when I was their age. They're not hungry the way I was, or as aggressive. The children of anybody who's in the limelight—a politician's son, for instance—have some special things to contend with, not all of them good. But I don't think this has been a serious problem for my kids, and they're doing fine.

Having children in the house meant that when I was trying to prepare myself emotionally for the next Sunday's game I had to remember to keep everything in perspective. If I was sitting there, getting myself ready to go out and stop Jimmy Brown, talking myself into being prepared to hit him a little harder and a little faster, it was hard to change directions and act interested when one of the boys came in to show me some little thing he'd made. But I tried. I did the best I knew how not to neglect the children because of those pressures that build up and build up each week before a game.

I didn't have as much time to spend with the children as I would have liked during the season. Sometimes they probably thought I was a kind of a funny guy, the way I'd act while I was waiting for the day of the game. But I tried to make it up to them in the off-season. I could spend more time with them then than the average father does.

During the season, I couldn't go out and play ball or take them fishing or hunting on Saturdays and Sundays, the days most fathers spend with their children. This was hard on my family sometimes. But they had to accept my schedule and appreciate that this was how it had to be.

When the boys were small, we didn't take them to the games because we knew they wouldn't sit still that long. But after John got to be seven or eight, he wanted to go to most of the home games. It was only then that he started to realize what his father did for a living and that people would yell and cheer when the old man grabbed a ball carrier and sent him crashing to the ground.

John could see then that playing football was one way to get recognition, but I don't think either he or his brother is going to grow up to be a professional football player, which is fine with me. Whatever they choose to do with their lives, I'll be satisfied if it's something they enjoy, something that gives them satisfaction—the kind of enjoyment and satisfaction I've found in football.

Every year I looked forward to having the season start again, and in 1966, when we finished our exhibition games, I started anticipating the competition with Johnny Unitas in the opener. All the previous winter we'd had to listen to Colts' fans claiming that Baltimore had been robbed of the title because of that close decision on Chandler's fourth-quarter field goal in the playoff. We wanted to go out and show that we could not only beat the Colts but that we could beat them when they had their regular quarterback.

Of all the quarterbacks I've played against—and in fifteen

years I've played against some good ones—Unitas was the best. Except for Bart Starr, and I only played against him in practice.

Unitas was the best among the opponents for his play-selection ability, his poise, the way he coordinated his passing with his receivers. He always had control of the game —that's the greatest thing I can say about him. He could pick you apart, little by little, piece by piece. He'd keep picking on you and picking on you, breaking you down here and there. He'd keep coming up with the right play on third down, which is the real test of quarterbacking. He was waiting for you to make one mistake. Then he'd pounce.

It was always a pleasure to play against him. You knew he wasn't going to beat himself, so you'd have to go out there and beat him. You couldn't afford to make mental mistakes when he was on the field. He knew where you were supposed to be. If you weren't there, he'd see it and take advantage of it.

A lot of quarterbacks don't pick up a mistake that fast. But if you were out of position when you were playing Unitas, he'd have a play ready to beat you. It was always fun playing against him.

Well, maybe fun isn't the word. But it was an opportunity to play against the best. If you could beat him, you got more satisfaction out of it than you did beating someone who wasn't quite that good. From the first day he came to the league, he was a poised quarterback, always in control of the situation. The game was never over as long as he had that ball in his hand. He didn't look graceful out there. You'd never hire old Johnny for your ballet troupe. But he did what he had to do. His job was to call the plays, hand off or throw the ball, be a coach on the field. And when the pressure was on, Unitas was at his best.

When Raymond Berry was catching passes for the Colts, the timing between him and Unitas was hard to believe, even when you saw it. Berry would have his back to the quarterback when the ball was thrown, and he'd turn around and reach up and the ball was there. Unitas anticipated Berry's movements with as much intuition as a wife who's checking up on a husband. He knew that so many yards down the field, in such and such a location, Berry would be ready to catch the ball. Then he'd get it there at that precise moment. I don't say it happened that way every time—there's no such thing as perfection on the football field or anywhere else. But it happened often enough because they'd worked on this timing until the execution was so close to being perfect that we could have two guys covering Berry and still he'd catch that ball.

The only way you could stop Unitas and Berry was to try to break down their timing. Sometimes we had some success at this, as in that 1966 opening game. The Colts got the first score, a field goal in the second quarter. But then Lee Roy Caffey grabbed a Unitas pass and ran it back for a touchdown, and a little later Bob Jeter intercepted another pass and ran for a score. So when the half ended, the Colts' offense had three points and the Packers' defense had fourteen.

Our offense scored another ten points in the second half, but it needn't have bothered. We were holding Unitas and the Colts scoreless. It was a fine way to start the long journey to the first Super Bowl. It entitled me to forget about

Unitas for a while and start concentrating on Jimmy Brown, because our next game was with Cleveland.

The Browns pulled out to a 14–0 lead before we got a score. With three minutes to go in the game, we were still behind by six points. But Starr was having a great year: When the season was over he'd passed for a total of almost 1⅓ miles and was voted the league's most valuable player. Like Unitas, Bart was able to control the game. Now he hit Taylor with a pass, and when the game was over the score was 21–20 in our favor.

We won our first four games that year. Then we lost by one point to San Francisco, which hadn't beaten anybody before. George Mira was playing quarterback for the Forty-Niners that day in place of Brodie, and we ran into him on an afternoon when he held a hot hand. So now we had a 4–1 record, and I went home and started concentrating on Gale Sayers, because the Bears were next.

Sayers was the finest instinctive runner I've ever played against. He ran like a rabbit, with a rabbit's quickness and ability to change direction while the hounds went thundering past. Once, watching the films when we were getting ready to play Chicago, I saw him make a play that I couldn't believe.

He went off tackle. He left the ground on his left foot. But he couldn't put his right foot down because there was a pileup ahead, and if he'd put that foot down someone would have reached out from the pile and grabbed it. So instead of landing on his right foot, he landed on his left foot—the one he'd taken off on—and it was only after he was clear of the pileup that he put that right foot down. Then he regained his balance and scooted away from there.

You wondered how it was humanly possible for Sayers to do some of the things he did. He made some moves when I was playing against him that seemed unreal. "How can the guy do those things?" I'd ask myself. To get hold of him, you had to be lucky. One player couldn't tackle him. When Sayers was in his prime and healthy, no one person was going to bring him down. You had to track him down with a posse, then surround him. The worst thing you could do with Gale was let him get outside your defensive perimeter. If he got around your flank, it was all over.

I loved to watch Sayers play football, but I hated to play against him because he was so elusive and so talented. He not only had all that quickness but he had more strength than he got credit for. On third down near the goal line, he'd run right through a lot of tacklers. Watching him on television or in the movies playing against some other team was a treat. I think I even watched him sometimes when I was playing against him, although then I didn't enjoy it quite so much.

Sayers had been sensational in his rookie year, and we'd been too aggressive in trying to defend against him. We'd get to him one step too soon, and he'd run by us. This time, we decided to try to turn him inside, to contain him, not to give him room to run on his sweeps.

I really prepared myself for that sixth game of the 1966 season—watching the films, talking to the coaches, thinking about Sayers and how to deal with him. To stop Sayers, the plan was to keep him in the middle of a perimeter of defenders. Each of us was to guard a certain piece of real estate when Gale had the ball, keeping him contained, then go in and everybody tackle him. Sayers was the kind of player who was probably going to get away if one man tried to take him without some help from his friends.

We were willing to give Gale a few yards inside. But we weren't going to let him get outside, where he could take off and score, as he'd done against so many other teams. "Keep him in a moving perimeter," Bengtson told us, and when the game started, that's just what we did.

It took team defense to stop a player like Sayers, and that's what we had that day. Everybody was in the right position. No one overran the play. We kept him trapped inside, and when the afternoon was over we'd held Gale to twenty-nine yards. Our defense had neutralized Chicago's main offensive weapon. We won, 17–0.

That was the sixth shutout since Lombardi became coach. It's interesting to notice that half of those shutouts came against our natural rivals, the Bears.

With Lombardi, you weren't supposed to look ahead more than seven days during the season—the game next Sunday was the only one that was important. Still, we did allow ourselves a thought or two about how the end of this season was going to be different. Always before, the Western Conference champ would play the Eastern Conference champ. Whoever won, that was it. The AFL had some sort of playoff, too, but we didn't pay much attention to what the other league was doing. The champion of the NFL was champion of football as far as we were concerned, and most other people felt the same way, even some of the AFL fans.

But the AFL and NFL were making peace, and this year the best teams from the two leagues were going to play each other. It wasn't named the Super Bowl yet—that was a last-minute choice—but it was going to show which league was really better. We were certain the NFL would win this showdown. But just to make sure there wasn't any slipup, we wanted our league to be represented by the best. That is, by the Green Bay Packers.

But first we had to win our conference title and then beat the Eastern Conference winner. So most of the time we followed the coach's advice and worried about one game at a time—the next one.

Donny Anderson got his chance in the game against Atlanta, which was an expansion team, and he scored two touchdowns, one on a seventy-seven-yard punt return. We also breezed by Detroit but then we lost to Minnesota, with Fran Tarkenton scrambling around. With a quarterback like that, it's more like a basketball game than football. But sometimes those scramblers manage to surprise you and win.

The next time we played the Vikings, late in the season, we kept Tarkenton's team from scoring a touchdown until the last quarter, and by that time we had a safe lead. We won all the rest of our games, too, including a close one with the Colts on the next-to-last Sunday. That gave us a 12–2 record. The two games we dropped were lost by a total of only four points. If we'd played just a little better we could have been the first team in history to win fourteen in a season.

To play in the Super Bowl we had to get by Dallas, and none of us thought this was going to be easy. The Cowboys had been an expansion team not long before, but they had improved fast under Tom Landry, who'd coached the defense for the Giants when Lombardi was there as offensive coach. He'd developed a fine team in Dallas, with players like Don Meredith, Don Perkins, and Dan Reeves.

Landry liked to use a lot of different formations. It was Lombardi's philosophy as well as Bengtson's to stick to basic football and not try anything too fancy. We felt that football is fundamentally blocking and tackling, and the team that does these two things best will win—it's simple arithmetic. So it was our plan in getting ready for Dallas to keep our defenses as simple as possible and concentrate on execution of the basics so we had confidence in what we were doing. Each player had some leeway to make his own adjustments, depending on the situation, so he could adapt to what happened faster than if we had a complicated kind of defense.

But in that 1966 championship game, Landry added some formations we'd never seen before. We'd studied a lot of movies getting ready for that game, but Dallas had never used some of those plays when the cameras were turning, and it caught us off guard. It really put Willie Davis and me on the spot, trying to adjust at a time when there was so much riding on how we reacted.

We stayed in one basic defense that whole game, however, adjusting it automatically to whatever formation the Cowboys pulled on us. So it was Dallas that determined what defense we were in on any given play. Still, we weren't really prepared to adapt to some of those things Landry showed us that afternoon. Dallas made some good yardage. In fact, it gained something like four hundred yards against us, and that didn't happen to our defense very often.

But Lombardi had some tricks up his sleeve, too. The day before the game, he'd showed the offense a new play variation, and on the first play of the game Elijah Pitts made thirty-two yards on it. We were ahead 14–0 before the game had gone very far. But then Dallas started fooling us with those formations, and before the first quarter ended the Cowboys had tied the score.

We knew they'd caught us off guard. But we felt that we could stay in the game with our automatic defenses, adjusting to whatever Dallas was doing. We knew we could win, playing the way we knew how to play. The other guy may outcute you. But sooner or later, if you stay cool and hold your poise, things will come your way.

In the last minute of the game, the Cowboys were a touchdown behind. But they were deep in our territory, first down and goal to go. Still, we stayed patient. We stayed with our own game plan. And then the moment came when they outsmarted themselves. They had a guy offside during one of those tricky formation changes, and that moved them back five yards. By the time they'd shoved on back to the two-yard line it was fourth down. A field goal wouldn't do them any good. This was the whole season, right here. We dug in. We made up our minds that they weren't going to get those two yards.

"We got to hold 'em," I told the other guys as we huddled behind our goal line. "And we're going to hold 'em. The offense got thirty-four points for us. We're not going to blow it."

The teams lined up. Meredith faked a hand-off to a back, then went out on a roll-out pass. That was when Dave Robinson made an all-pro play. He got past a Dallas guard. He grabbed the quarterback. The ball was thrown up in the air, and Tom Brown intercepted it.

We'd won the ball game, and we'd won it because we were patient enough to stay in our own defense, to play our own game. Now we were going to represent our league in the first Super Bowl.

There was a lot more at stake in that game than the difference between the players' winning and losing shares. But that first bowl game was built up out of all proportion, really. Our league had a lot of tradition, and we were going against the representatives of a younger league. If we could beat teams like Dallas and Baltimore, why couldn't we beat the Kansas City Chiefs? I felt they were a pretty good ball club, but not really in our class, regardless of the buildup the game was getting.

We watched movies of the AFL champions, and I saw nothing to change my confidence that we could take them. We didn't know much about their players, but they didn't know much about us, either. When we ran out on that field, our league's prestige was on the line, but I didn't think the NFL had anything to worry about as long as the Packers were on hand.

It turned out to be a real close first half, however. Kansas City really came after us. I was blocking for a kick—an extra point—and one of their guys came up and gave me the elbow. That really got me mad. I've got elbows, too, and I've used them. And here I was getting hit instead of doing the hitting, and I didn't like it. When guys come in there burning even on an extra point, you start to wonder what's going on. You don't give a guy the elbow on an extra point, which is usually pretty automatic, so I got sore. But it showed me the Chiefs had come there determined to play us on the football field and never mind our reputation.

Kansas City had stacked its defense against our running game, and when the Chiefs got the ball their players were trying a lot of fancy stuff. The Chiefs had their quarterback in a moving pocket, which was then the rage in the AFL. I could see this was another team like Dallas, one that tried to outcute you. We liked that type of team. We really did. We felt they could go ahead and be as cute as they wanted to and we'd beat them with basic football.

But at the half, we were ahead by only four points, 14–10. We weren't feeling too proud of ourselves when we got to the dressing room.

"Hey, you guys, you better wake up," Lombardi said. "The game will be over and you'll be on the short end. What the hell's going on out there? You forgetting you represent not only yourselves but the league and every other player in the league? Now get out there and play."

So we woke up and started to play some football in the second half. In the third quarter, Willie Wood intercepted a pass after a good rush by Henry Jordan and Willie Davis. He ran the ball to the Kansas City five, and then the offense came in and scored. From there on, it was a runaway. Starr started passing more—Max McGee caught seven of them, including two for touchdowns—and we won the second half, 21–0.

But in that first half, Kansas City played us almost even up, and it was a credit to them. It was a big game for both teams. Talk about pressure—during that first half, the pressure was thick enough to slice.

We felt it and I'm sure they felt it. But when we finally got back to playing the way we knew how to play in the second half, everything worked out fine.

CHAPTER VIII

By now, pro football had really come into its own. Sixty-five million people watched that first Super Bowl on television. Everywhere you went, people were talking football. They felt they knew the players from seeing us on closeups—and not just the quarterbacks and ball carriers, either.

There was a time when if you were a lineman, nobody knew you except your relatives, and some of them weren't sure how you spent Sunday afternoons. If you were on the defensive team, all that most people knew about you was that you were one of eleven anonymous guys who ran around trying to tackle people and knock down passes. But by the mid-1960s, a lot of Americans who hadn't known much football a few years earlier were getting educated. They could see it took as much skill or more to be a good defensive man as it did to run with the ball.

I was one of those who felt the change in attitude. I look like a different man when I put in my teeth and walk out of the stadium with my horned-rim glasses and bald head. But by now, I couldn't go anywhere—not only in Green Bay or Milwaukee, but any place in the United States—without people coming up and wanting my autograph.

I don't go around looking for that kind of recognition, but I've never tried to evade the public the way some players do. The way I see it, if a man's too weak to write his name on a piece of paper, he's got to be hurting pretty bad and had better take up some other sport instead of football, such as tiddlywinks. It bothers me when players give the brushoff to somebody who's friendly enough to want an autograph—especially if it's a kid. Being pleasant to the public is part of the price of being in the limelight. If people weren't buying tickets to see you play, you wouldn't be drawing your paycheck.

The only time I'd get a little irked was when somebody'd come up when I was eating in a restaurant, and by the time they left my steak was cold. Other than that, I've never minded. It's an honor to have them want to talk to Ray Nitschke.

"Why take the time to bother with these people?" other players asked me.

But I like people, and I try to treat everybody the way I want to be treated myself. If they respect me, I respect them. If they don't want to treat me right, then I try to stay clear. But if somebody wants to be friendly, I don't care whether he's got a million dollars or thirty cents in his pocket. I can remember times when I had trouble finding a nickel and a quarter to jingle together myself.

I don't say I've always felt this way about people. It used to be, when I was drinking, if somebody gave me the big smile I'd figure he was laughing at me and I'd be tempted to go belt him one. But I finally grew up.

Being in the public eye is one of the things a lot of young players aren't prepared to deal with. By the middle 1960s, with football so much in the limelight, the pressures were much greater than they had been when I got to the league. I was used to such things by then, and I could handle them.

But a young player who suddenly got a lot of money and a lot of fame when he was twenty-one or twenty-two years old discovered there were temptations he wasn't ready for.

An athlete can get to thinking he's pretty important. A player needs an ego that's bigger than normal. He has to believe he's better than the other guy, or he's in trouble. But that doesn't mean he can't be the kind of man people can like away from the field. Since I wised up and realized "I" wasn't the only letter in the alphabet, it has been important to me to have people respect me not only for being a football player but for being Nitschke, that friendly fellow with the bald head.

Football has given me a lot. I've achieved things that athletes who were more capable physically and mentally than I was didn't achieve because they didn't have the same commitment to the game. I think if you're going to be a professional you should try to give the game everything you have, and not only on the field, but off.

I have no complaints about players who get involved in outside activities in the off-season. It makes sense that they should. Any athlete knows he's going to quit while he's still comparatively young. Most people don't think much about retirement until they're close to sixty-five. A football player knows he'll give up his career before he's forty—quite a bit before, in most cases. So he has to get involved in something during the off-season that he can continue when he can't play any longer.

But those who get involved in outside interests that affect them adversely during the season not only hurt their team and their teammates but themselves. If you're going to be a part of something, go all the way or drop out. There's no place for people whose minds are on something else when they're being paid to play football.

Outside interests are more of a problem now than when I first came to the National Football League. Because of the new enthusiasm for the game, there are more opportunities and consequently more temptations. People are always telling you how to spend your money, especially after you've won some extra thousands in a championship play-off. Those big bonuses young players get for signing get them involved in investments. I avoided that problem: The only investment I made with my five hundred dollars was a used car. But I suppose if the Packers had made out the check with three more zeroes on the end, I would have had to spend a little more time figuring out what to do with my bonus.

Some young players get so wrapped up in their business problems that they can't really give the sport that brought them all this money a fair chance to use their talents. I've been involved in a lot of things myself, including some investments. I've gone all over the country making speeches and personal appearances for pay. I've done commercials, like the one where I put on a helmet and rammed my head into a wooden piling for Georgia Pacific to show how tough the stuff was. I've been involved in everything from a rope-skipping contest in Bloomer to a movie in Hollywood with the Monkees. But I only did such things in the off-season. Once the season began, I didn't worry about anything but football.

Bloomer, Wisconsin, claims to be the rope-skipping capital of the world, and somebody set up this competition between me and a disc jockey from San Diego, a fellow who spends a lot of time skipping rope. He was a lot smaller than I am, so they gave him a regular jump rope. The one they gave me looked like it was for anchoring a sailing ship. He beat me, but I blame it on the rope.

The Monkees were a teen-age singing group that was famous at the time, and this was the first movie they'd made. They invited me and Sonny Liston for walk-on parts. It was a war scene and there I was, playing a shell-shocked football player, wearing the green and gold of the Fighting Irish. It was kind of a weird movie. It didn't take long: One day and my scene was shot. There were plenty of Hollywood types around who were ready to tell me all about how to be a football player, so I didn't have any trouble with my role.

If you'd told me back at Proviso High that I'd go around making speeches to perfect strangers, I would have said you were nuts. But after I tried it I found out I didn't mind standing up and talking about football. The fees people were willing to pay helped the family budget. The way I approach that sort of thing is to stand up and talk, without planning ahead of time what I'm going to say. Once in a speech to the Touchdown Club in Columbus, Ohio, I said that when Lombardi called us together in the huddle before the first Super Bowl he didn't say the Lord's Prayer, he said, "Money," and it inspired us. Then I told them they'd heard of the Fearsome Foursome and the Eleven Angry Men, but the Packers were the Greedy Forty.

We joked about how rich all of us were getting when the winning shares started going up so high—winning those postseason games in 1966 gave every Packer an extra twenty-five thousand dollars. We could even kid about religion. Lombardi and, I hope, everybody else knew such remarks were meant as a joke. Actually, a lot of us took the subject seriously. Some people couldn't understand how a group of rough football players could pray together before a game. But we did, and I think this really brought the team closer together.

Lombardi was truly a concerned Christian. He felt there was a place for religion in his work, which happened to be coaching football. As a boy, he'd thought for a while that he wanted to be a priest. If he'd become one, some of us said, it would have changed the history of the Roman Catholic Church, because it's never had an American as pope. But when he went into football he felt that an athletic squad is no different than any other group where people meet together. Christians can be football players, and vice versa. The coach thought that when a group meets, it's helpful to pray together. He brought religion into the locker room, which is where it belongs, with the people. No matter what kind of religion we had—Lombardi was Catholic, I'm Lutheran, other players had various beliefs—we all had one God, and we could each pray to him in our own way. Religion was there because a lot of players as well as the coach believed it belonged there.

Praying together was one of the ways of giving the team the kind of unity we needed to deal with the problems and pressures that build up over a season. Pressure is something you have to learn to live with every season, but it was worse than usual in 1967. When your team is the champion, every other team is up for each game, hoping to knock you off. After all that publicity we got for winning the first Super Bowl, the Packers were the team everybody in the league wanted to beat. Besides, we knew how much the coach wanted those three straight championships. It's true that Green Bay won three straight under Curly Lambeau from 1929 through 1931, but Lombardi said that didn't count because in those days football was a different game.

"The Little Sisters of the Poor could have won then," he said.

Over the years, Lombardi rarely played an inexperienced man unless we were twenty points ahead or unless he was forced to substitute because of an injury. But when we started that 1967 season, he had some important cogs in the Packer machine that were missing and had to be replaced. Taylor had played out his option and gone to New Orleans. Hornung, who'd missed his only chance to play in a Super Bowl because of a pinched nerve in his neck, had been picked by the Saints in the expansion draft and had retired.

Grabowski and Anderson had been hired to replace that Taylor-Hornung combination that had scored so many points for us, but they were only second-year men. The coach had Elijah Pitts, who'd done a good job for us when Hornung couldn't play the previous year, and he picked up Ben Wilson from Los Angeles as another back. He talked Max McGee out of retiring. He had a good crop of rookies, but those of us who'd been there through so many tough games were the ones he depended on most. There were only fourteen of us left in Green Bay who'd been there when Lombardi won his first conference title in 1960.

When the 1966 season ended, it had seemed as if the Packers were unbeatable. But this was 1967, and what we'd done the year before no longer mattered. Detroit tied us in the opener. We barely got past Chicago. We won from

Atlanta, but then we had to play the Lions again, and in the third quarter we were tied, after being behind earlier in the game.

Dave Robinson and I were blitzing when Milt Plum went back to try a pass. When the quarterback saw us barreling down on him he tried to throw to his fullback. But he got the ball away a little low. Robby batted it in the air. When it came down, I had it. I get paid to knock down people carrying footballs, not carry them myself. But I took off for the end zone twenty yards away and made my first touchdown since the Dallas game in 1960.

When you intercept a pass and make a touchdown, it's a big play, and a defensive man likes to get some points. But it seems as if every time I carry the ball I'm apt to get hurt. I pulled a muscle scoring that touchdown against the Lions. In high school and college, I wanted to star on offense. But then I got older and smarter. I'd rather go after the fellow with the ball and hit him with a good, clean tackle than be out there with all those guys on the other team chasing me.

We won that Detroit game. The Vikings were next, and they hadn't beaten anybody so far. But they won from us. Lombardi was worried. Even in the games we'd won, he felt we hadn't looked like champions. He called his fourteen veterans to a meeting. He asked us to help him with the younger men.

"Frankly," he said, "I just don't know what the hell to do."

That didn't sound like the coach. Of course, we promised to do everything we could. But if the coach didn't know what to do, who did? It was quite a relief when Lombardi showed up the next day and started yelling at people. That meant things were back to normal.

Starr had been hurt in the Atlanta game, but now he was able to play again, and that helped. We took on the Giants next. They were ahead 14–0 at the half. Then we started to play football. We scored forty-eight points in the last two quarters to beat them, 48–21.

We came from behind again to beat St. Louis when Travis Williams returned a kickoff ninety-three yards—he set a league record that season by making four touchdowns on kickoff returns. The next week we played Johnny Unitas and his Colts. Baltimore had lost its last five games with us, and I imagine there was some feeling in the Colts' locker room that they didn't want to make it an even half dozen. They came out hitting.

But our defense was hanging tough, too. Neither team was able to score a touchdown in the first half, and with two quarters gone we were leading by a field goal. It was still 3–0 at the end of the third quarter, although the Colts came close to a touchdown late in that period. It was fourth and one. Unitas wasn't going to give up without trying for a touchdown. As we waited for the snap, I made up my mind that the man to watch was Lenny Moore. A quarterback will go with a favorite play or a favorite player on a crucial down, and with Moore on your team, he had to be Unitas' favorite to pick up that one yard. Over the years, Johnny has had a lot of success giving the ball to Moore. But this time I was ready. Sure enough, Lenny got the ball, and I hit him hard and fast, and instead of a first down, Baltimore had a one-yard loss and we had the ball back on downs.

A similar situation came up in the fourth quarter, and once again the ball went to Moore. I was expecting it for the same reasons as before. I didn't throw Lenny back this time, but I stopped him for no gain. After the game, Lee Roy Caffey said those were the two greatest fourth-down plays he'd ever seen. I was a little proud of them, myself. There's a special kind of challenge in a short-yardage situation, and you have to defend against it differently.

Normally, all a back has to do is take the ball and fall forward and he'll gain a yard. So if a yard is all he needs, it's a matter of getting to the line a little faster than he does, meeting him there before he has a chance to fall forward. One step is the difference between making the play and not making it. A false move and he's made the gain. It's a guessing game. He's trying to outguess you and you're trying to outguess him and sometimes, as in those two fourth-down plays against Baltimore, you get lucky.

But even though we scored a touchdown in the fourth quarter of that game and went ahead 10–0, Unitas was still in control of his game. Late in the fourth quarter, he passed for a touchdown. The kick failed and so it was 10–6, and a field goal wouldn't tie it for the Colts. They had to have another touchdown, and so they tried a desperation play, an onside kick. It rarely works. But it worked this time, and after Baltimore recovered the ball, Unitas knew exactly what to do with it. He threw his second touchdown pass within sixty seconds of play, and we lost, 13–10.

In the next two games, our defense allowed a total of just seven points. Cleveland got one touchdown while we were scoring fifty-five points. The Forty-Niners were shut out.

So if we beat the Bears, who were next, we'd cinch first place in our division.

Caffey was hurt for that Chicago game and Tommy Crutcher, who lacked experience, took over as right linebacker. Quarterbacks love to test a new man. They feel very friendly toward a new face. Right away, they make him feel like an important factor in the game. So Jack Concannon started sending his backs into the right side of the line, and he said later that this was how Chicago outrushed us, 180 yards to 71 yards. But he added, "after a while, Green Bay made some adjustments—they toughened up."

What happened was that I started offsetting to the right to give Crutcher a little help. Not that he wasn't hanging tough himself. At one point, the Bears had the ball on our six, but Tommy made two fine tackles, and we held them at the two. They had to settle for a field goal.

Concannon could brag that they'd outrushed us, but he couldn't brag about the final score. It was 17–13, our favor. The reporters were surprised we didn't do more celebrating about winning the Central Division title—there was no whooping around in the dressing room or squirting champagne. But we knew that with the league divided into four sections, we still had a good way to go before we'd be ready to pour bubblewater on each other and claim the championship.

Even though we'd won our division, it was important not to relax and lose momentum. The next Sunday we ran into Minnesota when Dave Osborn was having the best day of his career. He made 155 yards on the ground, and the game was tied late in the fourth quarter. But Joe Kapp fumbled on his own 28, and we recovered. Don Chandler won the game with a field goal with 8 seconds left.

Osborn hasn't had the publicity that some backs get, but he's always in the game, always giving his best. He keeps coming at you. He's the kind of back who wins ball games, and he almost won that one.

Every team you play has players with speed and power. All the backs are good. It's a matter of some of them having better men to block for them. If you have a great back playing behind a poor line, he's not going to get far. You can have a mediocre back with an outstanding line, and he looks like a star.

Each week, a middle linebacker has a different challenge, which keeps the job interesting. Each opponent has certain things he does better than others. One may go off tackle better than he runs the sweep. Another may go up the middle better or block better or catch the ball better than somebody else. Because a back can run certain plays better than others, his team will take advantage of that ability. Take Sayers, for example. He had certain talents, and the Bears would utilize them—or some of them. I could never figure out why they didn't throw to Gale more. With his ability as an open-field runner, they could have given him the ball on screen passes where he'd have room to run.

If you're on defense, you note what the other man's special abilities are, then try to take the best part of his game away from him. But all those backs are big. They can all hurt you physically. If you're not careful, they can hurt you on the scoreboard, too.

After we barely beat Dave Osborn and the rest of the Vikings that year, we went to Los Angeles. The Rams were fighting it out with Baltimore for the Coastal Division title, and for the first time in history Memorial Coliseum was completely sold out for a football game—76,637 fans, all yelling for the home team.

I'd spent the week before that game thinking about Roman Gabriel. He's a good representative of the new breed of quarterback. When I first came to the league, a quarterback ran with the ball only from fright. But Roman's as big and tough as a fullback and just as hard to bring down. It makes him effective on the option, where he has the choice of passing or keeping the ball himself. It gave me one more thing to guard against. If I saw somebody like Unitas with the ball, all I had to guard against was the pass. But when Gabriel had it, you could never be sure he wouldn't come barreling through the line, ready to sting and be stung.

The Rams had to win that game to stay ahead of the Colts. The only reason we wanted to win was for our pride, but that was enough to make it a great contest. First one team went ahead, then the other. In the third quarter, we were behind by seven points. But then the Road Runner, which was what the writers were calling Travis Williams, caught a kickoff four yards inside our end zone and ran it back for a touchdown. The Rams broke the tie with a field goal, but then Chuck Mercein gave us the lead with a touchdown.

So we were ahead by four points late in the game when Donny Anderson went back to punt and Tony Guillory got his hand up in front of the ball. Then Gabriel hit on his third touchdown pass of the afternoon and we lost, 27–24.

Losing a game like that was no disgrace. But the next week was different. Pittsburgh, which hadn't won from us since 1954, beat us in the last game of the season. That gave us a

9–4–1 record for the season, compared to 11–1–2 for the Rams. We were scheduled to play them in Milwaukee two days before Christmas of 1967 in the first of two playoffs to decide who'd represent our league in the second Super Bowl.

The experts studied the season's statistics and gave some thought to how we'd lost our last two games, including the one with the Rams, and they decided our chances weren't good. Los Angeles had lost only one game all year, and the headline writers claimed they were the "team of destiny," whatever that meant.

We'd had problems all year with injuries, and we still weren't in good shape. Ben Wilson had rib and ankle troubles. Pitts had a torn Achilles tendon. Grabowski had twisted his knee in the Colts game, then reinjured it against the Bears. Donny Anderson was hurt, although he could still play. We were getting short of guys who could carry the ball, and the coach had picked up Mercein from the Redskins' taxi squad, so for this big game of the year our starting fullback was going to be a player who hadn't been considered good enough to play for Washington.

But the boss man didn't buy that "team of destiny" stuff about the Rams. Neither did I, although I couldn't forget how the Los Angeles team had beaten us by blocking a punt and then scoring on a Gabriel pass. I had a lot of respect for Roman. He's an inch taller than I am and weighs almost as much, which made him the biggest quarterback in the league. There was no question about his strength, his poise, or his ability to read defenses.

The Tuesday before the game, Lombardi made us a speech. He gave us a slogan.

"Everything you do this week," he said, "you run to win. On or off the field, you run to win."

All that week, Lombardi kept reminding us: "Run to win." The words were burned into my brain. I kept saying to myself, "I'm running to win, I'm running to win." But it wasn't until the morning of the game that the coach told us where he'd found the phrase. It was St. Paul who first advised that you should "run to win," he said. Lombardi didn't claim Paul had been thinking of the Rams at the time. Still, it was nice to know that our strategy was based on not only the coach's authority but the saint's.

I was really keyed up for that game. When I started tackling people, I was running to win. When Gabriel was backing up looking for passers, then headed downfield because he couldn't find them open, I'd go after him, running to win. I was really reckless that day, but it was all right because I was running to win.

I wasn't the only one. Henry Jordan had one of the finest games I've ever seen a defensive man play. He caught Gabriel five times. The Rams scored first on a fumble, but that touchdown was the only score they got all day. When Travis Williams broke loose, he started running to win, and he made it over the goal line forty-six yards away. When Carroll Dale caught a pass, he started running to win, and he scored another touchdown. Then in the second half, Chuck Mercein ran to win and Williams ran to win and we had two more touchdowns, so the team of destiny from L.A. lost to the Packers, 28–7.

All during that cold December afternoon, the fans shivered in their blankets and cold weather gear. Even the beer sales fell off at County Stadium, and when that happens in Milwaukee you know it's cold. But down on the field we were so fired up we hardly noticed those icy breezes. I was hitting people like Les Josephson, the Rams' halfback—he made only sixteen yards on nine carries—and when we'd get back to the huddle we'd start hitting each other. Jordan would pound my shoulder pads and yell, "Come on, let's go get 'em," and I'd whop the next guy in line. No matter what the fans thought, it wasn't cold out there on the field at all.

Lombardi had an explanation for everything, and after the game he explained why we'd gone after Los Angeles with so much abandon.

"Everybody's been saying we were dead, that we'd won in a patsy division, that we weren't the Packers we once were," he said. "We had something to prove."

We proved it, too. As Willie Davis said afterward, "it was like those other people were going to come into our house and break up the furniture."

Lombardi had used that "run to win" slogan to remind us we had to play hard because here was our chance to make all those painful practices pay off. We could do something no one had ever done before—win three championships in a row for Green Bay, then go on to win the first two Super Bowls. And that's why all week he was saying, "Okay, you guys, let's go—you're running to win."

I still carry that little slogan in the back of my mind because I believe, as Lombardi did, that if you're in a contest you give it everything you have. The coach was proud of that phrase. He made sure we wouldn't forget it. He had those three words, "run to win," engraved on the inside of the championship rings we got that year.

Some of the sportswriters said our 28–7 victory over the Rams that frigid December day in Milwaukee was one of our greatest games under Lombardi. Red Smith said Jordan never played a finer game. He said I was "a living flame." I don't know about being a flame, although it was cold enough so the team could certainly have used one, but I know that a lot of us were playing with that abandon the coach was always talking about.

I really enjoyed myself that afternoon. I felt like going out there and being even meaner than usual. I wanted to hit people and watch them bounce. When it was the offensive team's turn to go on the field, I hated to leave. Once when the Rams were close to a first down, the referee called time out for a measurement, and I told him not to bother.

"Don't measure," I yelled. "Give 'em first down. We're not ready to stop."

Except for a fumble and then a fifteen-yard penalty against us, that "team of destiny" from Los Angeles would never have scored at all in this game for the Western Conference title. Another fumble had stopped our opening drive and, as Lombardi said, "We had to make two fumbles for them to score seven points."

Until that day, the Rams were the highest-scoring team in the league. But, of course, Gabriel was operating under a handicap. He didn't have St. Paul on his coaching staff the way we did.

CHAPTER IX

There's no problem getting yourself emotionally ready to play a game like that 1967 playoff with Los Angeles or the even more important game that followed, the one with Dallas, which beat Cleveland 52–14 to win the right to represent the Eastern Conference of the NFL. The Dallas game was going to be the biggest game of Lombardi's career, maybe the biggest one in the long history of the Packers. It would decide whether we'd take our third straight league championship and have a chance at our second Super Bowl. So we didn't need St. Paul or even St. Vincent to tell us we'd better be ready to play the Cowboys when we ran out on that field.

But every game of the season is important. Before every game I've ever played, I'd get a knot in my belly. If I didn't, I'd know something was wrong. It's not that I was afraid of those other guys in football suits. My fear was that I wouldn't play as well as I was capable of playing. Anyone with pride in himself is going to be tense before a game, whether it's with the Cowboys for the championship or only an exhibition.

Being mentally prepared to hit people is something you can't turn on and off, like pulling a switch. It has to be built up during the week. If you've brought yourself to the right emotional pitch, you get butterflies when you run out on the field for the first play. Then you hit somebody. You hit somebody with everything you've got. And if you hit him hard enough, those butterflies go fluttering away.

There was a penalty for being so tensed up for each game. Monday and Tuesday, win or lose, I'd feel a big letdown. If I'd built my emotions up especially high for a game, I'd have a bigger letdown. It's true that all the games are important, but why kid ourselves? Some are more important than others. It's not always just a question of whether you're playing for a title or trying to beat one of the top teams. Anytime we've played the Bears, for instance, it's been a big game, and I built my emotions up for it because all my old friends would be watching and I didn't want them to see Nitschke out there not doing his best. Whenever we were playing at Lambeau Field it was a big game for me. My family and friends and neighbors would be there, and that made a difference. Knowing that all those people in the stands had their hopes wrapped up in the Packers' winning made a difference. Any home game is a big game, never mind what the standings are.

Even though that 1967 playoff with Dallas would decide whether we'd get our third championship in a row, we prepared for it about the same as for every other game during a season. Week after week, season after season, my schedule has gone something like this:

Monday: A day off. Stay around home, trying to unwind from Sunday, feeling depressed. It was like somebody'd stuck a pin in a balloon. Even if we'd won the game, even if I'd played well, that's how I felt afterward. There was a big letdown from the emotional buildup that had led to Sunday afternoon. Now I was mentally fatigued, gloomy, down. The whole season was like that, my emotions going up and up as the game approached, then down and down after it was over. That's one reason I was so much better off when I quit drinking. Alcohol accentuates your mood. When I'd get depressed after a game and start drinking, I'd just get more depressed. But even under the best of circumstances, Monday during the season is sort of a nothing day.

Tuesday: Now it's time to bottom out from the postgame blahs and start building toward the game next Sunday. It's also time to go back to work. A short practice. Lots of stretching exercises to get the kinks out. Then a movie of the last game so you can see what you did wrong and what you did right. Next, you hear a scouting report about what to expect in the upcoming game. Now you were starting to think about that team you'd be playing Sunday, not the one you played last.

Wednesday: By now, my emotions would have started to build toward the next game. The coaches kept us busy. We'd review what to expect from the next opponent, splitting up into offensive and defensive squads and talking about the individual players we'd be seeing next Sunday, their strengths and weaknesses. We'd talk over the other team's plays and how to defend against them. After about an hour and a half of this, we'd go to the practice field and have a two-hour workout. We'd demonstrate the other team's defense for our offensive team, and they'd demonstrate the opponent's offense for us. For a linebacker, a good share of the practice consisted of trying to defend against the kind of passing game we'd expect to see on Sunday. The whole secondary might practice against the offensive receivers, backs and quarterback. Then everybody would get together and we'd practice against the running game, with the offense demonstrating the opponent's ground attack and with us demonstrating the other team's defensive habits.

Thursday: Another hard day of practice and study. You tried to put yourself in the right frame of mind to go out there Sunday. If you were on schedule, the emotion had started to build pretty well, but not too far. You wanted it to peak on Sunday.

Friday: It was time to ease off a little physically, though not mentally. A shorter practice. More attention to working on finesse, perfecting the fine points of your game, getting used to last-minute changes, making final adjustments on your assignments. After that practice, you were supposed to be ready for Sunday afternoon. Even the meetings were short on Friday. You'd seen movies of your opponent's last two games, so you were aware of his weaknesses and strengths. On Friday, you reviewed what you'd learned, and made any final changes in your plans.

Saturday: A travel day if the team was playing away from Green Bay. In any case, it was mostly a day for resting, for putting your feet up, for getting your mind keyed up to go roaring out there the next day, ready to play. Usually we had a fifteen-minute practice that day, at home or away, but it was just to loosen up the muscles. All day, no matter what was going on around you, your mind would be on the game. It had to be. By now, you had to be ready. If you waited until Sunday, it would be too late to turn on those emotions that had been gradually building up during the week. If we were playing in Green Bay, I'd come straight home to my house in Oneida after the morning workout and cool my heels. Saturdays during the season, I was just

166

a nothing. Like Howard Hughes, I'd stay away from everybody.

Sunday: The hard part of the process was over. Now I was ready. I wanted to go out there and show those guys on the other team why it was a mistake for them to leave their locker room when the Packers were on the field. I was not only ready to play, I was ready to have fun because the week's drudgery was over.

The only part of football most fans see is the game on Sunday, but that's only the tip of the iceberg. The game may very well be decided several days before by the kind of effort the players put out in practice, the amount of study they do on the opponents, the way they build up their emotions toward the moment when the contest begins. It's in practice that you learn to react to a stimulus without having to think about it—if somebody does this, you do that. If you really get yourself involved in practice, really concentrate, it will make the game itself so much easier. Practice is work. You have to take it seriously. There's time for a little laughter once in a while, but not too much. Football is not a laughing game. The fun is in the game itself, when you get out there and put it all together. If you joke around in practice, that's the way you're going to look on Sunday— like a bad joke. If you're kidding around during the game, somebody's going to come up and knock your block off.

The ones who practice hard are the ones who'll play well. The ones who goof around don't usually help the team much when game time comes. A few guys are loose in practice and stay loose in the game, but they're rare. Most of us really have to bear down and work at what we're doing.

I've always been one of those who had to work hard at the game.

One bad practice can affect how you'll play the next Sunday. You try to build up a psychological edge for the game in easy steps, starting with Tuesday. One bad day throws you off. If you've had a whole week of bad practices, you'd be better off hiding under the bench on Sunday.

The player who applies himself and disciplines himself during the week has the advantage. The one who thinks his natural ability will carry him finds out it'll carry him only so far. I've seen players with a lot of ability who just went through the motions in practice because they didn't really like football but were good enough physically to get by for a while. They fooled themselves. Sooner or later, a man like that loses out.

In getting ready for a game, a middle linebacker can't concentrate on getting ready for just one opponent. Some players can—a guard, for instance, knows he'll be dealing mainly with one man on the other team. But I always had to worry about a lot of different people. Everybody except the center has an angle on the middle linebacker—the guards, the tackles, the tight end, the flankers, the backs, any one of those players may be assigned to block him on a particular play. The middle linebacker doesn't know ahead of time which will be coming after him, so he has to watch them all.

That's one reason why a man playing my position has to be a different breed of athlete. He has to be able to take a lot of contact, a lot of physical abuse, and he has to be ready to give it out. He has to be a fellow who totally enjoys contact. He needs a tremendously competitive personality, a natural instinct for football, the ability to react instantaneously to what happens on the field. He has to be able to adjust to developments without having to stop to think about it.

One of the things I've enjoyed about the job was the challenge of not having a set pattern, never knowing from one play to the next who's responsible for butting heads with you. A middle linebacker must contend with the whole offensive team at one time or another, so his spot is a very interesting place to spend Sunday afternoons.

In baseball, a team tries to be strong down the middle—catcher, pitcher, second baseman and shortstop, center fielder. A football team has to be strong down the middle, too, because a straight line is the shortest distance to the goal. If the offense can move the ball straight ahead, it doesn't waste time going to the flanks or running sweeps. You're there to see that no one's going to move straight ahead, because your body's in the way.

As a middle linebacker, I've never felt I was having a good afternoon unless I was in on 60 or 70 percent of the running plays. Playing there in the middle, it was easier to see these plays developing.

Once the ball was snapped, I didn't have to look in the backfield to see who had the ball—I could tell from the man who was trying to block me where the ball carrier was going to be. One of the hardest things for a middle linebacker to learn is not to watch the backs. He wants to get the man with the ball, so it's a natural instinct to try to see who he is. But once you start looking in the opponent's backfield, you get in trouble. Your first job is to evade that player who's been assigned to try to block you.

What you do is watch the snap, then move in the direction indicated by what the opponent you're keying on does. It might be a back. If he moves right, you go right. If he goes left, you go left regardless of whether he has the ball. Your initial key is that back, and he dictates what you do when the ball is snapped.

But then you forget about him and start looking for the blocker who's after you. The player you've keyed on has given you your direction. Now the blocker tells you where the ball is going to be. If the blocker's helmet is on your right hip, for instance, you know the ball carrier is to your right. The blocker is usually in front of the ball carrier, and your job is to get past that blocker—"go through that man's helmet," as they say. You do that any way you know how within the rules. I'd use my forearms. I'd try to keep the blocker from making contact with my legs, because once he hit my legs I'm on the ground and I'm not going to get to the ball carrier.

That's the object: Find the ball. But there's usually a man connected with it, so you have the courage to hit that man.

Of course, the blocker has another objective in mind, and he isn't going to be helping you any. He has one kind of job to do, and you have another. He may outweigh you by forty pounds or more. He's as strong as you are. You aren't going to overpower him. What you usually try to do is push his head. Being connected, the body has to follow. A man's balance and equilibrium are determined by the head. Push it down, he'll go down. Knock it to one side, he'll go to that side.

While you're trying to outmaneuver the blocker, you stay in the football position, with your knees bent. He's usually coming at you low, his body thrusting up at you. If you can't push the guy down, you try to straighten him up. Once you've straightened him up, you've defeated his strength, and you can usually throw him aside and go after the ball and that fellow who's attached to it. Your goal is not to let the blocker drive you back. If you don't get to that ball carrier until he's five yards down the field, you aren't successful at your line of work. If you beat your blocker and get to the ball at the line of scrimmage, you're accomplishing what you're being paid to do.

The blocker is usually bigger than you, so you have to be quicker than he is. You have to work at your game so you'll be agile. If you do have to use strength instead of agility, you learn how to use it most effectively. You do this by being aggressive and getting the blocker before he gets you. You have to beat that blocker the instant the two of you come together.

It's like tackling. In tackling, you hit the ball carrier harder than he hits you. You go at him with more velocity, a more aggressive attitude. If you're not going to hit the blocker or the runner with more enthusiasm than he hits you, he's going to defeat you.

That's why learning all the fine points of tackling is important for a defensive player. After the season starts, there's not much chance to practice tackling except in the games. You're supposed to know how. It's taken for granted. But I disagree with this theory. I think tackling is something that ought to be practiced all the time. It's not only technique, it's attitude. You should work on it, and I think that's something the coaches often overlook. Most of the time, the only way you can practice the various techniques of tackling is to get together with a teammate before practice. Once the drills start, there's no time for that kind of actual contact.

It's true, we get a chance at the tackling dummy, a round cylinder that springs back and comes right at you like a runner—like Leroy Kelly or Dave Osborn. You practice your tackling with the dummy if the coach feels you need it, but there's never any time to practice against a live target running full speed. That's something that is saved for the game. The theory is that you might hurt somebody, so when we do practice tackling it's at half or three quarters speed. But when you get into an actual game, the backs don't run that way.

Defending against the ground game is only part of a middle linebacker's responsibilities, of course. On a pass play, he has other things to worry about. In the zone defense, which is what most teams play now because of the greater speed and agility of today's receivers, you take anybody who comes into your assigned area. That area varies. It could be straight back, so you'll cover the part of the field where a tight end comes downfield ten or fifteen yards, then hooks. In another defense, your zone might be on one side of the field. At other times, a back who comes out to catch a pass is your responsibility no matter where he goes. Coaches try to keep the middle linebacker from too many man-on-man situations, because normally the outside linebackers are faster. But if the back is your man, it's your job to take him.

Even after fifteen years in the pros, I haven't learned too many tricks. But I did learn to study how various opponents tried to block me. One blocks high. Another blocks low.

Some leg-whip you. Some take you head-on. Some try to overpower you, wipe you out. So I'd try to adjust to each individual. I came to realize that the blocker wasn't just a guy with a big jersey with a number on it. He was a human being with certain abilities. Coming at you, the blockers may look a lot alike. But each has different strengths and weaknesses. So I'd try to avoid his strengths and take advantage of his weak points, if I could find any.

That's why I had to start playing each game long before I ran out onto the field on Sunday. I'd study the other man's moves in the films—really study them. I'd remember how he played me the last time we met. I'd try to outthink him, not just outmuscle him.

"You're a middle linebacker, so how can you be thinking?" somebody may object.

But I knew I'd better be thinking, or he'd take advantage of me. I had to use brains as well as brawn on every play. If a linebacker is doing his job well, he's going to have his mind in gear before a play starts and while it's developing. People say the job is all instinct. They're wrong. A lot of preparation is involved, a lot of adjusting is going on from minute to minute. A lot of thinking under pressure.

In some games, certain people are going to defeat you. I've had problems with certain guys over the years. But you try to figure those problems out so that those opponents don't defeat you the next time. I've been beaten. I've been blocked. But I'm glad to say there haven't been too many of those defeats. If there had been, I wouldn't have been in the league for fifteen years.

My biggest problems were usually with opponents I didn't have a book on, people I hadn't seen much. And sometimes

I had problems because that week I wasn't up for the game. When you get beaten by an opponent, it's usually because you weren't prepared as well as you should have been.

The game's nature is emotional. At times, you lose your emotional edge. You don't take an opponent seriously enough. At practice, you go through the motions instead of bearing down. Maybe you don't have the proper respect for the other team. And then when you go out on the field you aren't ready mentally.

Every practice makes a difference in how you play on Sunday. If you don't concentrate on what you're doing during the week, you can't go out there and play well. But besides the practice and study, you have to get ready emotionally.

"Ray," I'd say to myself, early in the week before a game, "you're going to be the best linebacker in the world Sunday. There's no way that guy's going to beat you because you're better. You're not going to let the team down. You're not going to let the fans down. You're going to do the best you possibly can. The very best you possibly can. . . ."

I couldn't let my mind wander to some investment I'd made. I couldn't start worrying about something that had nothing to do with the game. I had to be dedicated to the game and my role in it.

"That center's not going to block me because he's not as good as I am," I'd tell myself. "That ball carrier—when I see him, I'm really going to belt him one. That all-pro back they've got—he may be good, but I'm going to show him who Ray Nitschke is. He's not as good as I am, and his team's not as good as my team."

And so on and on, all during the week before the game.

It was how I worked at getting ready. There were always temptations to start thinking about other things when I should have been concentrating on football. But when I gave in to them, I'd have a bad Sunday.

Lombardi has been quoted as saying you have to hate your opponent. I don't know about that. I didn't hate the guy. But I will say this: Those days leading up to Sunday, I didn't like him very much.

The other weeks of the year, he might be a friend of mine. I really like a lot of players on other teams. But not if they're carrying the ball. Not if they're trying to block me.

Even in an intersquad game, where the opponent is another Packer, I've taken the attitude that he isn't going to walk over me, because I'm not going to let him. Those intersquad games were the hardest ones to play because you hate to go out there and belt a good buddy. But if he's throwing a block or running with the ball, you let him have it because there's only one way I know to play football, and that's all-out.

It's pride. It's survival. And I hope the other guys feel the same way. I hope when that back comes at me he's thinking, "That Nitschke is going to try to get me but I'm too good a man to let him do it."

In football or anything else, we all have some of that competitive spirit. I don't think it's hatred for the opponent. But you're trying to do the best you know how to surpass the other fellow, just as he's trying to beat you.

With a professional, trying to excel is based partly on money. But the most important rewards aren't financial. They're things like knowing you can compete against another man and you can win. They include the chance to show you have some skill, some ability, along with the courage to take part in the game and the discipline to prepare yourself to do it well.

Football is not an easy game. But it demonstrates that a man has self-discipline, that he has control of his emotions, that he can rise to an occasion and perform before a big audience against the best the other team can throw his way.

To be the best—that's the biggest reward. Being able to say to yourself, "I'm the best," and believe it—that's the drive behind what we do on Sunday afternoons. It isn't just the money.

CHAPTER X

To have control of the game, yourself, your team, the situation—that is what quarterbacking is all about. And of all the quarterbacks I've known, the two who lived up to that ideal best were Bart Starr and Johnny Unitas.

They knew when to call a play and when not to call a play. They knew where the defense would be and where it wouldn't be. There's a best way to attack every defense, and Starr and Unitas were the most successful I've seen at figuring out what it was. When the pressure was on, they could come up with the big play.

One indication of Bart's greatness as a quarterback was the way he'd save a play for a particular point in the game —waiting, setting it up, holding it back. For instance, in the 1967 playoff with Dallas for the league championship, we had a play we knew would work. From studying the movies, we knew the Cowboys' defensive lineman, Bob Lilly, would move quickly when we ran a sweep. So we planned what we call a "give play"—you make him think you're running another sweep with the halfback, but when the defensive man pulls, you give the ball to the fullback, and he goes right through the hole the lineman left and on down the middle of the field.

Lilly was following our guard, Gale Gillingham, when he pulled out to lead the sweep. So we were going to have Gale pull out. Lilly would follow. Chuck Mercein would go through the opening he'd left, and we'd have a sure gain.

It was a play we were sure would work, and some quarterbacks might have tried it right away. But not Starr. It's the kind of play that's going to work only once with an all-pro like Lilly. Bart wanted to save it until he needed it most.

He kept saving it until the game was almost over. But when he did use it, it was the finest call I've seen a quarterback make in fifteen years of watching the best of them. It was an example of how well Starr kept control of a game, instead of letting it control him.

The 1967 game with Dallas was the most dramatic of any during my time with Green Bay. Anyone who watched it will never forget how that game finished. The last play of the game is the one everybody always talks about. It was shown over and over on television. It was a great play. But that call that fooled Lilly at exactly the right stage of the game was a greater one.

The playoff with Dallas was held on the last day of 1967 in Lambeau Field. You don't expect tropical temperatures around Green Bay on December 31, but the weather that day was ridiculous. It was thirteen below zero. The icy wind was so strong that it made it seem three times that cold. It was the kind of day when anybody who isn't getting paid to go outside should huddle next to a roaring fire. But there wasn't an empty seat, of course. This was the afternoon when the Packers had a chance to win a third league championship in a row. Any fan with a ticket who chickened out could never again have held up his head within a hundred miles of the banks of the Fox River.

People put on ski masks and parkas and lined boots and

two pairs of mittens. They piled blankets on themselves and brought Thermos jugs of coffee. And still some of them nearly froze, so you can imagine what it was like for us down there on the field. The only way football should be played on a day like that is with both teams wrapped in goosedown comforters, but nobody wanted to suggest a costume like that to Lombardi.

Playing in a climate like Wisconsin's, I've had a chance to experience some bracing weather. I've never grown to like playing in the cold, although I usually prefer it to playing when it's so hot that the heat absorbs your energy and you have a tendency to get lazy. When it's cold, you keep looking for something to do to keep your muscles warm—tackling the opposing quarterback, for instance. You keep moving when it's cold, and it seems as if you don't get tired. Some people say it hurts more when you run into somebody if it's below zero, but I don't think you feel the hit any more than usual—it hurts anytime.

But when I say I'd rather have it too cold than too hot, I don't mean the kind of cold we had that December 31, 1967. The wind-chill factor was forty or fifty degrees below zero. Six of my toes froze before I'd been outside very long. I didn't think about how bad they felt until after the game and Jackie and I went out for supper. I got in the restaurant and I couldn't keep my shoes on, the toes were so swollen.

The Cowboys complained that evening about how their players had frostbite and how they came from a warm climate so they were the only people affected by the cold. But it wasn't any warmer on our side of the scrimmage line. A lot of our players got frostbitten, too. But we didn't mention it. We didn't have to. We'd won.

The buildup for that 1967 NFL championship game was like nothing we'd experienced before. Fans all over the country wanted to see if we could win three in a row. The Packers had captured the interest of people who'd never been within five hundred miles of Green Bay. We were representing football followers in Tupelo and Walla Walla, Paducah and Sioux Falls—all those fans who were proud of living in a small city and identified with a team from another small city that had proved it could whip the big-city boys.

There was another big reason for all the interest, and its name was Vincent T. Lombardi. When he'd arrived to take over the Packers, he was Vincent Who? Nobody pays much attention to assistant football coaches. At the age of forty-five he'd never been anything more than that. Less than nine years had passed since he showed up in Green Bay, but now he was one of the best-known men in the United States. People were talking about running him for Vice President, making him head of the FBI, or backing him for governor. There was never much chance of any of those things happening—Lombardi knew the name of his game, and it wasn't politics. But the fact that he was being mentioned in connection with jobs like those indicates how this coach from a small Wisconsin city had caught the nation's attention.

The 1960s were a time of turmoil in our country. A President had been shot. Cities had been set on fire. Generations had discovered a big gap between them. The old ways seemed to be changing, and a lot of Americans were uptight and worried. That's one reason so many of them started watching football for recreation. In football, you can see what's going on down there on the field, and after the day is over you know for sure who won. In a lot of other areas, people had lost track of what was going on, and they didn't know whether their side was winning or losing. So football was getting to be something more than a game, and Lombardi was something more than the league's most successful football coach. He was talking about some of the old values that most people still believed in and proving they brought success.

I believed in those values, too. So I was flattered when a Chicago *Daily News* columnist, Bob Billings, said I was a leader of "the theological school founded by Vince Lombardi."

"When Lombardi started preaching his doctrine of love, respect and brotherhood last year," Billings wrote, "snickers were heard from coast to coast. The whip, cynics said, was mightier than the sword. But Nitschke is a believer. . . .

"The Cowboys are only a football team. The Packers are a practicing religion."

That's what my high school English teachers would have called hyperbole, but I could see what the guy meant. Under Lombardi, we really had become something more than a collection of forty oversized egos, each man out for what he could get for himself. I've talked about how I changed and matured. Well, the team had changed and matured and become less selfish, too. We had a unity. We had a family feeling. We were trying to accomplish things as a team that we could accomplish only if we had a measure of that brotherhood the Chicago writer was talking about.

For instance, in the week before the Rams game where we won the right to play Dallas, Fuzzy Thurston had spent a lot of time with Gale Gillingham, who'd beaten him out of a starting job as our offensive left guard, going over the strengths and weaknesses and moves of the people Gale would be playing against. Thurston had been one of the stars of the team. His pride had to be hurting now that he was getting a little paunchy and was no longer a starter. But he was a great student of football, and he kept going over the assignments with Gillingham, filling him full of information he'd gathered rather painfully over the years. He really got Gale ready to play a great game.

Somebody asked me when the Packers started thinking about the playoff with Dallas, and I said, "in the shower, right after the Rams game." We knew the Cowboys were young, strong, and fast. Some people said the Packers were getting too old. But not everyone agreed. As one writer pointed out, "when they take off their money belts and start to play in a big game, they're still tough."

The week before we played Dallas, I studied our game plan, which included details on the Cowboys' offense and how each player was apt to react in a particular situation. I had my own book on the runners and quarterbacks, too. I had an idea from past experience what each would do on a given play.

As always, our game plan was based on what the opponent had done the last few weeks, not last year. Teams change. Somebody might be injured, or a young player might have broken into the lineup so we couldn't depend on anything but recent information. Besides, Landry was a smart coach, and we knew he was staying up nights trying to think of ways to outmaneuver us. We'd beaten him in a tough game a year ago. He'd had twelve months to think about that and think about how to beat the Packers.

By now, I was the defensive player assigned to watch Bengtson's hand signals and pass along his instructions to the defense. But that was only part of the responsibility. Like offense, defense is a game of audibles. If the other players changed formation at the last minute, they had to pause for one second before they snapped the ball. So that gave us one second to change our defense. Calling the audibles makes you a key guy on the defense, the way the quarterback is the key to offense. In recent years, a lot of casual football fans have come to realize that, so the middle linebacker has been getting credit for the role he plays on a football team.

How many times we changed our signals depended on the tactics of the team we were playing and our own overall game plan. To some extent, the showdown with Dallas was going to be a guessing game between me and their quarterback, Don Meredith. He'd be trying to fool me. By calling defensive audibles at the line of scrimmage, I'd be trying to stop him from doing it.

The year had been a difficult one for our defense. We'd had a slow start. We hadn't played up to par because of injuries. Some of our fellows were playing hurt. They deserved credit for being in there at all, but you can't be 100 percent effective when you're hurt. You can't play with abandon. But we'd started coming into our own in the Detroit game, except for some third-down plays. Even though I wasn't satisfied—I'm never fully satisfied—I thought we were ready for Dallas.

When we ran out on that frozen field, I looked up in the

stands when those 50,861 fans started yelling for the Packers. You could hardly see any faces. Everyone was bundled up so much. But there was no doubt that they were there to cheer us on, and I decided if they'd come out on a day like that, the least we could do in return was go out and win the game for them and send them off to the pneumonia ward happy.

Starr took to the air in the first quarter and threw a touchdown pass to Boyd Dowler. Dowler caught another in the second quarter to make the score 14–0. But then one of our guys couldn't hold onto the ball with his numb fingers, and Dallas grabbed the fumble. Before long, it was 14–7. We couldn't move the ball, and the Cowboys got it back and started going down the field again, but we stopped them, and they settled for a Danny Villanueva field goal, which made it 14–10.

Then both teams settled down to some tough defensive football, and it looked for a while as if that four-point lead was going to be enough. We couldn't score. Neither could they. It got to be the fourth quarter. Then Landry and Meredith reached into their bag of tricks.

The quarterback handed off to one of the backs, Dan Reeves, who started running to his left. Our cornerback, Bob Jeter, moved up to guard against the run instead of sticking to Lance Rentzel, the man he was supposed to cover. Reeves stopped and threw to his left, and they had a fifty-yard touchdown play.

That was really the only offense they had against us in the second half—we didn't defense it properly—but it was enough to put Dallas ahead, 17–14. With three minutes to play, we were still losing.

But we had the ball. We had Starr. And Bart still had that give play that he'd been saving.

When he got around to using it, it wasn't just the right time. It was the perfect time. We'd been moving the ball a little, and the defense was all fired up to stop us, the way they'd been stopping us most of the afternoon. Standing on the sidelines watching, I wondered if Bart was ever going to use that play. The hands on that scoreboard clock were moving pretty fast, and if we didn't do something soon it would be too late. But I figured Starr knew what he was doing. He always did.

Then the ball was snapped and Gillingham started to pull out for the sweep, and big Bob Lilly fired off that line and pulled with him. Only instead of a sweep, Mercein was running right up the gut, right up the alley where Lilly should have been. Nobody blocked anybody. It was beautiful. It was a play we'd been working on all week for the one big down where we needed it most. We'd taken advantage of that fine defensive player's habit of being just a little too aggressive, and it was the best play I've ever seen Starr call.

Mercein didn't score. But he got us down in Dallas territory. Now we had a chance for a field goal, and that would send the game into sudden-death overtime. Considering how cold my feet were, staying out there to play in overtime didn't sound like too great an idea. But it would be better than losing.

Starr still had ninety seconds to go, though. We had the ball on their thirty. There was a time when he could have handed the ball to Taylor and Jim would have put his head down and defied anybody in a Cowboys' uniform to stop him. There was a time when Bart could have given the ball to Hornung and Paul would have smelled all that winner's money and would have slipped past tacklers and been on his way. But Taylor was in New Orleans and Hornung was up in the stands without his shoulder pads. So Starr had to think of some other way to win.

He sent Mercein through the line and flipped a short pass to him and Chuck, who hadn't been able to stay with the Giants or Redskins, proved Lombardi had known what he was doing when he signed him. He didn't go down under the Cowboys' attack until he was on the Dallas eleven. On the next play, he was stopped on the three. Then Donny Anderson earned some of that six-hundred-thousand-dollar bonus by taking it two hard yards to the one. That gave us another first down.

I looked at the stadium clock. Less than sixty seconds of the regular season left. But we were so close, how were they going to stop us now? We were the Packers. We were the guys who always won the big ones. My feet were so numb it was like they weren't attached to me, and I'd never been so cold in my life, but who cared about that?

A quarterback like Starr always has a reason to call a particular play. He's always thinking ahead to the next one and the one after that. He wants to get the defenders to start anticipating what he's going to do next, so he can cross them up and do something different. Here we were, down to our last few seconds, and he was still cool, still thinking. He ran one of his backs at the line, which is what everybody expects you to do with a yard to go, and the defense stopped him. So now it's second down and he ran another play with a back into the line, and the defense stopped him on the

JOHN BIEVER PHOTO

VERNON J. BIEVER PHOTO

Opposite page: Ray Nitschke as a 6'2" 200-pound fullback at the University of Illinois.
This page, top: Nitschke terrorizing the Kansas City Chiefs in Super Bowl I.
Bottom: In 1971, Coach Dan Devine replaced Nitschke with 23-year-old Jim Carter (left).

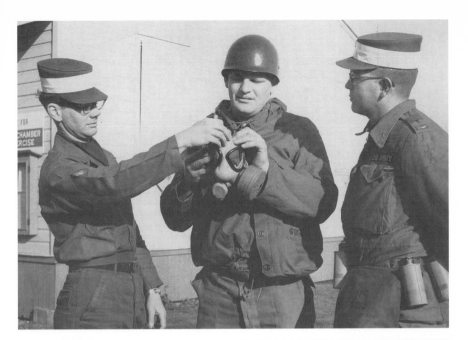

VERNON J. BIEVER PHOTO

Opposite page: Nitschke holds back an intense Coach Vince Lombardi. "Lombardi's special asset," said Nitschke, "was his ability to handle men." *This page, top:* During the summer of 1959, Ray was called to active duty in the Army Reserves, thus missing Lombardi's first training camp. *Bottom:* Packer Jersey No. 66 is retired. Ray with son Richard, daughter Amy, and wife Jackie.

Ray Nitschke, family man

Above left: Ray and Jackie on "Ray Nitschke Day," 1972. *Above right:* Ray and Jackie at daughter Amy's wedding to Jon Klaas, 1993. *Left:* Ray as beardless Santa, with Jackie and sons Richard (left) and John (right). *Opposite page:* Dad helps John up ladder to backyard tree house.

Above: Three retired Packer
jerseys: No. 15 Bart Starr,
No. 3 Tony Canadeo, and
No. 66 Ray Nitschke.
Right: Ray Nitschke's
induction into the Professional
Football Hall of Fame, 1978.

one-foot line. There were thirteen seconds left when Starr called time.

He looked over at Lombardi. There might be time for only one play. A field goal was almost sure from here, and three points would tie the game. Then we could take our time, going out there and making sure we scored first in overtime. Sending Don Chandler and the kicking team in was the safe and sensible thing to do. The coach believed in conservative football. He didn't believe in taking a chance of not coming away with some points in a situation like that, and this was the biggest game of his career.

Afterward, Lombardi said he'd taken pity on all those freezing people in the stands and decided to go for broke so the game would end, one way or another. You can believe that if you want to. But I think he kept Chandler on the sidelines and gave Starr one last chance to win the game to show his love and respect for the players. Some of us— me and ten other guys—had been on his team when it played and lost its first championship game in 1960. All of us had listened to him yell at us during grass drills. Over the years, we'd played well for him and been proud, and we'd made mistakes and been sorry. We'd gone out and played when we should have been in traction sometimes and we'd proved that, win or lose, we were a unit, a brotherhood. In one sense, we were Lombardi's family. Black or white, young or older, hairy or bald like me, we were his sons. If he had sent the kicking unit in when we were twelve inches away from the biggest victory we'd ever had, a victory we'd strained and worked for and dreamed of, nobody could have criticized him. But it would have meant he didn't have confidence in our ability to take that last step, to rise to the limits of our ability when all the chips had been shoved into the center of the table.

So Chandler stayed on the sidelines. The whistle blew. Bart took the handoff. The Dallas line, which had dug its heels into that frozen sod twice to stop the Green Bay backs, dug in once more to stop them again, knowing if they could do it they would have won the game. Over the years, Bart has hardly ever carried the ball himself. They couldn't expect him to carry it now, even with only a foot to go.

But when Ken Bowman and Jerry Kramer shoved big Jethro Pugh aside far enough to open a momentary crack in the Dallas wall, it was Starr who threw his body through that opening and scored.

This was my tenth season with the Packers, and we'd had triumphs before. Lots of triumphs and some defeats. If you went all the way back to Proviso High when I was a ninety-pound weakling trying to play freshman football with kids who outweighed me and outmuscled me, I'd spent a good share of my life around a football field. But in all that time, I'd never had a feeling like the one I had when I ran into that dressing room after we'd beaten Dallas, 21–17, and had given the coach that third championship in three years that he wanted and we wanted so much.

Lombardi was in tears. But so was everybody else. It was something to see, that locker room full of big, tough guys, hugging each other and slapping each other's backs and crying from happiness. What a feeling there was among us. What a great joy it was to be there.

And don't think it was just those other guys who got all emotional. I was so shook up that I forgot six of my toes were frozen. That was one of the greatest moments I've ever experienced.

There was no way that celebration could be spoiled, but a former Eagles' player came close. The dressing room filled up with reporters and television people and Tom Brookshier, who used to play for Philadelphia but was now working for CBS, stuck a microphone in my face and told sixty or seventy million people:

"Here's Green Bay's madman, Ray Nitschke."

He was smiling. I think he meant it as a compliment. But I didn't like being called that, and I didn't do any smiling.

"I'm not a madman," I told him. "I just enjoy football."

I didn't appreciate what Danny Reeves told the reporters after the game, either.

"He went wild after we had gone ahead, 17–14," he said, referring to me. "He actually kicked at Don Perkins after Don had gained five yards. He's an animal. It made all of us mad when he took a kick at Don like that, right in front of everyone, and no one called it."

I'm not a madman. I'm not an animal. And, when it comes to that, I didn't kick at Don Perkins. If I'd been aiming at Perkins' butt, I would have hit it.

What happened was that I was mad at myself after Don made that run. He was a fine back, and the year before he'd gained over a hundred yards against us and a lot of that had been my responsibility, so I took it as an insult to my ability. Before the 1967 game began, I'd made up my mind that Perkins wasn't going to make anything like a hundred yards this time if I could help it. When the game started, I was playing as hard as I could to stop him from going anywhere, and on this particular play I hit him right on the line of scrimmage.

But he wouldn't go down. I couldn't get my arms around him. He bounced back off me and made a nice gain, and after the whistle blew I kicked the ground because I was disgusted with myself. I didn't have anything against Perkins. I wasn't angry with Perkins. I was sore at a fellow named Ray Nitschke because he'd had his chance to make a good play and he'd blown it.

But as it happened, the camera angle was such that it looked to all those millions of people watching TV as if I'd been trying to kick Perkins. So a lot of them decided I must be a real dirty ballplayer, when all that happened was I was mad at myself and disappointed and kicking the ground in disgust.

And then after the game, Tommy Brookshier went on national television—with my family watching, my friends watching, people back in Maywood, Illinois, watching—and insulted me. I didn't like it. I'd been trying to play as hard and aggressive and smart as I could out there. And then this guy called me a madman.

When he called me that, I wasn't thinking so much about how I could take it but how my family and friends would take it. Calling me a madman didn't make them look any better, and I didn't appreciate it. I told him I was no madman. I was trying to do my job, which was to play as hard and as well as possible.

A madman has no place on the football field. I never try to go out there to hurt somebody. That isn't the way I was taught to play football. Playing middle linebacker, you're doing a job that requires a lot of contact, and I enjoy contact and enjoy playing my position. But I've never played it like a wild man who ought to be locked up in a cage when the game's over.

Football is a violent game. If you play in a violent game, you know that the possibility of injury has to be taken for granted. There've been times after I've hit somebody when I've been afraid I had injured him seriously. There've been times when I've knocked a man out and I've been sorry about it, but you think the same as he would if the positions were reversed: "Better him than me." He knew the dangers and so did I, so it's a matter of letting the chips fall where they may. You hope nobody gets hurt seriously, so he's out for a long time. But you know injuries are part of the game because it's a tough, physical sport, and there's no use kidding yourself about that.

But I don't go out there trying to hurt anybody. If he's got the ball, I want to stop him. If a blocker gets in my way, I try to get rid of him. But you don't do that by being a madman on the field, and I resent it when anyone uses a term like that.

As for me being an animal, Reeves knew better than that. A man says a lot of things when he's just lost a game like that one. I've never been an animal on the football field or a dirty player.

I didn't stay angry with Reeves very long, especially after I read the other things he'd told the writers. He'd said I was the key to stopping the Cowboys and that there was no comparison between my ability as a middle linebacker and that of Butkus of the Bears or Tommy Nobis of the Falcons. He said I was in a class by myself. How are you going to stay mad at a guy like that?

I'd tried not to pay too much attention to those arguments about who was the best player at my position; in my own mind, I've always felt I was the best, but I didn't expect everybody to agree with me. But that season I'll admit my pride had been hurt a little bit when I wasn't named all-pro for the first time in four years.

Butkus and Nobis were fine young players and they were getting a lot of publicity, which was okay because they deserved it. But when one of them got picked as the best middle linebacker by the Associated Press and the other by UPI, it did hurt a little. But Lombardi didn't agree with those sportswriters.

"Nitschke's the best middle linebacker in pro football by far," he said, which made me feel pretty good because the coach had never seemed to feel I needed many compliments to boost my ego.

Lombardi was backed up by another man with a good right to express an opinion on the job of playing middle linebacker. Dick Butkus suggested that the ones who could settle the argument were the quarterbacks.

"They'll tell you who gives them the most trouble," Butkus said. "They'll tell you who really makes them eat that football. It's people like Ray Nitschke and Sam Huff. They're the best in my book."

Butkus went on to say that he and Tommy Nobis had been getting a lot of publicity, but they didn't have enough years in the league yet to outrank some of us who'd been around longer.

"Experience is the big thing," he said. "After Tommy and I get some experience, maybe if we're lucky we'll be regarded as the best. But I figure we're both young and have lots of time.

"Right now, though, all linebackers—left, middle, and right—can learn from Mr. Nitschke and Mr. Huff."

It's always nice to have a young man show a little respect for his elders, including calling them mister. I appreciated what Butkus said because he's a good one and knows what the game is all about. And he wasn't the only one on his team who came to my defense. After that rhubarb about Reeves calling me an animal and Brookshier saying I was a madman, several Bears' players spoke up.

"If Reeves can't take it," Ed O'Bradovich said, speaking like a loyal Proviso boy, "he ought to hang it up and quit."

"He's always rough," Mike Pyle said, referring to me, "but he has always played clean against me. I've never had any trouble with him."

Mike's a center and I hope he's had a little trouble with me over the years, because I've been trying my best to give him some when we played Chicago. But I knew what he meant. He went on to say he'd never seen me play as aggressively as in the games against Los Angeles and Dallas.

"He must have seen nothing but dollar signs," he said.

Butkus remarked that he'd remember that Reeves had ranked me as superior to him and Nobis the next time the Bears played Dallas. Then he went on to talk about that TV broadcast.

"Nitschke is just rough and tough. I nearly fell over when Brookshier said that to him."

O'Bradovich and I have known each other since we were boys, and he told the reporters that the way I play football is the only way to play it.

"I think I know what he objects to about that madman thing," he went on. "He's afraid people are going to think he's the same way off the field. He doesn't want somebody pointing to him on the street and saying, 'There's that madman.' I know how that feels because it's happened to me.

"I can see where some coaches and players might not like what he does. Ray kind of annihilates you when he makes a tackle. That's his style—just like Butkus. You're not supposed to be a nice guy out there. That kind doesn't make it in this game. You notice the middle linebackers more because they make their tackles out in the open. Ray just does it with a little more vim and vigor."

By the time I got back to my ten acres in the country at Oneida, five minutes out of Green Bay, and could put my feet up and thaw out my toes, I was over being sore at anybody. Brookshier may have meant to say "wild man" instead of madman—people have called me that for years, although I never got to like it because it showed they didn't understand what I was trying to do out there. I'm not a wild man —although, as somebody pointed out once, I'm not the third chorus boy from the left, either.

As for Reeves, he was a pretty fierce competitor when he got his helmet on, and I decided I'd take his remarks as a compliment, all except for that part about being an animal. But come to think of it, he didn't say what kind of an animal. I suppose he could have meant a pussycat.

The chill I got in that Dallas game in Lambeau Field gave me a bad cold, and I wasn't ready physically to play against Oakland in our second Super Bowl. I lost about eight pounds sitting around the house, sniffling and blowing, but even though I wasn't ready to play my best game physically, I was ready mentally, and maybe that's more important. I was determined that I was going to play sixty minutes of hard football—or whatever part of those sixty minutes the defensive team was on the field. There was no way they were going to keep me out of a game like that, sick or healthy.

The first Super Bowl had been played in Los Angeles, and even though 61,946 people paid to see it, there were some empty seats. But there weren't any vacant spots in the stands in the Orange Bowl in Miami that day early in 1968. The year before, a lot of people had figured no AFL team was going to give the NFL champions much competition. But the two leagues were getting closer to even now. The crowd in the stadium totaled 75,546. More than two-thirds of them had paid $12 a seat. Even the worst seats, which went for $6, had been sold out ten days before.

This was the first football game ever to gross more than three million dollars: It took in $3,296,822, including $2,500,000 for the television rights, which made it the richest single athletic event in the history of the world.

The turf was dyed green to look pretty for color TV. At halftime there was a 688-piece band. There'd been times in the Packers' early history when they didn't have 688 people watching, including the ones who sneaked in for free. Each winning player would get $15,000; each loser would get half that. We'd already collected $8,000 each because Starr made that last foot in the final thirteen seconds of the Dallas game, which figures out to $666.66 an inch.

The Packers were favored to win their second Super Bowl, of course. But a lot of Oakland backers really believed their team was going to win. In fact, four thousand of them flew all the way to Florida to watch the game, instead of staying in California and seeing it on television for free. The year before, Kansas City had the reputation of being a wide-open offensive team, the kind the Pack had been teaching lessons in fundamental football to for years. But Oakland went in for basics, like us. It was the kind of team that could nickel-and-dime you to death and keep moving.

Getting ready to play in Miami, I spent a lot of time studying their fullback, Hewritt Dixon. He was a strong runner, very aggressive.

Some experts claimed Oakland might pull an upset because some of us had been playing football quite a while. Forrest Gregg was thirty-four and getting gray. Henry Jordan and I were bald. But as Hank pointed out, that was just a sign that we'd survived a lot of high-pressure games under Lombardi.

Bob Skoronski, thirty-three; Jerry Kramer, thirty-one; Boyd Dowler, thirty; Starr, thirty-three, and Gregg had all been starters on offense when the Eagles beat us for the NFL title on December 26, 1960. On the defensive team, Willie Davis, thirty-three, was still at end, as he'd been then, and Jordan was still at tackle, along with Willie Wood and me, who were both thirty-one years old now. A couple of other guys who'd been starters in 1960, the last time the Packers lost a title or playoff game, were still around—Thurston, thirty-three, and Max McGee, thirty-five.

But we weren't over the hill, the way some of the writers had said we were before we started winning so many tough games that year. We'd played together so long that we had confidence in each other. Experience was what Lombardi wanted on that field when the pressure was on, and a lot of us had it.

Besides me, the linebackers were Dave Robinson and Lee Roy Caffey. Tom Brown, the youngest member of the defensive secondary, said we were the best linebacking combination in football, and who were we to argue with a teammate? Brown played opposite Wood at safety, and he said he and Willie could "just forget anything within ten or fifteen yards of the line of scrimmage," adding: "No other defensive backs can get away with that."

The Raiders had Daryle Lamonica at quarterback and guys like Fred Biletnikoff to catch the ball. But we knew that Dixon led the Oakland receivers with fifty-nine catches during the season, which meant that Lamonica liked to throw to his backs. When a back goes out for a pass he's often my responsibility, so I made up my mind I was going to be ready.

On the first play from scrimmage, I slammed into Dixon and, if you can believe *Time* magazine, I "flipped him cleats over clavicle," although that isn't the way we usually describe that piece of action in the locker room. Anyway, he didn't make an inch, and I figured it gave him a pretty good introduction to the NFL brand of defensive football.

Starr went out there with his game plan in mind and started out by demonstrating that the Packers could move the ball on the ground. Later on, he opened up our attack and threw more passes.

We scored six of the first nine times we had the ball. George Blanda was the kicker who'd been getting all the publicity, but it was Don Chandler who kicked four field goals that afternoon. Four out of four. Blanda got a chance to try only one. He missed.

Chandler put us ahead in the first quarter with three points. In the second quarter, Starr hit Dowler for a sixty-two-yard pass play and a touchdown after Don had kicked his second field goal. That made it 13–0, but Bill Miller caught a pass for an Oakland touchdown to make it 13–7. Chandler hit on a forty-three-yarder before the first half was over to give us three more points.

The Miami *Herald* had hired George Mira, the Forty-Niners' quarterback, to help cover the game, and he said the Raiders made a mistake in tactics in the first half by trying to run outside.

"You don't run outside on Ray Nitschke," he said. "He's tough and he reads plays a lot. Oakland frequently pulled its guards to lead the interference, and Nitschke simply shot the gap where the guards had pulled and caught the ball carrier from the backside."

In the third quarter, after Starr had started a drive from our eighteen and moved the ball downfield in eleven plays for a touchdown that put us sixteen points ahead, Lamonica must have decided Oakland was never going to beat us at our own type of game. He went to the air. He threw one toward Biletnikoff, but it was Herb Adderley who caught it. The rest of us started throwing blocks, and Herb ran sixty yards for a touchdown.

I enjoyed that. Nobody outside of the team knew it, but Adderley had been injured in the fifth game of the season, the one against the Vikings, and for a lot of the year he hadn't been able to lift his right arm above his shoulder. His right bicep looked as if it had been hit with a club. But he hadn't alibied. He'd kept his mouth shut even when he got criticized for letting people score touchdowns against him. Through no fault of his own, he'd been the goat a few times, and now it was good to see him have a chance to be the hero in the Super Bowl.

As had happened the year before, the first half was fairly close, but the second half was all ours. In fact, along toward the end of the game, some of the crowd started booing us because they wanted Oakland to score one more touchdown. The gamblers had made us 13½-point favorites, and if the Raiders could make 7 more points they'd be only 12 points behind.

They didn't make them, though. We won, 33–14. Our defense had held them to 107 yards rushing. Dixon made 54 of those yards, but after the game was over I felt like we'd had a pretty good afternoon on defense. I'd made 5 unassisted tackles and helped on 4 others, besides blocking a pass.

After the game, my legs were covered with welts. Dried blood was caked on my knee bandages. Somebody came up to me and asked me when I knew we were going to win, and I wasn't in the mood to be diplomatic.

"The first time we got the ball," I told him, which was the truth.

Starr didn't throw an interception, and nobody on the Packers fumbled. The Raiders fumbled twice, and Lamonica threw that interception that Adderley turned into a touchdown.

I hadn't been feeling too well before the game, but I felt fine afterward. Maybe I'd discovered a cure for the common cold—go out and smash into a lot of other sweaty bodies in the Super Bowl. One columnist claimed I'd "dry gulched enough unwary glamour boys to rank with Wyatt Earp and Bat Masterson as the fastest guns in the game" and claimed I'd played the game "with such joyous abandon one wonders whether it is really fair for him to demand a salary playing a game he obviously loves."

Well, I intended to go on demanding a salary, at the top of my voice in Lombardi's office, if necessary. But maybe he had something. Here I was, thirty-one years old, bruised and bleeding and battered, and I still thought I'd spent a very pleasant afternoon in the Miami sun.

CHAPTER XI

There was a time when a defensive player was lucky if he saw his name in print three times a season, but that had changed. People had come to realize that defense is at least half the game and that we weren't just eleven anonymous guys out there. By the nature of football, the middle linebacker gets in on a lot of action out in the open where people can see the numbers on his back. So by the time we'd won our second Super Bowl, old No. 66 was being watched, and I was getting called a lot of things that, I guess, were meant as compliments. "One half of a collision looking for the other," for instance, and "the guy who plays middle maniac."

Now that we were champions of both leagues, the reporters kept coming around, and sometimes the one they talked to was Jackie. She was quoted as saying that I was a very gentle man.

"He's very tenderhearted. He never uses any mean words, and he helps me with the dishes and helps me clean house. And when it comes to disciplining the children, Mommy has to do the spanking. It just breaks Raymond's heart. He babysits and he changes diapers and he loves to get down on the floor and roll around with the kids."

It was a little embarrassing to see things like that in print, even if they were true. But when I had my teeth out and my helmet on, nobody ever came around and made any cracks about my tender heart.

Jackie told one reporter about how our son, John, had been watching a sports fishing film on television and said, "Dad, you never took me fishing since I was born."

It was a Wisconsin spring day when that happened, and around Green Bay that meant there was a foot of snow on the ground, so it was no time to go fishing. But two weeks later we were all down in Florida, where the fishermen don't have to strap their rods to a snowmobile. If the kid wanted to go fishing, I decided, we might as well go where the fishing was comfortable.

The second Super Bowl had been a big game, all right. We'd known we were representing the league, and we wouldn't take the championship until we got by Oakland. But the pressure wasn't as great as the year before, when everybody wanted to see what would happen when the best teams in the two rival leagues met for the first time. Actually, after that Dallas game, the one in Miami was kind of an anticlimax. We'd beaten two great football teams, the Rams and the Cowboys, in two pressure games in a row, so we figured we could beat anybody.

We were confident, and Lombardi must have been, too. But before the second Super Bowl, I noticed he was starting to show the pressure he was under. He wasn't the same guy he'd been a few years before. He wasn't as healthy as I thought he should be. The way he coached took a lot out of him. He got to the point during that 1967 season when he was shaking from nerves.

Between the Dallas game and the Super Bowl, some of the fellows started speculating that this might be Lombardi's last season. He had his three championships. After we beat Oakland, he'd have the only two Super Bowls ever played. He had an 89–29–4 record in nine seasons and a 10–2 record in postseason play. Under Lombardi, we'd won ninety-nine games, not counting forty-two exhibitions. We'd placed first in the Western Conference six times, second twice, and third only in 1959, his first year—the year after we'd come in dead last under Scooter McLean. We'd won the league title five times in Lombardi's nine years as a head coach.

Winning was what he demanded, and winning was what he mostly got. But, as he said, to win you have to pay a price, and the coach had paid more than his share. I didn't want to think about him stepping down. I wanted him to be there, yelling at us and demanding we give 110 percent when training started in 1968. But when I saw his hands shaking and saw what those nine years had done to the man, I knew he must be giving some thought to retiring.

Everybody reaches that point eventually. For some, the thought comes early. A player gets to making big money, outside opportunities open up, he makes the right investments so he isn't hungry any more and he gets so he doesn't want to go out there and play a game with all the tremendous pressures of pro football. He gets to the place where he decides: "I've had it. I don't want to keep on making the kind of personal commitment I have to make in this game." Because you've got to be committed to go through what you have to go through. When you're not, it's time to leave.

Lombardi had proved everything he set out to prove. He had plenty of money now. He was world-famous. There's always a letdown after a season, win or lose, and that 1967 season built up so high that the letdown was greater than usual. Lombardi had talked of quitting before, but he never meant it. This time he did.

To understand what the announcement meant around Green Bay that the coach and general manager of the Packers was going to give up the coaching half of his job, you have to remember the way people regarded him in 1968. I could look down on the top of his head when we were standing on the sidelines. Almost every player in the league was half a head taller than this little guy from Sheepshead Bay. But around the league and among the Green Bay fans, our coach was ten feet tall.

You remember some of the jokes they told about him. How it was a good thing he hadn't led the Italian army, or Italy would have won World War II. About the winter night he went to bed and Marie said, "God, your feet are cold," and he answered, "Around home, dear, you can call me Vince." How he'd had an accident while taking a stroll—he'd been hit by a motorboat while he was walking across the Fox River. Or the one about the football player who died and went to heaven. He noticed a team of angels scrimmaging while a short fellow stood on the sidelines and yelled at them, so he asked St. Peter:

"Who's that?"

"Oh, that's God. He thinks he's Vince Lombardi."

The coach had made a training film to inspire the military —it was still being used to inspire them in the 1970s—and he'd made one for business groups. He was being quoted on a lot of things that had wider implications than football, such as the time he said it was time to stand up and cheer "for the doer, the achiever, the winner, the leader."

He was no longer just a coach. As somebody wrote in one of the highbrow magazines, he was a folk hero. A lot of us were uneasy about what was going on in the country, and here was a man who was willing to stand up in public and declare that the old values still meant something, after all.

If he'd been a loser, if the Packers were in last place, nobody would have listened. But we were winners. Lombardi was a winner. So they listened. That's one thing that hadn't changed: People still respected winning.

Two days before we played the Raiders in Miami, the coach said this might be the last time we'd be together, and then he choked up and couldn't finish his talk. But you never knew about Lombardi. He was a psychologist. He might be saying something like that so we'd go out and win one last game for him and then change his mind when he started thinking about winning the first game of the next season—and the second game, and the third.

But it turned out that the second Super Bowl really was the last game we played under Coach Lombardi. On February 1, 1968, he stepped down. He was still general manager, but Phil Bengtson would be running the team.

Green Bay had a special day for him. One of the streets next to Lambeau Field was renamed Lombardi Avenue. Somebody asked him if he'd ever expected to have a street named after him and he said, "Yes—Broadway," grinning when he said it. You remember that Lombardi grin—it scared a lot of opponents, who claimed all those teeth were made of stainless steel.

A lot of his old friends showed up for the ceremonies, including Hornung. Brown County Arena was jammed and

Paul made a speech, predicting the Packers would win a fourth straight title.

"In fact," he said, "I'll bet on it."

It got a good laugh, but Bengtson wasn't laughing very hard. He was on the spot now. It was a big set of shoes he'd agreed to fill. If we won, people would say it was Lombardi's team going ahead on momentum. If we lost, people would say it was Bengtson's team.

Phil was not Lombardi, and he'd be the first to admit it. But he was a leader who believed in the same kind of discipline, the same careful advance preparation. The only thing he didn't have was Lombardi's way with words. Lombardi was very articulate, and Coach Phil was a quiet fellow. He'd think things out—I'm not saying Lombardi didn't do that, too, because he did—but Bengtson would be a lot quieter about it.

After the 1968 season, people said there'd been a letdown when Lombardi stepped out and that we would have done better if he'd stayed on as coach. I don't think so. Everything else being equal, I think that 1968 would have been the same kind of frustrating year it was even if we'd had the same coach.

It was frustrating because we were better than our record showed. We had a good football team that year. Before the season, I said it was as good as any I'd played on. But that was before Chandler retired. Without Don, we didn't have much of a kicking game, and that hurt. A field goal at the right place can change the whole complexion of a game. If you're ahead by ten points, it's a lot different than being ahead by seven. For that matter, if the offense knows it's got to get all the way to the twenty-yard line to have a chance for a field goal, it's a lot different than when it knows it has a kicker like Chandler, who can score from the forty.

In 1968, the Packers tried twenty-eight field goals and missed all but thirteen. The year before, Chandler tried twenty-six and made nineteen. That's a deficit of only six field goals, but if those six had come in the right games in 1968 we could have had a record of 10–4, good enough to give us the championship for a fourth year in a row if we won the playoffs. If Chandler had been around and still kicking as well as the year before, it might have been an entirely different coaching career at Green Bay for Phil Bengtson.

Another reason we had trouble that year was that we'd become to football what the New York Yankees were to baseball in the days of Ruth and Gehrig. People were getting tired of us winning so often—not people around Green Bay, of course, who hoped we'd keep winning championships forever, but the others around the league. They were tired of hearing about nothing but the Green Bay Packers.

Everybody on opposing teams was getting keyed up before they played us. When you're the champions, everybody plays real tough against you. All through the off-season, they prepared to play Green Bay. The coaches and the players were determined they weren't going to let us beat them again. Every game we played, the other team would be playing over its head because it wanted to knock us off.

Another thing: In 1968, our division was getting stronger. There'd been talk of it being an easy division, but now it was being called the black-and-blue division, and with a lot of truth. Minnesota was getting better and Chicago and

Detroit were improving. We were on top, so they were shooting at us.

And maybe we weren't quite as hungry for victory as we had been. I felt I still had the hunger. So had some of the other Packers. But not all.

There's another factor that we didn't talk about because it would have sounded like we were making excuses. But in that 1968 season there were some calls by the officials that could have gone either way, and it seemed like they always went against us. It's human nature to be for the underdog. After those great teams of the past few years, anybody playing the Packers was automatically the underdog. I don't mean that the officials took that into consideration intentionally. But if you've got a borderline call it's natural not to favor the team that's been winning all the time.

If I'm watching a game, I'm just like everybody else: I want to see the underdog win. If I were officiating, I might give the benefit of the doubt to the team with less ability. But that's one additional hazard you have to contend with when you've made a habit of being the champs.

Our 1968 record was made with basically the same players we had in that great year of 1967. After 1968, we had some key players retire, but aside from losing Chandler, there weren't many changes in Bengtson's first season.

I'd been pretty well beat up after those 1967 playoffs. Jackie noticed that my back and my legs were completely black and blue. She thought I might be about ready to hang up my helmet.

"The way Ray looked after last season, I'd say he'll play only one more year," she told one reporter. "Every year,

208

you can see it's taking him longer to recover from his bruises."

But I wasn't really giving much serious thought to retiring. Sure, I wasn't twenty-one years old any more. But I felt I was still in my prime. I bruised, but I healed quick. Or anyway, quick enough.

One of the Green Bay radio stations, WNFL, had a contest where the fans voted on which player had been most valuable to the team in 1967, and I won. After being overlooked in the all-league and Pro Bowl selections, it was nice to know the home folks still thought I was earning my salary.

In the off-season, when the football writers have to find something to put in print, the argument about who was the best middle linebacker was revived. *Sport* magazine asked five former all-pro players at that position to choose.

Bill George voted for his teammate, Butkus. Chuck Bednarik of the Eagles picked Nobis. But the other three—Joe Schmidt of the Lions, Pat Richter of the Rams, and Bill Pellington of the Colts—made a pitch for the bald-headed vote. They picked me.

Pellington said I always came up with the big play, which is "a kind of leadership." Then he went on to say that "Nitschke takes it one step further. He's the core of the team. He directs it. He inspires it."

Richter agreed that I was a leader. And Schmidt, who's one of the players I've tried to model myself after, talked about what he called my "amazing lateral quickness and mobility."

During his playing days, Schmidt was a middle linebacker I really admired. He was a little smaller than I am, but he was always at the right place at the right time, especially against the run. He was a very intelligent ballplayer. He had the kind of leadership that inspired his teammates.

Butkus is another middle linebacker who belongs up there with the best. He's big and fiery and does things that are really unbelievable for a man who's 6 foot 3 and weighs close to 250 pounds. It's amazing to see a big guy so consistent and so active for a whole game.

Those two players tell the whole story of what middle linebacking is all about: Butkus, the big, bruising player; Schmidt, who was real quick and a good student of the game. I've tried to put my game somewhere between those two types of players.

The magazine also asked Johnny Unitas to decide who was the best middle linebacker, which was putting a quarterback on the spot. He knew that the two he didn't pick would come after him with a little more enthusiasm the next season to show he'd made a mistake. And the one he did pick would hit him a little harder to show him the choice was justified. But Johnny has never been a fellow to duck and hide when things get tough, so he stood right there in the pocket and threw the ball.

"They all hit me hard," he said. "They're extremely close in ability, but I'd have to say Nitschke's experience sets him above the others. He just seems to get the job done more consistently. . . . All I know is, Nitschke was the toughest one I played against last year."

Reading that gave me a friendly feeling toward old Johnny. I made a note to thank him, right after I'd knocked him loose from the ball the next time.

I don't pay much attention to most informal polls about who's the best, but it was nice to know that I'd won the votes of three of five guys who had played my position so well themselves and knew what being a middle linebacker was all about.

The men who play a particular position on a team are usually the same kind of people. Their personalities are similar. The linemen are big, strong, with a lot of raw power. The guys in the secondary are aggressive players with quick feet, and their personalities are built to match. The quarterbacks are a breed apart. The ends all have similar characteristics.

It takes a certain personality to play a certain position. You can walk into a room of strangers and, if they're football players, you can make a good guess what position they play just by watching them and studying their personalities. You can look at a man and think, "he's a lineman" or "he's a back."

In a room like that, if you wanted to find out which stranger would be playing middle linebacker, you'd have to decide which one really wants to play football the most. If he isn't the middle linebacker, the coach made a mistake. That's the job for the one who really loves to play.

The middle linebacker gets blocked by every opponent except the quarterback—and on a reverse, even the quarterback might try to sneak up on him. He has to decide which opponent is going to try to block him on a particular play, then figure out how to defeat that blocker and get to the man with the football.

A middle linebacker not only has to be quick enough to be able to react to a screen play, to get in the right place to help out on a sweep or a draw or to get back fifteen yards to guard a pass receiver, but he has to be strong enough to withstand a three-hundred-pound tackle who's coming at him to block.

It's asking a lot of a player. And when he gets to where he's going, he has to be able to do something. So when you're picking a middle linebacker, he has to be a special kind of guy, and there aren't too many around.

I've been fortunate to be gifted with enough strength and speed. Speed in a straight line is one thing, but speed going laterally is something else. There's an angle of pursuit, a cutoff point. I've been able to adjust the right way on a football field instinctively. What I've lacked in natural speed I've been able to make up for by being in the right spot. There have been times when I wished I was a little faster, but you can't have everything.

Playing offense in high school and college helped me on defense. Because I was a high school quarterback, I understood something about what the man in that job was trying to do. Having been a fullback in college helped me in defending against the backs.

"Hit the other guy a little harder than he hits you"—that's always been my football philosophy. Hit him first. Hit him with a little more enthusiasm. That attitude helped me. I've gone on the field with the intention of giving the game everything I have. God gave me a strong body and some natural ability, and I felt I'd be foolish not to take care of those natural assets and use them.

When I talk football to young people, I tell them: "If you want to play, you've got to love to play. A football field is the worst place in the world to be if you don't really want to play. You have to get yourself involved, or you're going to get hurt. If you duck your head, you're going to get hurt.

If you don't concentrate and watch what you're doing, if you don't bend your knees into the football stance, you're going to be in trouble. In tackling, you've got to go in there and put everything into it, or you're going to get hurt."

The fellows who get hurt are often the ones who shy away, the ones who ease up. Start trying to evade contact, and that's the time you'd better leave the game while you can still do it on your own power.

The fact that I've been seriously injured so seldom in fifteen years with the pros hasn't been all luck. Being able to relax helped. If you don't have your knees bent and get hit from the side, something's got to give. When you're in a pileup, you can't be tense, or you come out with a broken arm or leg. It's important to be able to control your body. I've worked on it. If this guy hits you and he has an angle on you, you've got to give a little bit. Through experience, you come to know when danger is there and when it's not. An old player reacts to danger better than a young one.

The people watching the game may just see a lot of big bodies running into each other. But if you really study football and get involved in it, you see there's a certain pattern to it. Everybody has a certain responsibility, and he's trying to take care of it. On a sweep, for instance, there will be certain opposing players leading it and certain ones blocking at certain angles. On an off-tackle play, there'll be a lot of bodies in on that because it's a quick power play. But a sweep is more wide open, with more finesse. On a screen pass or a draw, you know what to expect, and you train yourself to react accordingly.

Before the 1968 season began, I had ten years in the league and I was doing some things I hadn't known about in 1958. I wasn't out of position so much. I was able to adjust my game much better to a particular opponent and his strong points. I changed my game from week to week to compensate.

If I was going against one of the better players, I prepared myself accordingly. For instance, the Forty-Niners had a big, strong center named Bruce Bosley; he joined the league three years before I did. He was kind of slow. But if you gave him the chance to overpower you, he would. I always tried to be real quick against Bosley. But if we were playing the Rams after Ken Iman went to Los Angeles from the Packers, I'd remember that Ken was always throwing himself at your feet, trying to cut you down. A player like him, you know he's trying to anticipate where you're going to be, and you try to keep him away from your feet. You have to watch your feet much more with him than with a player like Bosley, who'd try to get position on you and then hold that position because of his great strength.

Experience helps you ward off blockers, improve your footwork, figure out the right angle to make a stop at the line of scrimmage or going back to defend against a pass. It's a matter of repetition. You improve with the years in reacting to such things as screens or draw plays.

There's no way you can stop the birthdays from coming every twelve months, but you can take care of your body so they don't bother you too much. In the off-season, I tried to keep myself in condition so I'd be ready when training camp opened. Each day, I'd go over to the stadium and run. I learned early that you'd better report to camp ready to play. I watched my diet, keeping away from starches and fats and eating less before the season started.

And by 1968, it was easy to see that all this was paying off. Some of the players who'd come to the league when I did had long since left, but those of us who kept in shape and continued to enjoy the game were still doing pretty well. At the NFL Players Association annual awards dinner in 1968, for instance, three of us on the Packers got mentioned: Willie Davis got the Whizzer White award for contributing the most to the league, his team, and the community; Forrest Gregg was named the league's best offensive lineman, and I was picked as the best linebacker. All three of us had been around Green Bay quite a while.

The Players Association was becoming a more important factor in football by now. A few months after that second annual awards dinner, the association and the owners began arguing about pensions, and the veterans were kept out of training camp until it was settled. The association wanted about $210,000 additional from each team for the pension fund; as Dave Robinson, our player representative, pointed out, teams had been paying that much to untried rookies during the NFL–AFL bidding war.

We worked out on our own at Premontre High School stadium until the dispute was settled, then joined the rookies at St. Norbert College. Under the settlement, a ten-year veteran would be entitled to $1,600 a month when he was sixty-five.

We settled down to get ready for Bengtson's first season as head coach. We knew the pressure he was under. We wanted to do a job for him. I really thought, getting ready for that 1968 season, that we had more weapons than we'd had the year before. But then Chandler retired. Starr got hurt. Other people got hurt.

215

We started out fine, beating Philadelphia in the opener. But then Minnesota and Detroit beat us. The Vikings' game wasn't close, but if we could have stopped the Lions' final drive we would have tied them. With less than ten minutes left, Detroit took nearly eight of those minutes to go seventy-nine yards and score the touchdown that put them ahead.

We got by Atlanta, then had another heartbreaker. We were leading the Rams until Bruce Gossett kicked a field goal with fifty-five seconds left to give Los Angeles the game, 16–14. That was a game that could have gone our way, but it didn't. The year before, we'd been winning the close ones. Now we were losing them. At one point, we had the ball on the Rams' four with a first down. In four plays we couldn't make those four yards.

The second time we played Detroit we tied them. Then we went back to the Cotton Bowl and beat Dallas, which had won its last six games. Starr had been hurt, but he came back for that game and threw four touchdowns.

Against the Bears, we were tied 10–10 with 32 seconds to play, and Cecil Turner made a fair catch of Donny Anderson's short punt. Chicago took advantage of a rule that says you're entitled to a free kick after a fair catch, and Mac Percival made a 43-yarder to beat us. That was another of those 1968 games that we could have won but didn't. It didn't make me feel any better in the locker room afterward when somebody pointed out that Gale Sayers had set a team rushing record with 205 yards. Sayers was a great back, but the Packers had been able to handle him some afternoons. Not that day, though.

Minnesota was next. We knew they were the team to beat for the division title. On Tuesday, I wrote "Beat the

Vikings" on the knees of my sweat pants. I usually did something like that to get me fired up for the next game, but I printed those words with a little extra determination, because this was a key game. If we won it, we might still salvage the season.

I spent a lot of time that week thinking about Bill Brown, the Minnesota fullback, who was not only a fine runner but also an especially good receiver among the backs. I went out there planning to see to it that Brown had a rough afternoon. But the afternoon was rougher for me than for him. Before long, I had two dead shoulders, the result of pinched nerves. It got a little hairy trying to belt a guy like Brown with nothing but my torso. I had to play, though. My backup man, Jim Flanigan, had a bad knee. At least I could move around all right, even if I couldn't feel anything underneath my shoulder pads.

Having both shoulders go numb at once was unusual. I'd had pinched nerves before, but only on one side. This time I got hit wrong, and it happened to both shoulders at once. It was a funny feeling. It was as if I didn't have any arms. I could see them, but they didn't feel as if they were still attached to me.

It happened right in the middle of the game. It would have been embarrassing to run off the field and tell the other guys, "Hey, I've got two numb shoulders." So I kept it to myself, hoping the numbness would go away. Such injuries usually don't last long. The blood starts circulating, and you get the feeling that your arms are fastened to your body again.

That's one thing people don't know when they're watching a game. They see somebody out there not playing up to his normal ability, and they think he's goofing off. But maybe he's hurt and even the coach doesn't realize it. You're being paid to perform, and besides, if you go out and somebody replaces you, maybe he'll take your job away. So you keep your mouth shut and play.

Bart Starr once played an exhibition game against Cleveland with a shoulder separation. As you might expect, he had one of his lesser days. Lombardi told him, "You're playing like a cripple." But Bart still didn't mention his bum shoulder. After all, as the coach was always pointing out, one of our mottoes was: "You're not hurting—you're football players."

There are lots of stories like that—for instance, the one about Tommy Nobis of the Falcons, who broke his finger in a game and never missed a play.

"Does it hurt?" somebody asked, and Tommy gave an answer worthy of a middle linebacker: "Only when I shake hands."

Lombardi contended that defensive players have to be tougher, mentally and physically, than offensive players. Maybe linebackers are especially tough. Nobis is one example, and Sherill Headrick, who played with Kansas City and Cincinnati, is another.

Headrick was known as "Psycho" after he told a reporter, "I'm a kook." During one game with the Oilers he went over to the sidelines and held out his arm to the Chiefs' trainer, Wayne Rudy. His hand was dripping blood, his thumb dangled limply, and there were broken bones jutting through the skin.

"You better fix this thing up," the linebacker said.

"You're going to the hospital. I'm not going to touch that until a doctor sees it."

"Damn it, grab onto it and hold it," Headrick yelled, and Rudy did. Psycho stepped back. His weight pulled the broken bones back inside the skin.

"Tape on one of the Popsicle splints," Headrick ordered. The trainer used a tongue depresser as a splint, and the linebacker ran back on the field without missing a play.

I think it was in that 1968 Minnesota game when my shoulders went numb that our defensive tackle, Bob Brown, played three quarters with a broken leg. I didn't know about it until later. I wondered why Bob wasn't moving around the way he usually did. He didn't tell anybody he was hurt. Maybe he didn't know the bone was broken, but he sure knew he was hurting.

Every player gets to feeling that the team can't get along without him. You have to be out there. If you don't feel that way, you don't belong in football. Even when he's hurt, a pro believes he's better than his replacement. And maybe he is. The other team doesn't know he's hurt, but if a rookie comes in to replace him, the opposing quarterback sees a possible weak spot and starts picking on it. Then the rookie's teammates try to help out, and maybe that leaves some other opening in the defense.

When coaches judge players to decide whether they're ready for the pros, one thing they ask is: "Will he play when he's hurt?" A willingness to do that is considered a big asset.

In that 1968 Minnesota game, we came close again, but we lost. We had first down on the Vikings' six at one point and couldn't score. They beat us by four points. And you know who scored both Minnesota touchdowns? Bill Brown, the fullback I was trying to handle with two dead shoulders. If I'd been healthy that day and we'd stopped just one of those scores, it could have made all the difference.

New Orleans was next and we figured to beat them, but I wasn't looking forward to the game. I knew I'd be spending the afternoon having to watch out for Monty Stickles, the former Forty-Niner who'd gone to the Saints.

Every game, he'd try to pick on somebody. He'd hit him behind the head or wait until the guy's back was turned and come up to block. He was a fellow you really had to watch out for, never knowing when he'd give you a blindside block. One game, he'd blocked me when my back was turned and injured my right knee. I finished out the game, but the knee slowed me down for the next couple of weeks. I'd had other bad experiences with Stickles, so I knew what to expect when New Orleans played us that day in Milwaukee.

Stickles kept trying to antagonize me, which was how he played the game. I tried to make sure I knew where he was on every play, but he kept pulling his usual tricks. I got to the point where I'd had it with all his cheap shots. Finally, he hit me once too often after the play was over. I just had to hit him one. I knew I shouldn't, but I gave him the forearm. Even then, I didn't go for his head, where I could really have hurt him. I got him in the chest. The referee was right there.

"No. 66," he yelled, "you're out of the game."

I'd never been thrown out of a game in my life—not at Proviso, not at Illinois, not with the pros.

"What are you talking about?" I asked the ref. "This

guy's been doing the same thing all afternoon. He's been giving us bad shots all day."

But I was out, and the Packers were penalized fifteen yards for unnecessary roughness. I felt bad about it. But if I had to be thrown out for hitting somebody, I'm glad it was that big tight end, Stickles. He was 6 foot 4, 245 pounds, fast, strong, a lot of ability. But I felt he always looked for the easy way, and I didn't appreciate it. He was always getting linebackers thrown out of games—fellows like Wayne Walker and Joe Fortunato. He'd keep goading them and when they'd retaliate, they'd be the ones who'd get caught.

Actually, there are advantages to playing against someone like Stickles. You give your game a little extra effort. An opponent like that makes you more alert. You have to be. Otherwise, he'll sneak up on you, and you may wind up getting carried off.

Getting thrown out of that game hurt me, and it hurt the club. Jim Flanigan wasn't able to play because of his knee, and with me out we had our only three healthy linebackers in the game: Robinson, Caffey, and Fred Carr. If one of them had been injured, Bengtson said later, he was planning to put in Doug Hart, who was then a reserve defensive back and stood 6 feet and weighed 190. But none of the three got hurt.

I wasn't the only one who had trouble with Stickles by any means. Walker of the Lions once complained to an official that Monty had jumped on him and kicked him.

"Take care of it your own way," the official said.

On the next play, Walker spun Stickles down and whacked him in the face.

"You're out of the game," the official said.

"But you told me to take care of him."

"I know. But I didn't mean it quite like that."

There aren't many dirty players in the league, and usually they don't last long. The way to play the game is to go after the ball carrier with everything you've got, but I don't go after him with the idea of gouging his eyes or trying to hurt him deliberately. After the whistle, when a guy's off balance, hitting him isn't called for. That's when you can really hurt him. His legs are out, and he's off guard. If you're down on the ground, a dirty player can step on you. On defense, where you can use your arms and hands, a dirty player can grab a guy's face through his mask or hit him below the belt or kick him. None of that is called for.

If somebody's got the ball, it was my job to get him, but I wasn't there to give him a forearm in the head when he wasn't looking.

To survive when a dirty player was on the field, you had to watch him at all times. If your back was turned or you were in a pile you never knew when he was going to take a cheap shot at you. You couldn't play as relaxed as you'd like to play—you had to worry about him stopping you from doing your job, not only for that game but maybe for several weeks thereafter if he took a cheap shot at you and you got hurt.

Sooner or later, most such players learn that it doesn't pay to play dirty. Other players are going to retaliate. It's degrading to football to have cheap-shot artists on the field. There's no place for a man who tries to injure other players.

There was something of a rhubarb in the papers after I got thrown out of that New Orleans game, with Stickles claiming he'd had a clean record for the last two years. But the way I looked at it, Stickles had that forearm coming.

Considering how much contact there is in football and how emotional a game it is, it's remarkable that there are so few dirty players. It's partly because the referee isn't the only one out there enforcing the rules. The players do some enforcing, too. If there's a dirty player around, they take care of him, one way or another. There's a kind of professional etiquette involved. Opponents who don't play by the rules are going to get hit a little harder.

Most of us realize we're all in this thing together. The average football player is a pretty good sort. He's no thug. Probably three fourths of us are married and have children. We're responsible citizens. We can't afford to get hurt, because football is our livelihood, and we don't go out of our way to hurt somebody else who's just trying to get along. Besides, those other fellows are just as strong and fast and mean as you are. A young player who starts out rough and dirty usually gets straightened out before he's been in too many games.

Part of playing within the rules is a matter of pride. It's like any other game—if you're playing cards, for instance, you don't want to peek at the opponent's hand because that would spoil the fun. You want to beat him but not by cheating, because what satisfaction is there in that?

In spite of Stickles, we won that game with New Orleans, although Starr had to leave with bruised ribs. The next week Zeke Bratkowski hit on eighteen of twenty-four passes, and we won from Washington. The Vikings lost to the Colts that weekend. So, after eleven games, we still weren't out of contention, even though we'd lost as many games as we'd won. Even with our .500 record, we were only half a game behind the Vikings.

Our next game was with the Forty-Niners, and we had the misfortune of running into John Brodie on one of those days when he was doing everything right. John is one of the really great passers—I've seen him complete passes that were hard to believe. If you were coaching a young quarterback, you'd love to see him throw like Brodie. He's a picture passer, a guy who can really pinpoint his receivers when he's hot.

Some days, John will force the ball and throw into areas where there are a lot of bodies, not all of them friendly. Those afternoons, he gets in trouble. But just for throwing that football, there's no finer quarterback.

Brodie has usually had good games against us, and that one in 1968 was an example. He made 319 yards in the air, including 2 touchdown passes. We were ahead 20-7 with 3 quarters gone, and it looked like we had the game in our pocket. But then John started throwing the way he can when he gets a hot hand. San Francisco made 20 points in the last 15 minutes and beat us.

The next week, the Colts held us to a field goal—the fourth straight game where Baltimore's defense hadn't allowed a touchdown. The score was 16-3 and we had our seventh loss, the most in any season since 1958.

There went our last chance to catch the Vikings, but the Bears could still do it if they beat us in the last game of the season. I've got good friends in Chicago, but if you work for the Packers you don't like to see the Bears win. We wanted to make sure that if Chicago took the division title they would earn it, but we had a large handicap going into that game: Starr and Bratkowski were both too hurt to play, and that left only Don Horn, who not only was young and inexperienced but had been in the Army since shortly after the Packers' intersquad game in training camp.

But Horn got back in time for the Chicago game, and he played like the rookie who comes off the bench in a B movie. He and Boyd Dowler played catch all afternoon. Dowler caught 6 passes for 182 yards. Even so, with a minute left to play we were ahead by only one point—28–27—and it was fourth down and Jack Concannon was backing up to throw. The ball came toward one of the Chicago receivers who'd come hooking into my territory. If that slogan, "Beat the Bears," that I'd put on the knees of my sweat pants early in the week was going to mean anything during the off-season, I had to do something about it. What I did was catch the ball. So instead of the Bears representing our division in the playoffs, the Vikings got the job.

Our 6–7–1 record gave us our first losing season since my first year in the league. But even so, we weren't far behind the division leaders. The Vikings were 8–6 and the Bears, 7–7. Minnesota went on to lose to the Colts in the Western Conference, and Baltimore beat Cleveland in the playoffs.

But then the Colts lost to Joe Namath and the New York Jets in the Super Bowl. I felt Baltimore let our league down. Having any AFL team win would have been bad enough, but I hated to have it done by Namath, which gave the media a chance to build him up into the superhero of the Super Bowl. No question about it, as a player he's outstanding. But I didn't feel he'd used good judgment in the things he did and said off the field. I wouldn't want Namath to be the quarterback on my ball club. I go more for the Starr-Unitas-Meredith type.

If that 1968 season was a frustrating one for the Packers' coach and players, you can imagine what it was like for the club's general manager. Lombardi had promised to let Bengtson run the team. He kept his word. He did come to practices a few times, standing on the sidelines, but he kept his mouth shut.

"Coach, wouldn't you like to chew us out once more for old time's sake?" Hank Jordan asked him one afternoon.

Lombardi knew it was meant as a joke and he managed to grin, but there was a lot of truth in the question.

He had a soundproof cubicle built in the press box, and that's where he watched the games. He came into the dressing room and talked to us a few times, but it wasn't the same. He'd made a mistake when he decided to quit coaching—he knew it by now and we could see it. But the only way he could coach the Packers again was to climb over Bengtson's back, and he wasn't that kind of man.

So it didn't really surprise me when he left Green Bay to get back into coaching. I suppose the money the Washington Redskins offered was a factor and so was the chance to buy a piece of the club, something he couldn't do with the Packers. But it was mostly that he missed the challenge of coaching. It had been his life. He found out he couldn't get along without it, no matter how much the strain of week-to-week competition took out of him.

I didn't blame him for doing what he had to do. But when he left, something went out of our lives. Lombardi had it right when he said the Packers had love for one another. It was something you couldn't explain to outsiders very well, but the attitude was there. When young players joined the club I'd see them falling in line and picking it up, wanting to be part of it. It was a unique thing in Green Bay. This was a small city and nobody owned the Packers but the public, so there was a special relationship with the fans. But it took Lombardi to bring it all together.

One of the few compliments Lombardi ever gave me when he was coaching was to say I was the kind of player who didn't need compliments. It was only after he got out of coaching in Green Bay that he told me it had been a pleasure to have me on his team.

"Ray," he said, "I've always liked and admired you. But you were not one I gave the big handshake or the pat on the back. You're one of those players I felt I always had to stay on. Always be critical toward. I had to do it. There were times when I didn't want to do it, but it was for your own good."

There were times when his attitude got me sore, but I think he handled me the right way. Some people need to be told they're good all the time, but Lombardi always felt I had enough self-confidence.

The coaches grade each play you make, and some players were always worried about what grades they were making. If they heard they had a bad mark on a play, it really bothered them. I think sometimes the coaches gave players like that a better grade than they deserved just to encourage them. But those grades were never important to me. I was just interested in how the game came out and whether I could give myself a good grade. If I'd tried as hard as I could and hadn't let anybody down, I was content. Lombardi didn't have to slap me on the back and tell me how good I was, because I knew how good I was. All I wanted to do was play up to the ability I knew I had.

"Nitschke is the rowdy and whipping boy of this team because he needs it and can take it," Lombardi said once. "He has the proper temperament."

Being called a whipping boy might not seem like much of a compliment, but I knew what the coach meant, and I had to go along with his thinking.

I got another compliment in 1968 that some people might not appreciate. The *Sporting News* picked me as one of the five meanest men in football. The others were Butkus of the Bears, Dave Jones of the Rams, Alex Karras of the Lions, and Dave Wilcox of the Forty-Niners. That's a pretty good crowd to be in.

I'd finished my eleventh season in the league, and along toward the end of that frustrating year of 1968 I'll admit I was getting tired. You take a lot of punishment in eleven seasons. Not only physical punishment. It's partly mental. It takes a special kind of man to withstand the pressures of pro football, year after year. Sure, the pay's good. But when you take a look at the size of your salary and think you've got it made, you're on a collision course with disaster. I've seen it happen around Green Bay. You can't get too interested in outside interests or spend too much time reading your press clippings about what you've done in the past. You've got to be able to go out there every game and prove you still want to play more than the fellow who's after your job.

I realized I'd been slowing up a little toward the end of some of the 1968 games, so I made up my mind that wasn't going to happen in 1969. I started going to the stadium and running every day, beginning in February. That would give me a head start on the running we'd have to do in April on an organized basis. The daily running was an extension of the aerobics program developed by Lt. Col. Kenneth Cooper, an Air Force doctor. A lot of the guys grumbled about all that running, but I believed in it. I felt better than I had in years. I was running two miles every day on my own, and after the season began I kept it up on Monday, our day off. It did a lot for my wind. In 1968, there had been times when I couldn't make the move I wanted to make or take that extra step that would get me into the play. It wasn't going to happen again.

I was still hoping to be on another championship team and play in another Super Bowl. It would have taken only a few little breaks in '68 to have given us the championship. And I'll guarantee that if it had been the Packers playing the Jets in that third Super Bowl, we wouldn't have laid an egg like the Colts.

We missed Lombardi. But that doesn't mean I didn't enjoy playing for Bengtson. He'd helped me a lot over the years. He'd helped me prepare myself so I knew what to look for in a runner, how to read keys, how to block a certain play. I was a better football player from having worked under a perfectionist like Phil. He knew we were going to get blocked on some plays and we were going to make some physical errors. The thing he stressed was not to make mental errors.

Experience helped, along with the training. I'd learned not to be fooled by such tricks as a back faking into the line on a pass play. I'd learned how one opponent would try to block me high, another low, and I was ready for them.

The defense had changed in many ways since I was a rookie. The opponents were bigger and faster. We were having to contend with such things as the moving pocket and the scrambling quarterback. The hardest plays for a middle linebacker are the draw and screen plays, because the other team is trying its best to confuse you. A linebacker normally looks first for the run, then the pass. But when they give you the pass protection fake and you drop back, trying to take care of your pass responsibility, and then they give the ball to a back, you've got a lot of empty space ahead of you to cover in a hurry. You've got to get where the ball is. These are the plays you can get hurt on. And I don't mean you can get hurt only by the other team picking up yardage. I mean hurt physically, too. You're apt to get hit from the side when you're trying to cover all that ground to get back in position. My knees have been banged up a number of times on plays like that.

Bengtson always contended that I had the right size, the right quickness, and an abundance of aggressiveness to meet a blocker or to tackle a ball carrier. He called me the best linebacker who'd ever played when it came to pass defense. But as all those strong, fast young men started coming into the league, year by year, I had to be sure I could contend with them. That's why I spent the off-season watching my diet and running to stay in condition.

It's not just physical contact out there—two big guys trying to knock each other down or a fast receiver trying to outrun a fast defender. While you're on that field, your mind better be in the game along with your body, because you can be sure the other team's quarterback isn't standing around wondering how his IBM stock is doing or what he'll order for dinner. He's trying to set you up. He's watching for you to make a mistake so he can take advantage of it.

Starr was great at that sort of thing. Time after time, I've seen him fool the defense by going for a pass when we had third down and short yardage and everybody was looking for a power play. But he had set it up earlier. On other third downs with short yardage, he'd called a running play. He'd try to get the defense so it expected a run in that situation. He even took advantage of the Packers' reputation of being an old-fashioned, grind-it-out, conservative sort of football machine. About the time the opponents started thinking Bart was kind of a stodgy fellow, that's when he was ready to surprise them.

Every quarterback is always trying to keep the defense in doubt about what he's going to do. Once the defense knows what you're planning, they're going to stop it. If you can keep them off balance, you'll be a successful quarterback.

Some teams do a lot of blitzing, trying to hurry the quarterback, but the Packers' coaches felt that blitzing took too much away from our pass defense. If the linebackers try to get to the quarterback, that puts a lot of pressure on the defensive backs. The receivers are so quick and knowledgeable that they can beat any defensive back, given the chance, especially if he doesn't have any help in the hook zones, which are usually the linebackers' responsibility. I like to blitz. It's a spectacular play when it works. But so often when we've tried it the quarterback has seen it coming and we got in trouble. So most of the time we've felt the defensive line could put enough pressure on the quarterback to throw him off his rhythm and the linebackers could react to the pass instead of running in there, gambling that they could get to the quarterback before he got his pass away.

Blitzing is fun, but it's a gamble where you can lose big. Defensively, it's a poor gamble unless you have to do it because you're not getting an adequate amount of pressure from your linemen. And gambles don't win games.

As a college player, I was disappointed when they wouldn't let me be a quarterback. I've always felt I had the right physical qualifications for the job. I could throw the ball. I could handle the pressure. But I think the position where I wound up in the pros was the right one for me. A quarterback can't show his aggressiveness. He has to keep it bottled up. On defense, you can get a little carried away —not too far, but you can be aggressive enough to set the tone. By hitting an opponent hard, I hoped I'd encourage my teammates to do some hitting, too.

For the second straight year, Green Bay fans picked me in 1968 as the Packers' most valuable player, even though, as Bengtson said, I wasn't in the best shape because of a chronic neck injury that had me playing under wraps.

"Seeing him in the training room every morning and knowing what he had to bear up under," the coach said, "I thought it was an excellent display of the attitude we must have on the Packers."

I appreciated what Bengtson said, and I was touched by the fans' vote, especially after a year like 1968. And then when I was picked by the league for the all-time all-pro team as the best middle linebacker in the NFL's first fifty years, it was a great feeling. To be recognized as one of the good ones, just to be included and to know I had the respect

232

of the coaches and players around the league—that really meant something.

It was quite a team that was picked as the best in the first half century. The only other active Packer who made it was Jerry Kramer, and he was about to retire. But there were some others who'd played at Green Bay earlier; Don Hutson, the great split end; Cal Hubbard, who played with the Giants, Packers, and Pittsburgh Pirates (the Steelers' predecessors) in the twenties and thirties before becoming a baseball umpire; and Emlen Tunnell, who made his reputation mostly with the Giants but came to Green Bay to finish his career when Lombardi got there.

Unitas was chosen as the all-time quarterback, John Mackey as the tight end, Jim Brown as fullback, Lou Groza as kicker, Dick Lane as cornerback, Leo Nomellini as defensive tackle, Chuck Bednarik as center, Gino Marchetti as end, Gale Sayers as halfback—all of them guys I'd played against. The only old-timers to make that team were Hubbard, Hutson, flanker Elroy Hirsch, and Jim Thorpe.

Five Packers made the thirty-man runner-up squad: Ron Kramer, Boyd Dowler, Forrest Gregg, Lennie Ford, and Herb Adderley.

Sayers beat out Red Grange, and Brown beat out Bronko Nagurski, which says something about how the nominating committee felt about modern players as compared to the great ones of the past. As for me, I won over Joe Schmidt of Detroit and Clyde "Bulldog" Turner of the Bears, which I considered quite a compliment.

It was nice to know that Unitas and Mackey and Sayers and some other pretty good players were now my teammates on the all-time all-pro squad. But I knew when the

1969 season started and I started chasing those guys, they weren't going to slow up just because we were on the same mythical team.

Now that I was going into my twelfth season, I was being called the Willie Mays of football—partly, I guess, because I'd been around for quite a while without losing my boyish enthusiasm for playing games. But once the whistle blew, I knew I was going to have to prove myself all over again.

And that was the way I wanted it. I was thirty-two, but I didn't feel a day over twenty-five. I hadn't expected to stay in pro football this long—not many players last as much as ten years. There were going to be some old friends missing from the locker room—Jerry Kramer and Bob Skoronski were among those retiring. But not me. I wasn't ready to quit. The Packers were preparing for their fiftieth season, and I was getting ready right along with them.

CHAPTER XII

As we started our final season of the 1960s, the Packers were no longer champions. But no matter what happened in 1969, Green Bay had dominated the decade in which professional football became the nation's No. 1 sport, a ten-year period when millions of Americans changed their habits to stay home and crouch in front of a television set every fall Sunday afternoon.

Besides the all-star team that was picked as the best in the NFL's first half century, forty players were selected as the best of the 1960s. I was the only Packer still active in 1969 who had made the fifty-year team. But eight of us still playing for Green Bay were included in the all-1960s team: Starr, Boyd Dowler, Willie Davis, Dave Robinson, Herb Adderley, Forrest Gregg, and Willie Wood, along with me. Paul Hornung, Jim Taylor, Jerry Kramer, Jim Ringo, and Don Chandler also made that honorary squad of sixties' stars. So the Packers placed thirteen men out of forty. And all thirteen had made their reputations under Vince Lombardi.

But we were going into the 1969 season without him. He not only wouldn't be on the sidelines. He wouldn't be in that soundproof cubicle upstairs at the stadium watching us and wishing he was still down on the field where he could chew us out.

In February 1969, Lombardi resigned as Green Bay's

general manager to coach and manage the Washington team. Some people were surprised that he would leave the Packers, particularly to go to a team like the Redskins, which had finished a typical 5–9 season in 1968. But I wasn't surprised. Maybe he'd become something of a legend around Green Bay, but I knew he'd never be content until he tried coaching again.

"I'm not a legend," he said when he got to Washington and people started wondering why he'd put his reputation in jeopardy, "because I don't want to be a legend. I'm too young to be a legend."

Seeing him during that 1968 season when he was a full-time general manager, he wasn't the Lombardi I'd known. He wasn't satisfied. He couldn't just sit up there in that office. He had to be doing something all the time.

The only action he got in on that year was golf. And the way he played, golf wasn't very relaxing for him. It wasn't relaxing for the people who played with him, either. He had to win at golf, just as he had to win at football and everything else.

Every athlete is naturally competitive. He'll try to beat you at anything you're playing, just to beat you. There doesn't have to be any money involved. But Lombardi had an unbelievable amount of competitiveness. He had to be the best. Nothing was going to get in his way. He was an extremely emotional guy. In dealing with his players as coach, he'd say things he didn't mean, and the next minute he'd be sorry. But when he was the coach he could say those things and we'd stand there and listen. But he was that way even when he played what was supposed to be a relaxing round of golf.

I'm a competitive fellow, too. But if I get beat at something like golf, it doesn't hurt my pride. I want to do the best I can at the game, but I don't have a lot of sweat invested in it the way I do in football. But if Lombardi didn't win at everything, it got to him. Golf was no way for him to get rid of those frustrations of having to keep his mouth shut when his team was down there on the field losing.

When he got to Washington and took charge, he was back in his element. He must have known it would take a miracle to make winners out of that team he'd inherited, but he had the reputation of being a miracle man. At a reception for him, somebody asked him his reaction to all that hero worship, and he gave that stainless steel grin of his.

"What the hell is a messiah to expect?" he said.

He was kidding. But he was serious, too.

Well, we wished him luck, except when we were playing Washington, and it didn't surprise us when Lombardi drove the Redskins to their first winning season in fifteen years. But we couldn't spend much time thinking about his problems. We had enough problems of our own.

I felt that Coach Phil had been criticized unfairly for our 1968 shortcomings. I wanted to see us go out and win for him, now that he had all the responsibility instead of sharing it with Lombardi. Our fans wanted us to go back to dominating the league. But those days were gone. The chance of any team dominating football wasn't good any more.

The league had changed. It had only twelve teams when I joined the Packers. Now, with its amalgamation with the AFL, it would soon have twenty-six—the union would be complete in 1970. Everybody was equal when it came to the player draft. There are only so many good players, and now they were spread around among twenty-six teams. There was no chance of one team being able to get more than its share.

A lot of the men who had made the Packers so great in 1967 were gone. Young guys were trying to take their places, but no inexperienced team was going to play like that collection of stars Lombardi put together and molded and developed into a machine that wasn't going to be beaten. Still, I was going to do my part for Bengtson. As one of the veterans who remembered what it felt like to win, I was going to do what I could to get us back into the habit of winning.

A linebacker is supposed to inspire his teammates by showing them how hard-nosed he is, but I guess my nose wasn't hard enough early in the year. In training camp, I developed a cut from where the front rim of my helmet jammed down on my nose. Every Sunday after the season began the scab would get knocked off early in the game and I'd start bleeding. The blood would get mixed with dirt and grass stains and lime from the lines on the field.

I was a living example of the old saying that linebackers have to bleed for a living. But that wasn't all bad. When we lined up, the opposing quarterback would look across and see Nitschke bleeding under his face mask and maybe he'd do a little thinking about how the next blood shed might be his.

We started off Bengtson's second season as head coach in the best possible fashion by beating the Bears. Chicago didn't make a point against our defense. The next week we held Brodie and the Forty-Niners to one touchdown and the Packers won again, so we went into the Minnesota showdown unbeaten. The Vikings were the team we had to get past if we were going to win the Central Division.

But we didn't beat them. The score was 19–7. We bounced back the next week and took the game with the Lions, but then we lost to the Rams. We took Atlanta and barely beat Pittsburgh. So we had a 5–2 record, and if we could get past the next three games, we'd be on our way.

But we lost to the Colts. The next week, Minnesota knew it was in a ball game, but the Vikings won 9–7. Then we lost to Detroit. Our record was down to 5–5. We won three of our last four games, but all that accomplished was to keep us out of last place. Our 8–6 record was good enough for third, behind Detroit and Minnesota. The Vikings won with 12–2. If we'd taken our two games from them, we would have been tied at 10–4 each. But we didn't, and the fourteen-point difference between Green Bay and Minnesota in those two games was enough to keep us out of the money again.

Minnesota won the playoffs but lost to Kansas City in the Super Bowl. So Green Bay was still the only NFL team to win that game. That was some satisfaction, but not very much when you looked at the standings and saw us in third place in our own division.

When the American Football League was beginning, its teams scored a lot because no one in the AFL had any defense. But by now the better teams in that league had reached the level of NFL teams. They added a lot of things to pro football: a wide-open offense, with such things as the moving pocket for the quarterback and a lot of speed that appealed to fans and added to the color of the game. In its early days, the AFL had the reputation of being the place where the quarterbacks threw the ball all the time, scrambling around and trying to hit a bunch of fast receivers. But as the AFL matured, that league went the way of the NFL, with its big backs and big blockers. The AFL teams found out you can't just have a fast man who can run with the ball. He has to block and keep people away from the quarterback, too.

When the merger of the two leagues was completed in 1970, the twenty-six teams were divided into two conferences. Green Bay was in the National Football Conference of the NFL, and the same four teams were in our Central Division. But three of the old NFL teams—Baltimore, Pittsburgh, and Cleveland—moved over to the American Football Conference. We'd had quite a fine rivalry going with the Colts over the years, and in a way I was sorry to see them go. But the change meant we wouldn't be seeing Johnny Unitas and his crew quite so often, a development that had its good points.

Our opener in 1970 was with the Lions. In the last game of the exhibition season, the week before that Detroit game, I hurt my lower back. It affected my running. I couldn't make the moves you should make to play middle linebacker. My agility was reduced. Probably it would have been better to sit on the bench for a while, but when the opener began I was in the lineup as usual.

There's pressure from your teammates to stay on the field even when you shouldn't be out there. Like that Thanksgiving Day game with Detroit when I hit somebody's helmet and broke my right forearm. And the games when I've been temporarily out of my skull, like the time we were playing the Cardinals in Miami and they had a guy named Thunder Thornton. Thunder was thundering and I had my head down and he hit me and knocked me dizzy. I'd still like to see the movies of that quarter. People told me I was on the field, but I can't remember a thing about it.

But I haven't been hurt too often. Only my hands are marked up from warding off all those helmets and shoulder pads so I could get by the blockers and get to the ball. The shoulder pads stick out and the helmets have sharp edges, so I've got a lot of scratches on my hands. I do have a pretty good scar on my face and people think it's from playing football, but I got it when I was a little guy. I was playing airplane in Elmwood Park and the airplane made a crash landing in a bush. It looks like a cleat mark, but it isn't. Nobody ever walked over me like that.

But the older you get, the longer those inevitable bumps and bruises last. The body doesn't heal as quickly. It's harder for an older athlete to recuperate, and we were seven games into the 1970 season before I got rid of that back injury that was slowing me down.

I think that injury had another effect on my career. When we got a new coach the next year, Dan Devine naturally looked at the previous season's game films. I figure he must have spent a lot of time looking at the movies of those first 1970 games when my back was hurting and I didn't have my usual agility or speed.

We had some other problems before the 1970 season started. Herb Adderley had blamed the coaching staff because he wasn't picked for the last Pro Bowl and had asked to be traded, which is how one of our best players wound up in Dallas. We needed him at cornerback, and replacing him was difficult. I was a good friend of Herb's, and I didn't want to criticize him. He did what he felt was right. But I couldn't see why he made such a big thing about the Pro Bowl. There are more important things than playing in the Pro Bowl.

In the off-season, we traded Lee Roy Caffey, Elijah Pitts, and Bob Hyland to the Bears for Mike McCoy. He and Rich Moore each weighed 285 pounds, which meant I was playing behind a couple of big ones. Henry Jordan and Willie Davis were agile rather than big. With two young guys there, I knew I'd have to work a little harder until they got some experience under those large-sized belts.

There was a hassle that year over whether the veteran players should cross a picket line established by the players' association when it went on strike for a better pension plan. Some veterans did cross, but I didn't. I'm for the association. When I came into the league, there was no such thing as a pension plan. But now we have pension rights, and it's a tremendous thing. You need to stay in the league at least five years before you qualify, and each year you play after that you're entitled to more. Because of the pension plan, some young players who might quit decide to stick it out for at least five years.

The Packers went through the 1970 exhibition season undefeated. But along toward the end of summer, some of us who played under Lombardi were having trouble keeping our minds on the game. The coach was dying. He was only fifty-seven years old, but cancer was one enemy he couldn't lick. We flew into New York for his funeral at St. Patrick's Cathedral. All the Packers were there and the Redskins, his new team, and a lot of other football players who'd respected and admired him.

But after we got back to Green Bay, the season had to go

on. We had to try to get ready for our opener with the Lions. Lombardi was gone and a lot of the faces that had been so familiar when he was coaching were gone. It was another year for us. Now, without St. Vincent, it was another era for football.

Our part of the new era did not begin very well. After the opener, Coach Bengtson said we'd accomplished a rare feat. We'd made every mistake any football team could possibly make.

The first half of that opener wasn't so bad. We held Detroit to thirteen points. Even though our offense couldn't score—it gained exactly twenty-seven yards in twenty-five tries—there was still a chance for a comeback. But the second half turned out to be worse than the first.

Lambeau Field had just been expanded, so the 56,263 people in the stands made up the largest home crowd ever to watch the Packers. As one fan put it, "Never have so many paid so much to see so little."

Before the game was over, the spectators were doing something a Green Bay crowd seldom does: They were booing. The boos were for the offense, not the defense, but that wasn't much consolation.

For the first time in history, we were shut out at Lambeau Field. The last time we'd failed to score in a game played in Green Bay was when the Packers played in East Stadium and the Bears won 17–0 in what turned out to be Curly Lambeau's last season. The most demeaning part of that 40–0 loss in 1970 was when Greg Landry made seventy-six yards on a quarterback sneak for a touchdown. It turned out to be the longest gain from scrimmage anyone made the entire season.

The Sunday night after that disaster was the worst of my life. There was no way I could get to sleep. I kept replaying the game, over and over. I wished I hadn't given up drinking, so I could drown my sorrows. Instead, I lay there in bed listening to the clock. It chimes every quarter hour. I heard those chimes each fifteen minutes all night long.

Everything just got away from us in that game. Detroit played well, but the Lions weren't forty points better than we were.

I hadn't been in a game like that since we went to Baltimore and lost to the Colts in 1958 by a score of 56–0, but then I was a rookie and it didn't bother me as much. I had never started off a season so poorly. Lying there, listening to that damned clock, I thought maybe it was time to retire. With my bad back, I couldn't run. I had no coordination. I was off balance all the time. I was trying to make tackles, and I was falling on my face. I got to wondering if I was kidding myself. Maybe my trouble wasn't my back injury. Maybe I was just getting old.

But if you claim to be a professional you have to come back, even after a loss like that, and get yourself emotionally aroused for the next game. The fact that it was with Atlanta helped—the Falcons were one of the weaker teams. Even so, we barely beat them. The score was 27–24, which is an indication that the offense did better at making a comeback from that 40–0 humiliation than we did.

But the next week, the defense showed what it was made of. We held Minnesota to ten points while our team was making thirteen. That put us back in contention. I still wasn't playing the way I wanted to be able to play, but we had proved we weren't as bad as we'd looked in that opening game.

We won from San Diego, lost to the Rams, then played Philadelphia in a Monday night game—the TV fans were now getting football on Mondays as well as Sundays. We beat the Eagles, but then we lost to San Francisco and Baltimore. We won from the Bears by one point, then lost to Minnesota and Dallas. We beat Pittsburgh, then got whipped by Chicago and Detroit. The Lions really had our number. They skunked us again, 20–0.

So we wound up with a record of 6–8, which gave us a tie for last place in our division with Chicago and meant Bengtson had his second losing season out of three. He was a disciple of Lombardi. He knew what happens to losing coaches. He'd been an important part of those great Packer years, molding a defense that was the toughest in the league. But winning really is the only thing that counts, as Vince kept saying. Phil was out.

We were the ones who'd been letting the other team score, and we were the ones who hadn't scored enough points ourselves. But Bengtson was the one who left town.

The new coach, Dan Devine, had a great record at the University of Missouri. Now he had to make the transition to pro ball and try to get the Packers back on the winning track.

After the first seven games of 1970, my back had healed and I'd finished strong. I felt I could help the club with my ability and my experience because I was one of the veterans on a team that was rapidly filling up with talented but inexperienced young players. I only hoped the new coach wouldn't spend too much time looking at the films of those first seven games, when I'd been playing hurt.

For the first time since Lombardi told me Tom Bettis was benched and I was his middle linebacker, I faced the possibility that I wouldn't be a starter. Jim Carter, a good, young player from the University of Minnesota, had joined the squad in 1970 and got quite a bit of playing time when Dave Robinson was hurt. Now he was going to try to take over my job.

I wasn't ready to let him have it. Somebody wrote that I was intending to quit after the 1971 season, but I'd never said that. In 1958, I might have predicted that I wouldn't last more than five years. But then we started winning titles and honors and the years flew by and here I was, bald and battered and thirty-four years old, but I still wanted to play. Even after that unhappy 1970 season, I knew I could still contribute.

I wasn't the only one who hadn't much excuse to brag about 1970. The Packers ranked ninth in the league in rushing and we had thirty-four fumbles, the most of any team in the National Football Conference. Our kicking game wasn't as bad as it had been in 1969, when we made only six of the twenty-two field goals we tried. But of the fifteen three-pointers kicked by Dale Livingston in 1970, only five were longer than thirty yards. Nobody on the defensive team was picked as an all-pro. Only Gale Gillingham made it from the offense. Things were changed from the old days, when the Pack always had a half dozen men who were judged to be the best in the league.

I'd reported to the 1970 training camp in good shape, in spite of the players' strike. When the veterans lined up for a two-mile run before camp opened, I came in first. I was in fine condition when the '71 camp opened, too. I knew I had to compete against youth, and I was determined to go into that competition in the same spirit as I'd always played the game. If you get clobbered, you get up just a little bit smarter. I felt that no matter who the coach was or how many rookies showed up in camp, a middle linebacker had to be a big, mean guy. And I felt that on the Green Bay Packers, I was still that guy.

But it was soon clear to me that Devine didn't feel that way. In the exhibition games, it was Carter who got most of the playing time. I could understand that he needed experience. But there was no use kidding myself. The coaches had made up their minds to go with Carter and put Ray Nitschke on the bench.

Every player knows his career won't go on forever. Some day, unless he quits before it happens, he winds up as second string. But I've always felt a man should earn his way into the starting lineup. The only way you can appreciate being a starter is to earn it. It seemed to me that they were just giving Carter the middle linebacker's job—my job—on a silver platter, and putting me on the second team.

It really hurt. I had a lot of pride. If I was going to be beaten out, I wanted to be beaten out by somebody who could show me he had more ability than I did. I felt I was still the first-stringer. I understood the coaches had a job to do in bringing younger people along, but I knew I could still play; and when you're second string, it's not the same.

Since high school, I'd always been a top dog. I'd never sat on the sidelines except when I was a rookie. It really bothered me. I felt that where I belonged was on the field, not pacing along the sidelines with a headset on, listening to the coaching staff upstairs in the press box and passing along their comments. When the exhibition season opened and Carter was the starter, I tried to persuade myself that it was because I'd been slightly hurt—although I remembered all those times when I'd played with a lot more serious injuries. When the second game came and I was still on the bench, except for a few plays, I still hoped the change was temporary. But as the season wore on, it was plain that I was no longer part of the first team.

I resented it. I felt Devine was dead wrong. At the very least, he could have alternated Carter and me at middle linebacker, giving Jim a chance to get some experience without having to carry the entire load. I didn't go along with the idea that we had to build for a winning team five years later; at my age, there wasn't going to be any five years later. I wanted to win in 1971, not 1976. I think that's how the fans felt, too. I think you ought to always try to win the next game, not worry about something five years away. Who knows what's going to happen in five years?

But I kept my mouth shut about how I felt. At home, I talked about it, all right. But I didn't talk to the press or go around griping in public. The Green Bay organization has been good to me. I wasn't going to do anything that would hurt it, no matter how hard it was to stand there on the sidelines and wear a headset instead of putting on a helmet and running out on the field where I belonged.

I'd never been a second-stringer, and I asked myself, "What are they trying to do to me?" Inside, I had some bitterness toward Devine. If this was what he wanted to do— forget about winning now and build for the future—maybe

248

that would be good for him. But it sure wasn't good for me.

He was a new coach with a new team, and I could understand that he wanted to develop it in his own way. But I didn't like the way he'd come in and moved me out. I didn't feel it was fair to the team or to me. I had something besides my playing ability to offer. The team was sorely in need of leaders. From my years and what I'd learned the hard way, I felt I had leadership to offer. A team needs four or five leaders, not just one. In the days when the Packers had been winning consistently, we'd had such leaders, and I think I developed into one of them. I felt I could still be one. But not while I was sitting on the bench. Not while I was walking around with a headset, relaying advice from upstairs.

Soon after Devine got to Green Bay, it was clear that he was a different type of coach than Lombardi had been. Lombardi would tell you what to do, and that was it. But Devine had a tendency to plead with his players. You don't have to do that with professionals. They should do what they're told. I felt he didn't penalize them often enough. He wasn't harsh enough toward the people who needed it. You have forty big egos on the squad, forty guys who want to do things their own way because they're used to being top dogs, and you have to gain their respect for your leadership—for what you say and for how you do things. A coach must be the strongest man on the field. If he says something, he has to follow up on it and make sure everyone understands that's the way it's going to be.

Coming into an organization like the Packers is a tough job. I had sympathy for Devine's problems. But after working so many years for Lombardi, I felt we ought to build on the tradition he had established and not make too many drastic changes in the way we'd done things with an organization that had been as successful as the Packers.

Devine's background was college coaching, and any college coach who moves to the pros has to make adjustments. Playing for Old Missouri is a little different than playing for Green Bay. A professional is basically in football for a livelihood, and you can be much tougher with him than with a college boy. You don't have to talk him into playing ball or sell him on the idea of upholding the honor of the city. A coach shouldn't worry about being liked by the players, but he must be respected. You sell the players on the idea that if they have any pride in themselves they'll go all out and do their jobs, because if they do well and the team does well they're going to benefit in cold, hard cash, not in some compliments in the college yearbook. They're not out there doing their all for the old Missouri Tigers.

You shouldn't have to ask professionals to do something they're hired to do. You give them rules, an agenda, a program, and that's it. If they don't follow the procedures a coach sets down, then it's time for discipline. A team has to be like an old-fashioned family, with certain rules that are obeyed and with everybody given certain responsibilities. If a coach doesn't establish himself as a tough boss, a lot of players will take advantage of him.

Without such discipline, guys will repeat the same mistakes over and over again. A pro should be told once, and that's it. If all that happens when you make a mistake is some more conversation, some players take the attitude: "Why should I play real hard when if I do anything wrong I'm not going to lose much by it?"

The attitude should be: "Play the way I say, fellow, and do things my way, or you're out. If you don't want to run down the field on a kickoff, for instance, we'll find somebody who wants to do it." There shouldn't be all this pleading with a pro to do something he's being paid to do. If a guy's out there to make a tackle, he should make it all out. If he makes a mistake, he should be reprimanded. If he makes too many mistakes, he should be encouraged to go into some other line of work.

And the reprimands should be kept within the organization. They shouldn't become common knowledge. It shouldn't be the head coach's habit to tell everybody in the world who's playing ball and who's not. I felt that Coach Devine told the reporters a lot of things in 1971 that should have stayed within the four walls of the locker room.

Some people claim that the Lombardi kind of discipline had its day but won't work now. I don't buy that. If anything, the rookies coming up now need more discipline, not less. A lot of them claim they want to play football, but they don't want to work as hard as you have to if you want to develop your body and yours skills to the utmost. It's understandable. Times are different. A lot of them aren't hungry the way I was hungry and some others of my generation of players were hungry. We knew we were going to get knocked back on the seats of our pants sometimes but that we had to be sure to get up a little smarter than we were before we landed there.

I believe in having a good time playing football. I enjoy the comradeship, the feeling of being part of a unit that goes out there and defies the other team to try to win. It's rewarding to learn how to compete, facing your opponent with your head up and your back arched, determined to play with every ounce of ability you have.

It's a great feeling to look around you at those big guys who are on your team and think, "We're going to make this the best outfit in the world because we have respect for each other and a kind of fellowship that has nothing to do with race or religion or anything else that divides people from each other."

The feeling you have is this: "I'm not going to deny you because you're black and I'm white or because you go to a different church than I do. I'm going to respect you because you're a human being and I expect you to do the same for me because we're all in this together, we're all trying for the same thing, we're forty guys with something in common: the desire to make our team the best, the goal of winning for our fans and our families and above all for ourselves, for the pride we have in using the talents and skills that have been given us."

Football is more mental than physical, no matter how it looks from the stands. You can't just turn your emotions on and off like a faucet. You have to work at it. You have to discipline yourself. You have to feed that body of yours and give it the rest it needs and take care of it because otherwise you won't give your best. And a lot of the young people don't seem to want to do that.

It isn't just the money you're paid. It isn't having people point you out on the street. If you really go all out, you become a better person. If you really dedicate yourself to something—football or anything else—you learn about yourself and about life. There are going to be times when you don't get what you want. You've got to accept the defeats and go ahead and work toward your goal. You learn that winning doesn't come to those who just go through the motions.

Nobody's ever given me anything. I've had to work to be a football player. There've been a lot of times when I've been tired and frustrated, even sad. But the youngsters miss something if they don't allow themselves to get caught up in the wonderful excitement of competing against another person with everything that's in them. If you learn that the important goal is to give your best, then you'll get satisfaction from the game.

And it carries over to other things. If you learn to motivate yourself on the field, you can motivate yourself in other endeavors. It isn't only in football that you have to learn to get along with the other guys on the team, have respect for the other people, be willing to accept discipline and to practice self-denial because you have a goal in mind.

Besides, whether you're getting paid for it or not, football isn't just hard work. It's fun. It's exciting. Sure, it's violent. But it's controlled violence, it's disciplined violence, it's violence within certain rules where you're not intending to hurt the other guy and he's not out to hurt you but you're trying to do one thing and he's trying to do another and you're matching yourself against the best that he has to give.

Football provides the kind of thrills that young men want, and a fellow who gets his excitement playing ball is not going to have to get it by driving a car too fast or looking around for trouble with drugs or drink.

Even after all these years, I still get that old excitement rising up in me when I hear that whistle that starts a game.

And that's one reason I paced up and down the sidelines, angry at the coach and sore at the world, when the ball was snapped and I wasn't in the game.

During the 1971 exhibition season, one of the things that kept me from feeling completely discouraged was the attitude of the people in the stands. When I'd finally get a chance to go in, late in the game, they'd start yelling and cheering. I remember when we were playing the Dolphins in Milwaukee and it happened. There was the same reaction at an exhibition game in Green Bay. You might put that down to hometown sentiment, but it happened in other places—in Cincinnati and Buffalo and Los Angeles. It was great to know that although I might be considered second-string by some coaches, the fans were still for me.

I started the season opener with the Giants, when we lost 42–40 in the kind of a game neither team could brag about very much. The next game was in Milwaukee, and I was on the sidelines. Things were fairly close for a while in this game with Denver, and each time the defensive team went in I'd expect to hear my name called. But it wasn't. The first half ended and I hadn't played and the third quarter ended and I hadn't played. I was hurt and angry. I couldn't understand why the coaches didn't feel they needed Nitschke any more.

Then came the fourth quarter and we were well ahead of Denver, so the game was no longer in doubt, and then the coach said to go in. I didn't want to go. It's one of the very few times in my life when someone's said, "play football," and I preferred not to do it. If the game had been close, it would have been different. But now it looked as if they figured we had a safe enough lead so they could afford to let me go out on the field.

But I didn't say anything. I jammed my helmet down on my head and I ran out and all of a sudden those people in the stands were on their feet and cheering as if somebody'd just made a ninety-nine-yard touchdown run. I got a feeling down my spine I'd never experienced before—not when people yelled for me after an intercepted pass or a goal-line tackle, not even when the roar went up when a playoff ended and we'd won another championship. I could feel my face getting red. There were tears running down my cheeks inside the helmet where I couldn't get at them to wipe them off.

One minute I was going out there because I had to, thinking how the coach wasn't doing me any favor to put me in at a time when we were beating the Broncos 34–13. The next minute, there was that ovation for old No. 66.

It told me something. It showed me that I might be getting old and Dan Devine might be shoving me aside. But he couldn't shove aside the great years I'd had with the Packers. The people still remembered.

CHAPTER XIII

The 1971 season was not only frustrating for me but for the Packers. The team finished dead last in the Central Division. Its 4–8–2 record was the worst for Green Bay since my rookie year, when Scooter McLean had his single season as coach.

Now that I was no longer a starter, I thought about retiring. But I decided I still had something to prove—not to the coaches but to myself. I wanted to prove I could play in this league for fifteen years, which meant I had to stick around through 1972. There aren't many of us who last fifteen years in pro ball. Most members of my class of '58 had been out of football for years.

But I still felt young—anyway, young enough. I still had the desire to play. I didn't want to look back when I was fifty years old and regret that I'd hung up my helmet too soon.

Still, if it hadn't been for the reaction of the fans, I might have given up football in 1971 even though I knew I could still play. My pride was hurt by being forced into the role of a second-stringer. When I was a rookie, I could accept it. But not now.

Here I'd been playing all those years, and all of a sudden a man who'd never played middle linebacker before was supposed to be better at the job than I was. All year I was torn inside. I knew I was as good as anybody on the field. I wanted to play so I could prove it. If it hadn't been for the support I got from the fans, I might have quit.

I had nothing against Carter. Jim is eleven years younger than I am, and there's no way either of us can change that. I didn't bellyache about being on the sidelines, but it was hard to have to stand there and see the team lose. It would have been hard enough to be out of things if we'd been winning. But with the kind of season we had in 1971, it was doubly difficult. I could see so many things going wrong, and there was not much I could do about it.

We were letting the opponents kill us with touchdown passes. We weren't aggressive enough. I felt that if I could go roaring out on that field and knock a few people down, it might inspire some of the other guys. I couldn't hit any-body while I was strapped into that headset.

We beat Cincinnati after winning that Denver game, giv-ing us a 2–1 record, but then we lost three straight. We tied Detroit and beat Chicago, then Minnesota won from us by a score of one field goal to nothing. That game could have gone either way, but it was still a loss. It was followed by losses to two weaker teams, Atlanta and New Orleans. We tied St. Louis, but by then we were out of contention.

So was Chicago, and the next-to-last game of the season would be meaningless as far as the standings were con-cerned. Even if we won, we couldn't climb out of last place. But this was the hundredth Packers-Bears game, which made it a landmark. And any game between Chicago and Green Bay is a tough one, even when there's nothing at stake but pride.

All that season, the fans kept cheering me when I'd come into a game. I was a familiar face from the good old days of a few years back, the days when people didn't have to go around with signs on their cars reading, "The Pack Will Be Back," but bragged about living in "Titletown, USA." But I hope the cheers were more than nostalgia for past glories.

Carter is an excellent player and, given time, he can be a better one, so I don't think the fan reaction was a reflection on him. I hope it had something to do with people in Green Bay knowing that I was a man who had matured there, had learned to control himself off the field, and give everything he had to give on the field. I wanted to think that the Packer fans were cheering for me, not downgrading anybody else.

They're quite a group, these Packer backers. If you can talk about professionalism among spectators, they have it. I've heard Green Bay crowds cheer an opponent when he makes a fine play, and that's something you don't find many places around the league. They don't boo the way fans do in some parks. They know football. They appreciate it. The game is more important in Green Bay. It's the thing that put the city on the map.

Some of those fans decided they wanted to do something about Nitschke besides yell when he finally got into a game. One day I picked up the telephone at home and it was Bill King. He's a retired police sergeant, a civic-minded person who's involved in almost anything around town that's designed to make Green Bay better. I've known him since soon after I joined the Packers. He handled the intersection at Mason and Walnut for years, then was assigned to the circuit court to work for one of the judges.

"Ray," he said, "we want to have a Nitschke Day at the Bears game. You have any objections?"

I thought about it. It was hard to believe that they wanted to put on a special day for me. In pro football, not many players get honored that way. The only other Packer who's had a special day in recent years was Bart Starr, in connection with a visit by President Nixon.

Bill said this was strictly a fan effort he had in mind.

"Then it's fine with me and I'm grateful," I told him. "But if you're going to have a Nitschke Day, Bill, I hope it'll be first class. I'd hate to see it fall on its face."

"Don't worry about that, Ray. There's a lot of interest in it already. I think you deserve it, and there are plenty of others around Wisconsin who feel the same."

So they went ahead. It was really heartwarming for a man who'd started out as a lonely kid in Illinois, a fellow who'd made some mistakes before he finally matured, to see how the fans responded. Starr's day was a great occasion for the Packers and for Bart, but it had political overtones and the people weren't involved the way they were this time.

When Jackie and I rode around town, we'd see bumper stickers saying, "We Love Ray." The committee sold buttons saying the same thing. My brother, Bob, said his son, Frank, wouldn't go to bed at night unless he had his "We Love Ray" button pinned to his pajamas.

The buttons cost fifty cents and the stickers a dime. About fifty thousand of the buttons and stickers were sold, so it wasn't long before the committee had raised quite a bit of money, and King asked what kind of gifts I'd like. A new car, maybe?

But I had a car. I had a house. I had everything I

needed. I told Bill I didn't want any presents. Just knowing that so many friends and people I'd never met wanted to pay me this honor was gift enough. I didn't want money or a bunch of expensive gifts, but as long as the committee was getting so much cash in its kitty, I did want something else. I wanted a scholarship fund established so the money raised for Ray Nitschke Day would do somebody some good. If young people, down through the years, were helped to go to college because of me, that would be a lot more satisfying than having another car in my garage that I didn't really need.

If it hadn't been for an athletic scholarship, I would never have made it to college. But the fund they established in my name wasn't just for athletes. It was for anybody who needed it and deserved it, which is exactly the way I wanted it.

The hundredth Packers-Bears meeting was scheduled for December 12. During the weeks before that game, my life was a strange sort of mixture. Everywhere I went I'd see those "We Love Ray" signs and buttons, and when I ran out on the field everybody would yell and applaud. But I was still second-string, and I didn't feel as much a part of the team as I had before. I felt lonely, standing there on the sidelines, watching the Packers play. I'd been used to being an important part of the team. Now I wasn't giving it much of anything, although I kept getting myself psyched up to be ready to go in. Next to my family, the Packers had been the most important thing in my life. Now I was still a part of them, but not the way I had been before.

I kept getting letters and telegrams. Some were from strangers and some from friends, including people I hadn't heard from since I'd been quarterbacking for Proviso. I kept being told so many nice things about myself that I got to wondering if my head would fit inside my helmet. But I figured if I got out on that field and made a couple of hits, the swelling would go down pretty fast.

Coach Devine had some good things to say about me to the reporters:

"I admire Ray because even though he is a highly competitive kind of guy, he has taken not playing with good grace. He's certainly had a lot of opportunities to pop off, particularly when he's out of town, but he hasn't."

The way I looked at it, why pop off? It sounds corny, but it's true—the game had been good to Ray Nitschke, so I wasn't going to start getting bitter about things now that I had another challenge to handle, the challenge of having to stand aside and watch a young player take over my job.

Without challenges, the game wouldn't have been as much fun. Most of them were ones I'd set for myself. I kept learning, because each game was different and each play was a little different from all those that had gone before. That was what had kept me from getting bored with football. Some players do get bored. They get tired of the constant pressure and get out. But I'd always felt that the team was important, the game was important, and my role was important. That attitude kept my incentive to play alive through all the drudgery of studying and practicing, waiting for the chance to run out there on the field on Sunday afternoon to start trying to prove myself all over again.

Devine said he was going to start me against the Bears, moving Carter to one of the outside linebacker jobs. So getting ready to play Chicago was easier than it had been to get myself prepared for those games when I knew I might not play much. This time when I printed "Beat the Bears" on the knees of my sweat pants, I figured I'd have a chance to do something about beating them, just as in the old days.

When I woke up on the morning of the game day, I started thinking about what I'd say when they gave me the microphone during the ceremonies. I decided I'd let my emotions carry me. I decided not to prepare anything but just to say what came into my mind.

It made me feel good to know that Jackie and our sons were going to share in the ceremony. John was eight now, and Richard was five. They were old enough so they'd remember Ray Nitschke Day, too.

We went out to Lambeau Field and I put on my uniform and the other equipment. There was one difference this time. Usually one of the things I do before I go out on the field is take out that partial plate I've worn since that guy from Ohio State knocked out my four front teeth. This time I left my partial in. I knew there'd be a lot of cameras.

After we got warmed up, I met Jackie and the boys and we walked out of the tunnel at the north end of the field and headed for the mikes near the fifty-yard line. Jackie was wearing red plaid slacks, and the boys were wearing bright blue snowmobile jackets. They looked great. I was proud of those three people who were walking along with this thirty-four-year-old senior citizen with No. 66 on his back.

All year, when I went on the field, it had sounded as if the stands were full of my relatives. But this time the cheers were even louder. It was a great feeling to know all those people were applauding for me, and as we made that long walk I thought about a lot of things. I thought of how proud my dad would have been if he could have known that the little boy he loved had grown up to be honored like this. I thought of how my mother would have felt if she could have been there. And I thought of all the other people who'd had a part in my being there: Andy Puplis, who'd encouraged me to make something of myself when I was a mixed-up kid who thought God had pulled a dirty trick on him by taking his parents; and Ray Eliot and Vince Lombardi and my brothers and all those others who'd believed in me and stuck by me and helped me.

I'm tough. I'm hard. I'm mean every Sunday when I walk out on that field. I've taken pride in being all these things. But while we were making that walk I had to reach up and brush away some tears.

We were getting close to the microphones now, and every blade of grass was familiar. Over the years, I've tackled somebody or been knocked down on every inch of that turf. As my friend, Joe Garagiola, said in describing that afternoon on the radio, over the years since I got to Green Bay some opponents had a few tears in their eyes, too, after they met me, and not from sentiment. But right now I loved them all—well, maybe not all of them, but most of them. Because those big, rough guys on the other teams were a part of what had turned out to be a wonderful part of my life, even though the fellow who'd been picked as the best middle linebacker in a half century was all of a sudden having trouble getting a chance to play.

The fans were still cheering. I hoped that they were cheering Nitschke the man as well as Nitschke the football player. I hoped that some of the sentiment they were expressing meant they understood that I'd never tried to be anything I wasn't, that I'd never tried to act like a big shot because I was an athlete.

Some of those people standing around the microphones had known me since I was a little boy. It was a great feeling to know they'd taken the trouble to be there, to be a part of this very special day in my life.

The ceremonies began. Elmer Johnson was introduced and Puplis and Eliot—three coaches who had helped me when I was young. Then Jackie and the boys were presented, and it was good to hear the people applaud these three who meant more to me than anyone else in the world.

Telegrams were read. I especially remember one from Marie Lombardi. "This is a very happy day for a man in heaven who is very proud of you," it said, and when Vince Lombardi's name went out over the loudspeakers, the echo came bouncing back from the stands like a cheer: "Lombardi . . . 'bardi . . . 'bardi!"

Then Bill King announced that the scholarship trust fund was on deposit at the bank. This fund established in my name, he said, was a token of the "respect and admiration and esteem we hold for you."

Then he added: "You are more than a football player. You are more than a professional athlete. You are a symbol of how all of God's children should live."

There was a big roar that lasted for what seemed like a long time and I knew it was my turn next and I stood there trying to collect my thoughts, wondering how I was going to tell 56,263 people what all of this meant to me. I intended to say that all I wanted was what other men want: to be an example to my children, a father they could respect. But I fell down in my thank-you speech. There was all the noise, and when I'd say something the echo would come back. Besides, I was a little shook up. I'd planned to have my emotions carry me, but they carried me away.

"This is the finest day of my life," I began. And the echo came back: "My life . . . life . . . life."

"I have been gifted by God (God . . . God . . . God . . .) to be an athlete ('lete . . . 'lete . . . 'lete . . .) and have played many games (games . . . 'ames . . . 'ames . . .) and am very proud to have been an athlete ('lete . . . 'lete . . . 'lete . . .) over these years (years . . . 'ears . . . 'ears . . .)."

I wished there was some way to turn off that echo that kept bouncing back and getting me mixed up so it was hard to remember what I was trying to say. But I went on to thank the people who had helped make my life something my children could respect—the echo mocking me whenever I stopped for breath—and then I said something that was as true as anything that could be said, even though it wasn't much in the way of originality: "Words can't express how I feel."

Even if I'd been reading from a script and even if that echo didn't keep bouncing back from the stadium walls, there weren't any words that would have been adequate. But it wasn't only the feedback from the echo that was making me stumble. I wanted so desperately to tell these people and all the others out there before their television sets how I felt about them. But my eyes had misted up again and my voice wasn't steady and I was blowing this chance to hit them with a speech that would repay them just a little for the support that had turned the most frustrating season of my life into this high point of my career.

Any two-bit politician who wouldn't know a blind-side block from a missed field goal could have been more eloquent. But I guess the fans understood what I was trying to tell them. I hope they did.

So then we walked back across the field, and Jackie and the boys took their seats on the sidelines on one of the three benches that had been put there for my relatives and friends. When the game began, I was a starter for the first time since September, and I ran out there determined to play like an all-pro. But I was still shaking from those pre-game ceremonies, and it took me longer than usual to really start hitting so I could forget everything except beating the Bears.

We did beat them, too. I wasn't satisfied with the way I played, but the other Packers were all fired up.

"We were trying to win as much for Ray as for the Packers," Willie Wood said later. "No one wanted to see this day marred by a loss."

Bob Brown said the game meant something very special to him, and Donny Anderson said that all the guys wanted to play their best. John Brockington, who needed only a few yards to have a thousand-yard season in his rookie year, made more than enough. The final score was 31–10 in our favor.

That was the first game we'd won since the seventh of November, when we'd barely nosed out the Bears in Chicago. We might be last in our division, but we'd proved we could still win from our oldest rival, and we hadn't really been humiliated by the other two teams in our division: We'd tied the Lions in one of our two games, and Minnesota, which won the Central Division championship, had outscored us by only two touchdowns over two games.

After the fourth quarter ended, Ed O'Bradovich, whose sister had been in my class at Proviso, ran over and gave me a real Bear hug—a friendly one, because the game was over.

Back in the locker room with the other players, I made them a little speech. This was football talk, and I think I did a little better with it than when I was trying to speak to the fans. There's no echo in the dressing room, for one thing. Even Coach Devine said it was a hell of a speech.

"Ray may be one of our oldest veterans," he said, "but he told everyone that he feels very much part of the team. He's not part of the younger generation and he's not part of the establishment either. He can relate very well."

I liked another thing the coach said—that I was a hitter and "I always have a warm spot in my heart for a hitter." I wished I'd been given more opportunity to do some hitting on the field that season, but it was nice to know the coach felt I could still hit. Because I was going to be back in 1972. I'd made up my mind to that.

I had to take some kidding about how I'd gone up to one of my sisters-in-law after we'd whipped the Bears and tried to kiss her, forgetting I was still wearing my face mask. Jim Carter started joking about how I'd accidentally knocked him down during the game after he intercepted a pass that set up the touchdown that put us ahead.

"Hey, Ray, tell 'em why you did it," he yelled, and I told him: "That was probably the hardest hit you got all day."

What the governor of Wisconsin had proclaimed as Ray Nitschke Day still wasn't over. There was a postgame party, with Bart Starr one of the masters of ceremonies. I'd asked that they forget about gifts, but I got some anyway. A Manitowoc teacher had gone to a lot of trouble to carve a mural depicting me and my career. A Wisconsin company gave me a big photograph of myself, taken during the '71 season. I told the crowd the reason I looked so glum in that picture was that I wasn't playing. Bishop Aloysius J. Wycislo gave me an award on behalf of the Green Bay diocese, and I said I was thankful to know that the Catholic Church was behind a Lutheran. Another company gave me a gold watch, and Evinrude made John a junior test driver, gave Jackie a snowmobile, and gave me a trailer so I could pull it for her. There were other presents and there were telegrams, including one from George Halas saying I was "a hard hitter but never a cheap shot artist," which was a friendly remark for old Papa Bear to make.

Somebody said that the TV special a Green Bay station had made of my life had been looking for a title but had rejected a suggestion to call it, "The Bald and the Beautiful." Governor Patrick J. Lucey and Green Bay mayor Donald Tillman spoke. Gene Foxen, a classmate at Proviso in 1954, gave me a scrapbook with messages from schoolmates. Elmer Johnson was there and Andy Puplis and Ray Eliot. There was a lot of joking along with the sentiment, and Jackie and I were having a great time. My brothers were there with their families, and after Eliot looked at the other two Nitschkes he said he must be a lousy recruiter. He'd picked the runt of the litter.

The best part about the day was that I was with so many people I loved and respected, and it was plain that they respected me. It gave me a wonderful feeling. The need to respect others and win their respect was something I'd learned the hard way.

All during that special day I kept remembering little Raymond Nitschke, that lonely kid I'd been, and how he'd been influenced by athletics and athletes. I thought about a game when I was a high school senior and how a player from the Philadelphia Eagles was said to be in the stands; I don't know for sure whether he was, but I know I played my heart out because a pro was there watching. And I thought about a banquet in high school when some visiting players up at the head table were kept busy signing autographs and how I kept looking up there, thinking: "It'll never happen to me."

But now it had. Now kids came up and wanted me to write "Ray Nitschke" on a piece of paper. It was hard for me to realize that my name could be valuable to anybody, unless maybe it was signed to a check, but it was. Once at a telethon on a Fond du Lac television station, I must have signed autographs for ten hours straight. If you'd told me when I was at Proviso that something like that would happen to me, I would never have believed it.

One of the things I got on Ray Nitschke Day was a plaque, bought by my high school classmates. A replica of it was hung in the Ray Nitschke Hall of Fame that had been established at the Proviso East fieldhouse. Knowing it would be there made me happy. Maybe some other mixed-up kid, who felt the world wasn't treating him right, might walk past there and take a look at it and think: "If Nitschke did it, so can I."

And I hope he can, whether what he wants to do is play football and hear the crowds cheer or his dream takes some entirely different direction.

CHAPTER XIV

There was one good thing about not getting to play much in 1971. I wound up the season in great shape. It was like a year off. I headed into my fifteenth season in the league ready to go all out, whenever I got the chance.

Before the 1972 season opened, I found myself the oldest of a diminishing group of Packer veterans. Bart Starr, who'd been unable to play much in 1971, gave it one last try in training camp and decided to quit as a player, moving over to become a coach. Zeke Bratkowski had gone to the Bears. So that left it up to Scott Hunter, who'd had to handle the quarterbacking most of the time during his rookie year and learn a difficult job under fire. Donny Anderson was traded to St. Louis, so the new backfield tandem was Brockington and MacArthur Lane. There were other changes and departures and switches, and now I was the senior veteran. Coach Devine made me cocaptain and put me in charge of the coin toss, so at least I'd get on the field before the game started, even if I spent the rest of the day on the bench. At the opener, which we won from Cleveland, my old friend of that 1967 playoff interview, Tom Brookshier, acted surprised when I came out and shook hands politely with the Browns' players during the coin toss ceremony.

"There's Ray Nitschke," he told the TV audience, "and he's not hitting anybody."

It wasn't the way I wanted to start my fifteenth year,

but I was still ready to give the team whatever I had a chance to give during the season. And I knew that whatever happened, it had been a good fifteen years. A couple of hundred games. Several thousand moments of standing there waiting for an opposing quarterback to take the snap so I could go after the man who was carrying or catching the ball, pitting my muscles and my brain and my experience and my desire against his skills. There have been so many games it's hard to keep them straight. Still, if you mention one of the big ones—and there have been plenty of big ones over fifteen years—I can tell you the score and who was doing the hitting and how we won or lost.

A player picks up quite a cargo of memories over fifteen seasons, including some he'd just as soon forget. Like the time a quarterback ran over me. It was the one you'd expect: Roman Gabriel of the Rams. He's not only a scrambler, but he's big enough so he doesn't have to dodge away from you. He can just weed out the tacklers and knock them down. He's the strongest quarterback of all those I've played against.

Still, a quarterback—Gabriel or anybody else—isn't supposed to run over a middle linebacker. The time it happened, I had a bruised shoulder. But that's no excuse. It was near the end of a game in the middle 1960s and we were winning, so I didn't go up there aggressively or as if I wanted him real bad. And he kept coming at me, and the next thing I knew I was down and he was still going. It was the most embarrassing thing that ever happened to me. It happened because I went up there figuring I'd take him with one shoulder, my good shoulder, and it didn't work.

Roman is an example of the kind of quarterbacks who've

come to the fore in recent years. When I first got to the league, most of them followed the Starr-Unitas pattern—guys who'd take charge of the game and pass from the pocket but never run except from fright. Now the coaches are looking for quarterbacks who can not only take it but dish it out. There aren't too many of them around—they're hard to find. Terry Bradshaw of the Steelers is one—he's so strong that he can run to his left and throw the ball fifty yards to his right with a flip of his hand while he's running. Being able to throw the ball back across the field without getting set is hard to believe, but a little flip and there it goes. Another example of the new quarterback breed is Jim Plunkett of the New England Patriots. That pro type offense he was taught at Stanford helped him, and he's big as well as agile.

Being big is a help. Some of those oncoming linemen are six foot seven, and they can really move. It's no place for a little guy.

I still think that in the long run the quarterback who stays in the pocket instead of scrambling is better off, but one reason there's all that running around behind the line of scrimmage now is that the defense is so much bigger and faster than it used to be. The young quarterbacks the coaches are looking for are the ones who can get away from the kind of pressure the defense is giving them.

From the standpoint of a defensive man, you like to see the opponent's quarterback running with the ball. You want him to take a lot of punishment. You're not out to hurt him deliberately, but you'd like to see him out of the game because the quarterback is the guy who can beat you. He's the coach on the field, the man with the game plans, the one who has the whole thing mapped out. If the No. 1 quarterback has to leave, it's usually easier to deal with No. 2 or No. 3. The first-string quarterback is the most valuable man on the offense so you want him to run, you want him to try for another yard. Because that gives you a chance to demonstrate why a quarterback isn't supposed to carry the ball.

If a scrambler like Fran Tarkenton catches the other team off balance, he can complete a lot of passes and he can beat you. But with all that running around, his team's timing and precision and execution are off. Even though he can wear out the defensive linemen with all that scrambling, he can be beaten.

In recent years, even Tarkenton has become more of a dropback passer. He's got quick hands, and he's always a threat to play against. He must have decided that scrambling isn't always the way to win games, with everybody running around and nobody knowing where they're going.

There have been other changes in football in fifteen years. There's more specialization now. People are playing football on the strength of their speed who wouldn't even have gone out for the sport fifteen years ago. They're track men in football suits, and their speed is being used for such things as running back kicks.

The sidewinders—the soccer-style kickers—are another modern development. It's not so much that they can kick the ball straighter but that they can kick it faster, and with all those fast defensive men bearing down on him, the kicker has less time to spare.

There's been a change in the relationship between players and owners in those fifteen years. It's both good and bad. There wasn't a players' association when I came into the league, and the association has given us bargaining power we didn't have. It's given us such things as a pension based on the number of years played, along with better medical and dental benefits. We have a pretty complete package. All those benefits are one reason why some players are deciding to go into pro ball. They not only get the quick money, they know they'll also get something long range out of a career. So the association is good from the players' standpoint. But it takes something away from football. It's not just a game any more, but a business. I'd like it to be a game. But it isn't: It's a big business, and winning and losing are all wrapped up in the dollar sign.

We're getting people on the teams now who wouldn't have made the pros fifteen years ago. When I came up, there were less than half as many teams. Expansion has given more people a chance to watch the games, but it has diluted the quality of play. It used to be that you'd find several players each year who were good enough to make the team. Now if you find one real good rookie a season, you've done well. The kids are bigger and faster than they used to be, but because of the expansion to twenty-six teams in the league, you don't have the same over-all quality.

The new players are a different breed of cat, too. You hear about people taking pep pills in the locker room to get up for a game, but it's not as prevalent as has been said. At least, I hope it's not. Some players with a weight problem started taking medication to cut down on their appetites, but a lot of the things that have been written about how common drugs are in locker rooms are wrong.

When I was breaking in, there wasn't much of that kind

of thing. I don't know what the younger players do now. It's a problem I've tried to stay away from, although I'm concerned about it if it affects the people and the game. Such things can damage football and the people who play it. I never needed any pills to get up for a game. I could get myself ready without that.

Pills are an artificial method. For that matter, so is the turf we play on in a lot of places. The players' association took a poll, and 85 percent of the players preferred playing on grass. But the other stuff is more economical in the long run. You don't have to mow it. You can practice on it without damaging it. So it's popular with management and with the colleges. The universities can fill their old practice fields with dormitories. With artificial turf, the team can practice in the stadium without worrying about chewing up the grass.

But as a player, I despise playing on artificial turf. You can run a little faster and there's harder hitting because of the speed, but the ball bounces differently and, no matter what anybody says, you don't have as good traction as on grass. You feel it more when you fall. You have to wear more protective pads because of the abrasions—knee pads, elbow pads. When offensive players try to make quick turns they don't have the proper footing, but the defense has just as much trouble in making turns while we're chasing them. I don't think it's to anybody's advantage.

The next step is playing under a roof, as in the Astrodome. But by controlling weather conditions on the field you take away from a basic premise of the game. Football should be played in rain, snow, sleet, heat, the whole bit. Part of the challenge is to adjust and defeat not only your opponent but the elements as well. When you control everything, you take away some of the things I like about the game. You should require people to adjust to conditions. It's all part of football: playing in perfect September weather, playing when it's one hundred degrees, playing when it's thirteen below and your toes freeze. You have to discipline yourself to ignore things like temperature and rain and snow and mud. It's part of the fun because it's part of the challenge.

Some changes that have come about in my fifteen years have been in tactics. Like the zone defense. As recently as the early sixties, it was mostly man-to-man. But when you're trying to defend against receivers who can run 100 yards in 9.5 seconds, you're worried about the bomb. You try to cover the whole field. You have defensive players 10 yards back. Everything is figured in fractions of seconds. The passer has so many seconds to release the ball. The receiver has so many seconds to get down field. The defense has so many seconds to cover him. In man-to-man, it's rough for a defensive back to cover a fast man. Because of the advent of so many young, speedy people, the kind who once didn't go out for football, we've had to go to the zone most of the time.

The middle linebacker's zone of responsibility is usually in the middle of the field. The three linebackers and a defensive back split the field into four segments, so if the ball is on the fifty-yard line you're responsible for a lot more real estate than if it's closer to your goal. The middle linebacker is supposed to guard against anything in an area fifteen yards deep and twelve yards wide. The secondary takes anything beyond those fifteen yards.

The opponent's quarterback knows this, of course, and he tries to hit the seams—the invisible line where two men's responsibilities converge. He's hoping each of you will let the other guy cover.

Most teams use the zone now except near the goal line, where you don't have to contend with the long pass. The Packers just started playing the zone in recent years. Whether you need it depends not only on the speed of the opponents but on the ability of the defenders. If a team has enough unusually gifted athletes in the secondary, it can do very well with a man-to-man defense even in these days of receivers who are trackmen. Given the right amount of talent, it's still the best defense. But your defenders have to be fast enough and agile enough to react to the receivers' moves.

There has been talk about the defense having the advantage now, which is why the league moved the hashmarks in the 1972 season to give the offense more room to maneuver. But if the defense has been doing better it's because the coaches came to realize that you win on defense. So in the last few years, they've been putting the top people there. Gale Gillingham, for instance. Here was an all-pro offensive lineman, but when the 1972 season began, the Packers moved him to defense.

Television has put pressure on football for higher-scoring games. If a fan doesn't watch too much football, all he likes to see is the long pass, the long run, the big play. But the person who studies the game and understands it wants to see an offense and defense really battling it out. To me, the low-scoring game is the good game, where it's nip and tuck for four quarters, with each team struggling for every yard.

But a lot of those who watch television only get a kick out of the game when there's a big play and the scoreboard lights up.

I can't knock the spectacular scoring play on TV, with instant replay showing it over again from a different angle. But if the rulesmakers make things too easy for the offense, football will get like basketball, with the team that goes the farthest over 100 points winning. I know some basketball fans who don't bother to tune into the games until the last 5 minutes. They don't find it exciting until all that preliminary scoring is over and the teams get down to deciding which one is going to get 120 points and which will have to be content with only 119.

Television may have put pressure on football to favor the offense, but it has also made a lot of spectators familiar enough with the game to appreciate its finer points. Football players are artists. I won't say many of us look like the boys in the ballet, but some players are very graceful, very precise.

The way I look at a game on television is to pick out one player and watch him for a series of downs—never mind where the ball is. On a passing down, I might look at a particular defensive lineman and watch how he tries to defeat the blocker to get to the quarterback, how he tries to outsmart that player, how he finesses him. Or maybe I watch a linebacker to see how he reacts to the pass—how deep he goes, how he moves his body, whether he covers a certain hook zone or goes out in the flat. If he's playing man-to-man, I want to see how he plays the receiver, how he reacts to his moves. On a running play, I may watch how a linebacker fills a hole or how a back comes up and meets the ball carrier.

To me, that's how to watch football. Don't merely follow the ball. Watch one player for a series of plays, then switch over to another. You find out who's playing out there and who's just taking up space.

There isn't just one football game going on. There are eleven separate contests down there on the field whenever the ball is snapped. Each play is a different situation. Every play is diagrammed to produce a touchdown for the offensive team. On every play, the defense is trying to stop it for no gain. If everybody does his job on offense, it's a good play, and the ball is moved. But if ten guys are doing their jobs and one falls down, it can be a broken play. The same thing is true on defense. If just one man gets defeated it may mean a big gain, and if several are defeated it can be a touchdown.

One man may make a mistake—usually a mental mistake, so he's not at the right spot. Or one man may simply be beaten by the opponent's physical ability, as when a receiver outmaneuvers a defender. In his prime, a player like Gale Sayers could run circles around a team by sheer physical ability.

Every offensive player ought to think when the ball is snapped: "This play is going for a touchdown." And every defensive player has to think: "I'm going to stop this play cold." If you start thinking, "They're going to make five yards, but that's all," you're in trouble. A defensive man who thinks like that isn't going to do his job.

It's a free country and you can pick out any one player to watch that you want to, but I usually wind up watching the middle linebacker. It's partly that I've made my living at that line of work. But if you want to follow the defensive half of that struggle that's going on down there, he's the best man to watch. You'll find where the ball is going because, if he's reacting properly, he'll be in the area of the ball 80 or 90 percent of the time. He's in a position to go either right or left and to follow the play. Because of where he's stationed in that defensive battle line, he can read whether it's going to be a pass, a draw, a screen, or a sweep faster than the other defenders. And he's going to try to do something about it.

As I've said, we're into an era of specialists in football, and that has added to the excitement of the game. You've got specialists who kick the ball and players who can run fast and passers who can throw the ball while scrambling around. You've got 280-pounders who are agile enough and fast enough to lead a sweep. You've got guys with enough brute force to push a man out of the way and get to the passer.

I think there's enough excitement in the game to keep television from killing football the way it did boxing, although there's a limit to how much ought to be on the screen. Sunday afternoon and Monday night aren't too much, but there is a saturation point. I couldn't get too much football myself, but I realize that a lot of people could. On the other hand, when you compare the game broadcasts to most of the alternatives on the tube, maybe we ought to have more football instead of less.

It involves violence, but not the kind of senseless violence that you see on a lot of TV shows. Most Americans don't go bear hunting or climb mountains or wrestle alligators.

They may have a lot of competition in their lives, but it's not the healthy kind of physical competition. So football is a substitute outlet even for those who only sit in front of the screen and watch the good guys—the players on their team—try to whip the bad guys from out of town. Maybe the man sitting at home would like to hit somebody, too, and take out the frustrations built up by a deal that went sour or a sale that didn't come off or a foreman who's hard to get along with. But he can't haul off and give somebody the forearm and knock him flat on his back. He has to be civilized and control himself and shake hands politely with his rival. But on Sunday afternoon or Monday night he can lose some of his frustrations watching his favorite team or favorite player. In his imagination, he can put himself right down there on the field and get rid of some of those tensions that have been building up.

Our nature is competitive. America is a competitive country. People are trying all the time to succeed. They're trying to be winners. But most of the time, they have to disguise their feelings.

You listen to those football fans in the stadium. They're all wrapped up in the team they're backing. They cheer and shout, and sometimes I've seen them cry real tears. When the game is over, they've gotten rid of some of their frustrations. They're ready for another week of bottling up their feelings.

I've had people in their seventies talk to me with as much love for the game as some kid who comes up, wide-eyed, and holds out a piece of paper to be autographed. That feeling cuts across all the things that divide us—age, sex, religion, color, education, and the rest. If you're for the Packers and I'm for the Packers, we've got something in common, not only with each other but with all those other people who are Green Bay fans. If you're for the Bears or Rams or Colts, you're part of another group that exults when its team wins.

Sure, football is a form of entertainment. But the fans don't just come to watch a show. They are there to see their team win. And I agree with them. I want to win every game. Every single game.

That's why I went into my fifteenth season in 1972 with all the determination of a rookie. Maybe the coaches didn't feel I was still a starter, but I was going to do as much as they'd let me to help the team. I wanted another championship—and I wasn't thinking of any five-year plan. I wanted to win now. I wanted that attitude to be contagious, because if you believe you're a winner, you can win. Everybody's got to think that way. Only the teams that truly believe in themselves are going to be winners.

I felt like George Allen, who went to the Redskins and started picking up the kind of veterans who put his team in contention right away. His attitude was like mine: "Worry about this year. Let the future take care of itself." It's fine to think about the future, but in this business a lot of unforeseen things happen. Pro fans are paying lots of money to watch the games, and you'd better win now.

With most of the great players of the Lombardi years gone, the Packers were a young team in 1972. We had to start the season with a second-year quarterback, backed up by a rookie, Jerry Tagge. A lot of the other players were still learning. There are special problems in dealing with young players that you didn't have fifteen years ago. They've got different backgrounds than players my age had. They're more independent. You're bound to be more independent if you've got a fat bank account before you even put on a uniform.

I'm not knocking these guys, and I'm not knocking the money they get. But there can be such a thing as getting rich too soon. It takes away the hunger. You can spoil an athlete by giving him too much money too early. It not only isn't fair to him, it isn't fair to the sport.

"Here's a hundred thousand bucks," you tell a kid. "Now we'd like to have you play a little football."

Such a player will go partway on his pride, but that only lasts so long. Then he'll say, "Hey, who needs this? What am I doing out here, getting knocked around? I've already got the loot."

With a young team such as the Packers, we fortunately haven't had agitators trying to create conflict within the organization. But in the 1971 season, the squad lacked leadership. Not only did we have a new man as coach, but the team hadn't developed enough leaders on the field.

This wasn't surprising, with so many young players on offense as well as defense, but it was one of the differences between the 1971 team and the one that represented Green Bay in 1972. In a squad of forty men, you need at least five who can carry out the responsibilities of leadership, and in Devine's first season with the pros, we had only one or two.

A leader doesn't have to be a star. But he has to be somebody who's carrying his weight, someone everybody respects, a first-line ballplayer. He has to be someone who's carrying out the coach's policies and isn't just interested in himself. He has to make sure all the players are working toward the same goal. If you have five leaders on a team, each one can help seven other guys.

In the great Lombardi years, we had more than five. A man like Starr—you couldn't find a better leader, on the field or off. And Willie Davis was a real leader, one who not only played the game well but was very articulate. We had men like Bill Forester, who was captain of the Packers during the early sixties. He was a slow-talking, tough player with an all-for-one attitude. He led by making everybody believe in him. Then we had fellows like Bob Skoronski and Forrest Gregg and Willie Wood. Willie was a fiery player who went out there with every ounce of energy that was in him. Henry Jordan was a leader from his play, the way he approached the game, the way he studied his opponents. Hornung was a tremendous leader on the field, a very competitive player—the bigger the game, the better he played. And Taylor was a leader from the way he played with everything he had.

You can continue the list: Boyd Dowler had leadership qualities, for example, and there were others, like Jim Ringo and Dave Hanner. I hope I did a little leading myself from my dedication and style of play. I like to think of how Lombardi or Bengtson would say, "Ray, set the tone," and I'd run out there all fired up, just aching to hit somebody. That was a kind of leadership, although as I matured and quit having the selfish attitude I had as a young player, I hope I qualified as a leader in some other respects, too.

The players we have now are harder for me to understand than the ones who were in the league when I arrived. They're more individualistic. In my younger days, most of us were just happy to be part of the team. Now many players don't seem to care what they can do for the organization. They feel it ought to be proud that it's lucky enough to have them.

They seem to feel the game owes them something instead of the other way around, that the people of the community owe them something because they're on the team. It was different when I came in. Players were more willing to make sacrifices. There was more of an attitude of "What can I do for the team?" instead of "What can the team do for me?"

But football can't be a game of individualists. It's a team game, where each man has to play his role to make the team a success. When the Packers were being called a football dynasty, what made us strong was people working together, not caring too much who got his name in the headlines as long as we won.

The thing we were looking for was the respect of the men we were playing with, because it's your teammates who know whether you're doing your part. A fan can stop you on the street and give you a compliment, or a sportswriter can put your name in the paper, and that kind of thing is all right. But it's the compliment from that big guy playing next to you that really means something. He knows whether you're working, whether you're doing your job. The average fan can't know. A lot of people get credit for a great play when somebody else deserves the cheers. If a back runs the ball for a long gain, he's a hero. But somebody was up there grunting and shoving and opening up that hole for him to run through.

When two teams line up and the quarterback starts counting, they're separated by the length of the football. Those few inches there at the line of scrimmage—that's where the game is won or lost. The guys in the pits who do the work don't get too much glory or money, but they're the keys to whether the team will be playing in the Super Bowl or sitting at home watching it on television.

It takes a fellow who's played football to understand what's really happening. He knows the hardships and frustrations. He understands how much preparation it takes before those teams run out on the field, the monotonous drudgery of doing the same thing over and over and over again until you react instinctively. He understands that if one man is going to be a great runner and get his name in headlines, somebody else is going to have to block. On the defense, one man may get the publicity and somebody else may be doing most of the work. You have to be able to accept such things, and only someone who has been part of it knows how it is.

In fifteen years, you learn a lot of things about the game, and the most difficult thing I had to learn was that in the coaches' minds I was no longer a starter. When the 1972 training camp opened, the Packers were younger on the average than all but two of the other twenty-five teams in the league. I'd look at those kids running around the field on Oneida Street and realize that some of them had been learning their ABC's in the first grade the year I drove my used Pontiac north to Wisconsin, first checking with Rand-McNally to find out where Green Bay was located.

There was one thing similar to 1958, though. According to the preseason odds, Green Bay was considered the underdog in all but three of the regular-season games we were scheduled to play.

When the season began, I was still playing behind Jim Carter and not liking it. But I was still part of things. And not just because I was named defensive cocaptain.

Getting that title gave me the chance to call the coin toss. It was funny. After all my years in the league, I was a little nervous when I went through that ceremony for the first time when we played the Dolphins in Miami during the exhibition season. I wanted to do it right. I wanted to win. But I flubbed it. I called it wrong, and Miami got first crack at the ball. In fact, we lost our first four coin tosses in the exhibition season, and it bothered me. I wanted to beat those other guys, even if it was just a matter of calling heads or tails.

At the resort hotel where we spent the week before the Miami game, the kids and tourists came flocking around. Somebody said I got in more candid snapshots than the rest of the team put together. Boyd Dowler used to kid me about such things, calling me "the people's choice." But I've never minded such remarks. I like people—unless, of course, they're running toward me with a football.

I like to play, too. Having to take second place on the field still stung. It was harder to convince myself that the change was only temporary.

Standing there on the sidelines after the season began, I could see my replacement making mistakes. Everybody makes them. When I was playing regularly, I'd see things I did wrong and try not to do them again. But he didn't seem to want to take advantage of my experience, even though he should have known I would have helped him for his own good and the team's. Except for a very few times, he never asked for my advice, so I kept it to myself.

It wasn't my place to interfere with the coaches or a ballplayer unless I was asked. We had a linebacker coach and a defensive coordinator. It was their job to point out mistakes, not mine. Still, I felt I could have helped the team by making a few suggestions about the job I'd held so long. When no one seemed interested, it was another reason I felt my fifteen years in the league weren't being used to help the Packers win.

All I could do was get myself up for each game so if I got in I could play well. And I felt I did play well when I got the chance. The team seemed to react with more enthusiasm when I went running out there. But most of the time, situations where I thought I could help came and went with me still standing on the sidelines, feeling frustrated.

When I didn't play, the tensions that built up during the week had no chance to find an outlet. Jackie said I came home after these games looking more tired than in the days when I was out there, hitting and getting hit. It's hard to have to stand and watch when you want to go roaring out and tackle somebody.

Sometimes the fans yelled things at Carter that indicated they thought the wrong middle linebacker was playing. He resented it. It put more pressure on him. But when a young player replaces one who's been around a long time and has built up a lot of fan loyalty, there's bound to be that kind of pressure, and he has to be man enough not to let it interfere with his play.

I felt that the way the fans cheered for me when I came into the games in 1972 was one reason why the coaches weren't playing me more. If I was given more playing time and if I played well, then the fans might demand I play even more. And that wasn't part of the coaches' long-term plans. They never told me why I wasn't starting, but I assumed it was because they wanted more youth and wanted Carter to build up experience for the seasons ahead. Hearing my friends yelling for me gave me a good feeling, but I wondered if it wasn't having just the opposite effect than the one they wanted it to have.

So as the Packers started winning games they'd been picked to lose, I didn't get too many chances to contribute. I tried to help by my attitude and to set an example by the way I went all-out in practice and prepared myself to play when I wasn't playing much. And once in a while I got a chance to go into a game for a play or two, and I did what I could. Like the Chicago game in the fifth week of the season. We were tied 17–17 with half a minute to play, and they sent me in to block on the left side of the backfield when Chester Marcol tried for a field goal. I noticed the Bears had only one man on the left side of the line, with the rest of them either in the middle or on the right. So when the ball was snapped, I wasn't on the left any more. I was in the middle, and when one of the Bears broke through, I cut him down. He didn't block the kick and we won 20–17, giving us a 4–1 record and first place in the Central Division.

It was no big deal. But it was one of those plays where having fifteen years' experience may have helped.

Being able to win as many games in the first five weeks of the 1972 season as we'd won all during 1971 surprised some people, but not those of us who'd seen how much difference a year had made in the Packers. Early in the training camp, I felt this was going to be a more successful season. There were changes in personnel: We added Marcol and Willie

Buchanon in the draft and such fine players as MacArthur Lane and Jimmy Hill through trades. But the biggest difference was in the players' attitude. The guys were playing together, playing like a team, without different factions trying to go off in different directions. There was more of an all-for-one attitude, the kind of feeling of comradeship we'd had under Lombardi. The players lacked experience, but they made up for it in enthusiasm and determination and togetherness.

Hill was a fine addition as a safetyman. He gave us some of the leadership we'd lacked in 1971. He set the tone for the defensive secondary. He helped make it one of the best secondaries in the league, one that should get even better in the years ahead. Willie Wood, who'd been the leader of the secondary for so many years, had retired, but Hill moved in and became the old pro and took over.

Buchanon, the No. 1 draft choice, turned out to be a remarkably talented rookie. It was his first year in the league, but he was as good a defensive cornerback as anybody in the business. He could cover any man in the NFL, man-to-man. You have to be strong at the corners, and with Buchanon on one side of the field and with Kenny Ellis having another year's experience, we had nothing to worry about there.

Lane, another great athlete, was obtained from St. Louis for Donny Anderson. Donny was versatile and talented, but MacArthur was a better blocker, and by teaming him with Brockington we had the two biggest and best backs in football for a ball-control type of game. Lane is the kind of halfback who runs like a fullback, and those two ball carriers could really sting the defense. Brockington had gained more than a thousand yards as a rookie, and now he had Lane's blocking to help him. MacArthur is a fine runner, too. He is also a leader. Like Hill, he helped fill our need for leaders.

Hunter had a year's experience as a quarterback when the '72 season opened, and that made him a better player and gave him added confidence. He also had the benefit of having Starr on the sidelines calling the plays. That kept some of the pressure off Scott. To his credit, Hunter listened to everything Bart told him about quarterbacking and took advantage of this chance to learn from a master of the game.

Starr can call as close to a perfect game as anyone you'll ever see, and Hunter was learning to execute the way Starr had. Watching the patterns develop on the field during a game, it sometimes seemed to me that it was Bart out there instead of Hunter.

But the biggest difference between the 1971 personnel and the 1972 team was Marcol. Picking him was the best draft choice of all those we've made in my fifteen years in Green Bay. I've come to realize that kicking wins or loses more games than any other part of football. A lot of games are lost by three points or even by one. If you have a man who can give you a field goal or even just good field position, it can turn the game around. Since Don Chandler had retired, the Packers' kicking had been a perennial problem. We kept losing games we could have won if we'd had someone who could kick the ball. But with Marcol on the squad, we had a good chance to get three points any time we were in the opponent's territory. And Chester's kickoffs were likely to go booming all the way out of the end zone. Ron Widby, who'd come from Dallas in a trade, was doing a fine job of punting as well as handling the ball for field goals. So at last we had a kicking game that was an asset instead of a problem.

It was one reason why we started out the season so much stronger than in 1971. In our first five games we beat Cleveland, Detroit, Dallas, and Chicago, and the only reason we lost to Oakland was an officials' decision that the NFL later admitted was incorrect. The sixth week, we lost by one point to Atlanta in a game played in the mud at Milwaukee. But even though Marcol missed what would have been the winning field goal, he made three others and was responsible for all our points.

Carter hurt his knee during that game, and I went in for a few plays. As I ran onto the field, I heard a big cheer. The Milwaukee crowd was just yelling for old Ray, but Jim thought the fans were cheering because he'd been injured, and it burned him up. Later, he realized he'd been mistaken. Quite a few people wrote him letters to explain they'd been cheering for Nitschke, not against Carter.

After losing to Atlanta, we were 4–2 for the season, but we were still leading our division. We had problems, though. Rich McGeorge and Gillingham, two of the most talented men on the team, were injured and out for the year. Most of the starters still lacked experience. Our reserves were thin at some positions, especially the vital one of quarterback.

But between 1971 and 1972, we'd become a football team with character, a team that is going to win a lot more championships for the Green Bay fans in the years to come if they continue to play as a unit instead of worrying too much about individual success. When the 1972 season ended, the future of the Packers looked great because of those talented young athletes and the way they are learning to play together.

Before the season began, nearly everybody had picked Minnesota to repeat as Central Division champions. The Vikings got off to a poor start, but when we played them in the year's seventh game they were playing well again. We lost, 27–13, in a game where they intercepted four of Hunter's passes.

That made our record 4–3 with another strong team, San Francisco, coming up next. After losing two games in a row, the coaches may have felt that a few changes were needed. Anyway, when the Pack took the field against the Forty-Niners, I was back where I felt I belonged. Devine moved Carter to outside linebacker, and Dave Robinson was benched. After the first quarter, Carter took over my spot and Robinson went in, but when the game was over and we'd won, 34–24, I could feel I'd been part of one of the season's crucial games.

Every game seemed to be crucial in the Central Division in 1972. We got past Chicago the following week by the margin of two of Marcol's field goals, but then the Washington Redskins beat us 21–16 and we were back in a tie for first with Detroit, with Minnesota close on our heels. And we were scheduled to play the Lions next. The team that won would be a game ahead, with two more to play.

The oddsmakers called us underdogs, but the Sunday we played was one of those bracing Green Bay days with a wind-chill factor of minus two, and the Packers dominated the game from the opening kickoff. Detroit didn't get a first down until the final ten seconds of the first half, and by that time we were ahead, 23–0. Late in the fourth quarter we were leading 33–0. One more touchdown and we'd whip the Lions the way they'd humiliated us a couple of years back. But in the final few seconds, Detroit managed to score on a pass play, and we had to settle for a 33–7 win.

Marcol kicked four field goals that afternoon, three in the first quarter. Ellis, who'd been hurt in the Washington game and hadn't been expected to play, made one of the early interceptions that helped put us so far ahead that the Lions had no chance to catch up. Against the Redskins, Hunter had done so poorly that Devine put in Tagge. But this time, Scott not only led an offense that was completely dominant for most of the game but scored a touchdown when he broke loose after Detroit thought he was trapped behind the line of scrimmage.

It was obvious to everybody early in the afternoon that the Packers were going to win. But nobody left those Green Bay stands. The crowd loved every point we scored. Even though we had the game wrapped up when I went in for Carter in the fourth quarter, they yelled with as much enthusiasm as ever. Half a dozen times during the afternoon, everybody jumped up to give the Packers a standing ovation, and it wasn't only because they needed the exercise to keep from freezing.

So we'd won a game we had to win to stay on top of the division, but there was no chance to relax and enjoy the victory, because Minnesota was next. The Vikings had been playing like a team that still hoped to go to the Super Bowl despite its early-season losses. If they beat us, we'd be tied for first, and our only hope would be that Minnesota lost its final game with San Francisco so we could back into the divisional championship.

There had been a lot of pressure on us for the Lions game. It built up just as high for this one, but the young Packers' team proved it could meet the challenge. The game didn't start out as well as the one with Detroit, however. When we ran into the dressing room at halftime to get warm, we were behind 7–0.

The thermometers around Minnesota read zero that afternoon, and the wind-chill factor dropped from eighteen below to twenty-two below during the game. Neither offense could do much during the first half.

But things changed in the third quarter. Lane got loose for a long run and Marcol, who'd missed a long field goal earlier in the game, kicked a thirty-seven-yarder. Then Fred Carr picked up a Vikings' fumble and ran it back to Minnesota's twenty-eight. Brockington, who became the first player in league history to go over a thousand yards rushing for his first two seasons, got the ball to the one-foot line a few plays later, and then Hunter took it over to put us ahead, 10–7.

That was enough to win because the defense was really hitting people out there, and the Vikings never scored again. But Lane scored our second touchdown after Buchanon intercepted a Tarkenton pass. A little later, Willie picked off another that led to a Marcol field goal, and after Minnesota got the ball back Ellis intercepted, and before long we had another three points.

Beating the Vikings 23–7 meant we'd won the Central Division title for the first time since Lombardi's last year as Green Bay's coach. The young team that most sportswriters had thought would finish third or even last in the Central Division had scored fifty-six points on successive

Sundays, while our defense was holding Detroit and Minnesota to one touchdown each.

Those victories meant that even if we lost to New Orleans in the last game of the season, the Lions or Vikings couldn't catch us. But we wanted to keep winning. There's no sense in putting on your shoulder pads if you don't go out there to win.

After all that pressure of the past two weeks, however, it was hard to get moving against the Saints. That game in New Orleans isn't one that coaches are likely to use in future years as an example of how football should be played. Neither team had scored when Marcol tried a field goal late in the first quarter. New Orleans blocked it. The ball bounced back to Widby, who'd held the ball for Chester.

A football player is supposed to react to what's happening, even if what is happening is a bit unusual, and I headed toward the sidelines. Ron saw I was open. He threw a pass— his second successful one of the year—and I grabbed the ball and headed for the goal line, making like an Illinois fullback again.

I didn't score. I got knocked down on the Saints' seven after running about thirty yards. But a few plays later, Hunter went over and we had a 7–0 lead.

The defense gave us another touchdown in the second quarter. This time, we blocked a New Orleans field goal try. Clarence Williams grabbed the ball and lateraled to Willie Buchanon, who sprinted down the field for a score. The Saints got that one back before the half, though, in one of the weirdest plays of what was turning out to be an altogether strange sort of game. Widby was trying to punt out of our end zone and, after what had happened earlier, we were trying to make sure the Saints wouldn't block the kick. They didn't, either. After the snap, Carter saw a New Orleans man bearing down, and he moved over to stop him. The ball hit Jim in the seat of the pants, one of the Saints fell on it, and New Orleans had its first touchdown of the day.

Archie Manning threw a couple of touchdown passes in the second quarter, but Tagge came in and scored a touchdown for us and Marcol kicked two more field goals to go with the one he'd made earlier in the game. So we won, 30–20. That gave Chester thirty-three field goals for the season, only one short of the record.

Winning that game made us 10–4 for the season and we'd qualified to play George Allen's Redskins, who'd won their division. Just as the fans' bumper stickers had kept predicting since the team started losing in 1968, the Pack was finally back. Walking off the field, I reached down and put my arm around Coach Devine's shoulders and gave him a big hug.

The other two NFC teams that had made the playoffs were San Francisco and Dallas, and we'd beaten both of them during the season. So if we could get by Washington, we felt there was no reason why we couldn't be back in the Super Bowl.

During our practices before the playoff in RFK Stadium, the sportswriters called me the team's "holler guy," and I guess I did raise my voice now and then. I knew the way it was for the young players to be going into a game like this— I'd gone through it when I was a young player myself, when Lombardi took us east to play Philadelphia for the championship. Everyone in the country seems to be looking over your shoulder. And in 1972, that included the President of the United States. Mr. Nixon, a Redskins' fan, tried to pressure the league into lifting the TV blackout in the Washington area but was turned down. He had to fly south and tune our game in from his Florida home instead.

Allen's team was being called the "over-the-hill gang," the way Lombardi's team had once been described. But in a playoff, there's a lot to be said for experience. Most of our players had never faced that kind of situation before. Other things being fairly equal, a veteran team has an edge on a younger team in a playoff game. We'd demonstrated that back in the middle sixties, but now the Packers were the representatives of youth instead of experience.

Washington had won its first title in thirty years, but a lot of Allen's players were experienced men who'd come with him from the Rams and had plenty of pressure games behind them. Billy Kilmer, the quarterback, was a veteran. Hunter had Starr to help him, but Bart couldn't get out there and pick those defenses apart the way he used to because now he had to stand on the sidelines.

The game turned out to be a defensive battle. Neither team could score in the first quarter. In the second, we recovered Larry Brown's fumble and moved the ball close enough for Marcol to try a long field goal. A couple of inches higher and he would have had it. But the ball hit the crossbar, and it was still 0–0.

The Redskins were using a five-man line and they stopped our main offensive weapon, the running game. So Hunter had to pass, and midway in the second quarter he hit Dale once and Lane twice, and we had the ball on the Washington forty-one.

Brockington carried to the thirty-eight, and then John Staggers made a good move on Mike Bass and caught a pass that gave us a first down on the Washington fifteen. But in the next three plays we gained only five yards and had to settle for a Marcol field goal to put us ahead 3–0.

That turned out to be the Packers' only score. Before the first half was over, Kilmer hit Roy Jefferson for a touchdown, and Curt Knight kicked a field goal. We went into the dressing room a touchdown behind.

No one scored in the third quarter, but the Packers had four penalties called against them, including a couple that helped keep a Redskins' drive alive and led to another Knight field goal early in the fourth quarter. He'd made only fourteen of thirty attempts during the regular season, but Curt booted a third field goal before the playoff game was over, making the final score 16–3.

It was the first playoff a Green Bay team had lost since 1960, when the Eagles beat us in Lombardi's second year as head coach. It meant we wouldn't get a chance to see if history would repeat itself, if the '72 Packers could get past the Cowboys and go to the Super Bowl the way the '67 team had done.

Losing to Allen's veterans was a disappointment. Still, we'd come farther than almost anyone had expected, and I was proud of those young guys who'd brought Green Bay its first division championship in five years. After suffering through four losing seasons, it was good to be on a winning team again. I hadn't been given as much chance to contribute as I'd wanted to, but I still felt I was a part of the 1972 success. I felt I'd helped by my experience and my attitude in making Dan Devine's fine young team into a winner, and that gave me some satisfaction after what had been mostly another frustrating season for me came to an end.

With that 1972 season, I had proved one of the things I wanted to prove: that I could survive fifteen years in a game that not only takes a lot out of you physically but subjects you to pressure, week in and week out.

Even after my playing days are over, I'd like to stay close to football. If I had my choice, I'd like to go into coaching. I'd like to stay in Wisconsin. Jackie and I want to be part of the Green Bay community the rest of our lives. We have three children now—Amy was adopted early in 1972—and we've found a home. The Green Bay area is where we'd like to raise our family.

But I'll take it one day at a time. One day, one game, one season at a time—that was Lombardi's gospel, and I'm a believer in it.

Still, after you've been around for fifteen years, maybe even St. Vincent would excuse me if I look back now and then as well as looking forward to next Sunday afternoon. In some ways, the game is the same. In others, it's a lot different.

In my first year in the league, total attendance at pro games was about three million. Now it's around fifteen million. In 1958, all you had to do to buy a Packer ticket was show up with your wallet out. Now people sleep on the sidewalk for days so they'll have a chance to buy a couple of seats. The lucky ones who have season tickets hand them down like heirlooms.

The American Football League hadn't even been organized when I signed with the pros, which had something to do with the fact that I had to settle for a five-hundred-dollar bonus. All a team had to do then was win one playoff game and it was champion of the world. Now there are twenty-six teams, and the playoffs go on for weeks.

There have been some smaller changes, ones most fans have forgotten. For instance, you might win a bet by saying it wasn't long ago when it was legal to grab an opponent's face mask, providing he was carrying the ball. That rule wasn't changed until 1962.

According to figures released by the federal pay board in the summer of 1972, the football clubs pay their players an average of twenty-eight thousand dollars a man, which is pretty good compared to what I made when I came into the league, but not so great when you compare it to the pro basketball average of fifty thousand dollars or even professional baseball's average of thirty-one thousand dollars for big-league players.

But I'm going to tell you something I wouldn't have told Vince Lombardi during those afternoons when we'd go into his office and close the door and discuss my salary until the windows rattled:

It wasn't money that kept me around for fifteen years.

I don't say I haven't tried to get what was coming to me or that I didn't try to win those salary arguments. Everybody wants to see his family live well. Besides, the size of your salary is one way you keep score.

But the money is secondary. The bruises and disappointments and drudgery and aches are secondary. The reason I've played football is that I enjoy it. Even practice. Even the lying awake playing a game over again. Even those mental gymnastics you have to go through to get yourself psyched up for the next game.

I've enjoyed every moment of my fifteen years—well, almost every moment. There is nothing I could have done with my life that I could possibly have enjoyed more.

There's only one thing I regret, looking back: I regret that it's not 1958 again, so I'd have it all to do over again.

EPILOGUE

By Gary D'Amato

When Ray Nitschke's heart gave out on March 8, 1998, family members, friends, and one-time foes alike were shocked. His heart? How could a heart as big as Nitschke's stop beating at age 61?

Nobody played football with more heart than did No. 66 for the Green Bay Packers. And as big as his heart was on the field, it was perhaps even bigger off it.

His willingness to go the extra mile to bring a smile to a fan's face was legendary. His love of Green Bay—the team and the community—was unmatched. He wore Packer pride on his sleeve, right next to his emotions. Nitschke struck fear into running backs, but deep down he was a soft touch, compassionate and sentimental.

In fact, as great a player as Nitschke was, his legacy may be that he was a better person than he was a middle linebacker. A Hall of Famer in the game of football, and in the game of life.

John Nitschke, the oldest of Ray and Jackie Nitschke's three adopted children, said it best in describing his father at the memorial service in Green Bay: "Team player. Warrior. Leader. Winner. Champion. Professional celebrity. Ambassador. True friend. A man of valor. A man of worth."

He was all of that, and more.

Nitschke was a man's man, a rough-and-tumble football player in the Lombardi mold who played hard and mean, but always within

303

the rules. His countenance on game days was frightening: prematurely balding, missing his front teeth, sneering, snarling—he was almost a caricature, except that caricatures don't hit like Nitschke did. Yet, he was, by all accounts, a devoted husband and a doting and protective father. Indeed, his cry-like-a-baby breakdowns at his daughter's wedding and the birth of his first grandchild surprised no one who knew him.

"He was a raving madman on the field," said former teammate Carroll Dale, "and a teddy bear off it."

When Amy Klaas thinks about growing up in the Nitschke household, football is not the first thing that comes to mind.

"When I was seven or eight years old, after dinner we would always have entertainment time," said Klaas, who was born March 2, 1972, and adopted by the Nitschkes one week later. "My dad would dance with me and then we'd do this acrobatic thing where I stood on his feet and he walked around the house. He always pretended he was ticklish; I don't think he really was.

"If we were at the pool, we had this game we did, where he would pretend to test the water, knowing full well that I was going to push him in."

When Amy was a teenager, Ray got a kick out of driving her and her girlfriends around town, never failing to honk his horn and wave at young boys, who stared back open-mouthed as the girls giggled in the back seat.

However, Nitschke could be stand-offish—though never rude—with Amy's dates if he didn't approve of them. On more than one occasion he growled, "I'm not going to like the man who marries this girl."

Of course, when Amy did marry, Nitschke welcomed Jon Klaas into the family as if he were a long-lost son. "He never introduced

Jon as his son-in-law," Amy said. "He always introduced him as his son. Jon just adored dad. They were crazy together."

At the wedding, big, tough, mean ol' Ray Nitschke bawled like a baby.

"My mom was holding on to his leg and trying to get him to control himself because he was crying so hard," Amy said. "He actually had bruises on his leg from her grip. That's how he always was. About two months after mom died [in 1996], I had my daughter. The first time dad held her, all he could do was smile and cry."

Amy and Jon named their daughter Jacqueline Rae, after Jackie and Ray Nitschke.

For John and Richard Nitschke, growing up with one of the most famous surnames in Green Bay was never a burden. John, born May 27, 1963, was old enough to remember his father's final days as a player. Nitschke's fifteen-year career ended in 1972.

"Dad retired when I was in the fifth grade," he said. "It was really neat to be able to bring him to school for show-and-tell. I was very proud of him. But, you know, Green Bay being the town it is, some guys' dads are plumbers, some are doctors . . . mine just happened to play football."

Richard, born January 25, 1966—twenty-three days after the Packers beat the Cleveland Browns in the NFL Championship Game—remembers pedaling his bicycle around Lambeau Field while his father worked out at the stadium.

"I was just a little kid. I'd kind of hang out with [equipment manager] Dad Braisher and [head trainer] Domenic Gentile," he said. "Sometimes, dad would bring me to St. Norbert's College with him for lunch [during training camp]. I remember going over to Willie Wood's house."

Both Nitschke boys played high school football, John at Green Bay Premontre and Rich at Pulaski, and both were good at it. But

Ray Nitschke never forced the fame on his sons, never coached them or critiqued their play, and he offered advice only when asked.

"Mostly, he just let us do our own stuff," Rich said. "I'm into fishing and hunting, and he was never into that. Nor did he push me into the stuff he was into."

After Nitschke retired, he remained a fixture in Green Bay, making appearances, giving speeches, hosting cruises, and helping charities. Wood called him the "quintessential celebrity," and, indeed, he made a handsome living just being Ray Nitschke. He capitalized on his enormous popularity, his arresting personality, and his ability to make people feel good. If you were opening a grocery store, you wanted Nitschke to be there. If you were selling furnaces or furniture, you wanted Nitschke's endorsement.

His unique appearance, raspy voice, and recognition factor made him a natural for television commercials, and he made many over the years. Perhaps the most memorable was his spot in the popular "Tastes Great—Less Filling" Miller Lite beer campaign in the 1970s.

"His intentions were to have fun all the time," said Wood, Nitschke's former teammate and one of his closest friends. "When he retired, he didn't have any other kind of occupation, so he made his living doing that. He knew how to play his part."

For a quarter-century, Nitschke marketed himself out of the basement of his home, situated on ten acres of land just west of Green Bay. Had he hired an agent, he almost certainly could have made more money. but that just wasn't Ray Nitschke's style.

"I believe he thought there was a bigger connection with the fan and the community that way, rather than just going through a middle man, said John Nitschke. "That's just who he was."

Nitschke knew, innately, that keeping in touch with Packer fans, young and old, was the key to his success. But there was nothing insincere about his devotion to them, or they to him. Each year, when he was introduced at the Packers' Alumni Game, he would charge onto the field to a thunderous ovation. People just naturally responded to him, and, unlike so many celebrities, he never tired of the attention.

"Coming from my father's background, coming from absolutely nothing, he never thought he would have that kind of adulation, to be cheered by sixty thousand fans," John Nitschke said. "That's why he played in the first place. He played for the adulation of the fans. It was his way of feeling appreciated as a human being."

Perhaps because of that, Nitschke never tired of posing for pictures, shaking hands, or recounting stories from his playing days for complete strangers. Nobody close to him could recall him turning down an autograph request. And he never just hurriedly scribbled his name, either; his neatly-penned signature is readable and instantly recognizable.

"Again, I think that goes back to his childhood," Amy Klaas said. "He never thought, when he was thirteen, that people would ask for his autograph. He never looked at himself as somebody important enough for people to ask for his autograph. So he certainly tried to accommodate everyone."

In the 1990s, Nitschke became a popular figure on the card-signing circuit. But if he was contracted to sign autographs for one hour, he would inevitably stay for two.

"That would kind of annoy the other participants, because it devalued their time," John Nitschke said. "But that goes back to the fans. That was his way of saying, 'Thank you.' His fans made him feel his self-worth."

In the mid-1990s, Nitschke bought a condominium in Naples, Florida, and spent a considerable amount of time there during the winter, enjoying the sunshine and playing golf; he was long off the tee and held a 5-handicap.

It was in Florida that Nitschke suffered his fatal heart attack. He felt chest pains during a drive north from Naples to Venice with Amy and his granddaughter, Jacqueline, and stopped at a convenience store for a soft drink. He suffered the heart attack shortly after Amy returned to the car with the drink for him.

Because of his seemingly robust health and his zest for life, his passing shocked his close friends and former teammates. When informed by a newspaper reporter that Nitschke had died, Hall of Fame tackle Forrest Gregg said, "Oh, my God. You just thought Nitschke would be here forever."

Days later, a crowd of nine hundred, including an estimated twenty of Nitschke's former teammates, attended the seventy-five-minute memorial service at Bayside Christian Fellowship auditorium, just east of Green Bay.

Arni Jacobson, the senior pastor at Bayside Christian who officiated, said Nitschke was "like Santa Claus with a cigar."

"I think Ray squeezed more out of his life than the oldest people that have ever lived," Jacobsen said.

"We will miss Ray Nitschke, we truly will," said Willie Davis, the Hall of Fame defensive end, who briefly shared his reflections on his former teammate. "There will be a lot of people who will play middle linebacker for Green Bay and in the National Football League.

"In my opinion, there will never be another Ray Nitschke."

Robert W. Wells (1918-1994), a Milwaukee newspaperman for many years, was also an award-winning writer of books, articles, and short stories, many of them written for teenagers. He is the author of *Lombardi: His Life and Times,* republished in 1997 by Prairie Oak Press. His other works include *This is Milwaukee, Fire at Peshtigo,* and *Daylight in the Swamp.*

Gary D'Amato, staff sports writer for the *Milwaukee Journal Sentinel*, has won more than twenty writing awards in his eighteen years as a newspaper reporter, including first-place honors in the prestigious Associated Press Sports Editors contest. He is also the co-author, with Domenic Gentile, of *The Packer Tapes: My 32 Years with the Green Bay Packers* (1995) and, with Cliff Christl, *Mudbaths and Bloodbaths: The Inside Story of the Bears-Packer Rivalry* (1997), both published by Prairie Oak Press.